D0712774

THE VENTURE CAPITAL INVESTMENT PROCESS

The Venture Capital Investment Process

Darek Klonowski

palgrave
macmillan

THE VENTURE CAPITAL INVESTMENT PROCESS
Copyright © Darek Klonowski, 2010.

First published in 2010 by
PALGRAVE MACMILLAN®
in the United States—a division of St. Martin's Press LLC,
175 Fifth Avenue, New York, NY 10010.

Where this book is distributed in the UK, Europe and the rest of the world,
this is by Palgrave Macmillan, a division of Macmillan Publishers Limited,
registered in England, company number 785998, of Houndmills,
Basingstoke, Hampshire RG21 6XS.

Palgrave Macmillan is the global academic imprint of the above companies
and has companies and representatives throughout the world.

Palgrave® and Macmillan® are registered trademarks in the United States,
the United Kingdom, Europe and other countries.

ISBN: 978–0–230–61288–4

Library of Congress Cataloging-in-Publication Data

Klonowski, Darek.
    The venture capital investment process / Darek Klonowski.
      p. cm.
    Includes index.
    ISBN 978–0–230–61288–4 (hardback)
      1. Venture capital. 2. Private equity. 3. Business enterprises—Finance.
    I. Title.

HG4751.K58 2010
332'.04154—dc22   2009047946

A catalogue record of the book is available from the British Library.

Design by Newgen Imaging Systems (P) Ltd., Chennai, India.

First edition: August 2010

10 9 8 7 6 5 4 3 2 1

Printed in the United States of America.

To Ela

Contents

Preface

Venture capital and private equity investing is a fascinating field. It involves providing capital to private businesses with an aim to accelerate their development. It is a form of risk-equity investing, where private investors support firms with a combination of know-how and capital in order to exploit market opportunities. In examining the meaning of this type of investing, it is important to distinguish between venture capital and private equity. Private equity refers to the provision of capital to develop new products and technologies, to enhance working capital, to affect acquisitions, to resolve ownership and management issues, or to strengthen the balance sheet. Venture capital, on the other hand, refers to capital co-invested alongside entrepreneurs for the purposes of providing capital and know-how to early-stage firms. Consequently, venture capital is often regarded as a subset of private equity. To simplify matters, this book uses the term "venture capital" as its primary description of investing into private firms.

The completion of a successful venture capital or private equity deal requires the deal to progress through a multistage process. This process is challenging to investors, as they must face a number of unique internal and external challenges along the way. This book provides a unique and comprehensive description of this process. The mechanics of processing venture capital and private equity deals are captured in an eight-stage model, consisting of deal generation, initial screening, due diligence phase I and internal feedback, pre-approval completions, due diligence phase II and internal approvals, deal completion, monitoring, and exit. The proposed model has a number of unique features. First, the investment process is described from the fund manager's perspective. Each description offers an inside look into a venture capital and private equity fund and defines the various approval processes that investors must undertake in consultation with their internal approval bodies (namely, the investment committee and supervisory board) in order to complete the deal and exit. Second, the model highlights the level of internal documentation needed throughout the life of any investment. Third, the model provides a clear definition of the differences between the specific stages that occur during the evaluation of an investee firm. Fourth, the model defines the investment process in terms of three interrelated channels of activity: document channel, information channel, and decision channel. Finally, it highlights the multidisciplinary nature of venture capital and private equity investing, which draws from many fields including finance, business law, strategic management, human resources management, psychology, and sociology.

This book is organized according to chapter. Chapter one provides an overview of venture capital and private equity by describing its objectives, stages of financing, and the organization of a typical fund. It also offers an entrepreneur's perspective on venture capital and private equity. Chapter two focuses on an overview of the venture capital and private equity investment process and describes the eight-stage investment model. In addition, this chapter also highlights the importance of the process in defining the competitive structure of the industry, and develops a typology of venture capital and private equity firms in the context of the adopted investment process. Chapters three–ten offer comprehensive discussions of each of the investment stages, while chapter eleven focuses on the challenges faced by the venture capital and private equity industry in the new millennium.

In addition to the primary content, readers will find a number of special features throughout the text. Each chapter begins with a brief description of a venture capital or private equity firm from a different geographic market, including Western economies and emerging markets. The funds were chosen in such a way as to provide readers with an understanding that venture capital and private equity firms may come in different shapes and forms, rely on different investment philosophies and target markets, employ various types of specialists, and focus on different financing techniques. These vignettes highlight the many differences between industry players around the world by providing key parameters and statistics (such as capital under management, number of deals and exits, most widely recognized deals, names of founding partners, etc.). In addition, information is provided to illuminate the fund's investment focus, operating philosophy, geographic orientation, management and staffing, and so on.

Other special features include the Practitioner's Corner, which provides readers with hands-on, practical perspectives on specific operating issues that occur inside of a venture capital or private equity fund. The practitioners' overviews specifically focus on "ratchet" mechanisms and exit. International Perspectives in Venture Capital is another feature found within, and focuses on providing readers with some exposure to issues faced in emerging markets. Three unique challenges—related to privatization deals, simplified forecasting methodology, and auditing procedures—are described in this feature. Last, the book includes a feature called Corporate Governance in Venture Capital, which aims to highlight the existence of numerous corporate governance challenges in the venture capital and private equity industry. Topics of discussion include the industry's code of ethics and specific cases where such ethics may be applied.

In addition to the special features described earlier, the book includes a number of unique descriptions of the venture capital and private equity process. Some of the most unique topics covered include venture capital and private equity negotiations (the book focuses on the dynamics of venture capital and private equity negotiations, and captures the essence of "value exchange" between entrepreneurs and venture capitalists beyond a description of trading zones and opportunities), business analysis (the book provides a unique framework for analyzing the commercial attractiveness of deals based on the 5M principles and targeted financial analysis), and corporate governance (it focuses on issues related to corporate governance in the venture capital and private equity industry).

This project could not have been completed without generous assistance from numerous "stakeholders." I would like to acknowledge the invaluable contributions made by over 30 investment officers from some of the leading venture capital and private equity firms around the world. Their assistance has allowed me to create a comprehensive, homogenous overview of the venture capital and private equity investment process that reflects investment practices from different geographic regions. I would also like to thank Douglas Cumming from the Schulich School of Business at York University and Thomas Hellmann from the Sauder School of Business at the University of British Columbia for helpful comments on the draft proposal for this book; Kyle Lougheed for editorial assistance; Heather Johnston for allowing time off from Brandon University; Will Schmidt for insightful comments on investment committees; and Jerzy Strzelecki for discussing industry trends. Last, I would like to thank the staff of Macmillan, especially Laurie Harting, Heather Faulls, and Laura Lancaster as well as Rohini Krishnan from Newgen Imaging Systems, without whom this project could not have been completed.

Darek Klonowski

Kohlberg Kravis Roberts and Co.

Key characteristics

Year founded:	1976
Founding partners:	Henry R. Kravis and George R. Roberts
Number of limited partners:	N/A
Geographic coverage:	North America (5 locations), Europe (2), Asia (5), Australia (1)
Headquarter location:	New York (USA)
Focus (if any):	Leveraged buyouts
Funds under management:	$59.3 billion
Number of completed deals/ IPO exits:	165/N/A
Private/public:	Private/public*
Most publicly recognized deals:	Duracell, Safeway, Yellow Pages, Toys R Us, Shopper's Drug Mart, Sealy
Number of investment professionals:	~80

Kohlberg Kravis Roberts and Co. (KKR) includes publicly held firms such as KKR Financial Holding LLC (NYSE New York: KFN) and KKR Private Equity Investors LP (Euronext Amsterdam: KPE).

Kohlberg Kravis Roberts is one of the world's most widely recognized private equity firms and an expert in leveraged buyouts. It is a true industry leader, with nearly $60 billion under management. The firm is committed to 14 private equity funds.

KKR's investment philosophy is based on seeking out high quality investments with strong management teams, predictable cash flows, leading and defendable market positions, and superior growth prospects. Such an investment approach allows it to utilize its expertise in leveraged buyouts. KKR's landmark buyouts include some of the largest buyout transactions such as Energy Future Holdings ($48.8 billion), RJR Nabisco ($31.4 billion), and Alliance Boots (£12.4 billion).

KKR is known for its active role in assisting portfolio firms. Its staff of over 80 professionals includes many former CEOs and CFOs from some of the leading industrial firms. This strong pool of in-house operational talent allows the fund to make their investee firms more competitive and profitable.

The firm's owners, investment professionals, and senior executives have shown a strong commitment to building the firm's private equity business over the years. The parties have jointly committed approximately $1.9 billion to the business.

Source: www.kkr.com.

Chapter 1

Introduction

The development of new entrepreneurial ventures plays a key role in shaping any national economy. Entrepreneurial firms are a source of growth and innovation in the industry for owners and provide jobs for the local population. They are also believed to offset economic declines and help to restructure existing industry. A healthy entrepreneurial sector is critical to any national economy and imperative to economic growth for several reasons. First, it is estimated that six out of every ten jobs are created by entrepreneurial firms. Second, young firms are spearheading the industrial transformation from traditional industries into high technology sectors. Third, entrepreneurial firms are at the forefront of developing innovations with a clear competitive advantage; they are known to commit more capital and resources to research and development when compared with more established corporate entities. Last, entrepreneurial firms are making significant inroads in developing global markets.

Entrepreneurial firms face two major problems. The first concerns access to finance, which places particular constraint on a firm's ability to increase the level of technology in their business. The second concern is access to know-how. Newly established entrepreneurial firms with founders inexperienced in a commercial environment may posses multiple shortcomings with respect to their managerial skills and abilities, while young firms struggle to run their businesses. Most young entrepreneurial firms—even those with sizable operations and sales—may not employ functional specialists, especially in the areas of finance and accounting; consequently, they rarely prepare business plans or formal budgets.

Another department often neglected by inexperienced entrepreneurs is marketing and promotion. Additionally, there are two key moments in a firm's life cycle when "know-how" is required. In the early stages of development, beginner firms are often "virtual" in their development; there is only an idea, concept, or invention driving the ultimate development of a full business. The key problem to address at this stage of development is business survival. Firms at a later stage of development require a different type of assistance and support. The key issue for these firms is management of growth and expansion with an aim to ensuring the sustainability of the business in the long term and the successful transition of the firm to another stage of development.

The problems of access to finance and the provision of know-how are closely related: access to finance is necessary to address operational challenges, and effective managerial skills assure proper utilization of capital. The provision of capital without proper managerial assistance is likely to result in a lack of development for firms (lack of know-how often leads to limited investment, which, in turn, leads to the limited growth of the business), more sensitivity to external factors, and a business potential that is unlikely to be captured. Providing know-how without capital is likely to lead to the immediate downfall of the business, a "freeze" of the private initiative, and lack of propensity for taking business risk. In short, the unintended consequences of these two challenges can initiate a chain reaction leading to business failure.

The aforementioned problems can be addressed through the introduction of special types of investors called venture capitalists. Venture capitalists can resolve the dual problem of inadequate know-how and access to finance; they offer funding, technical and managerial support, and networking capabilities, and have become central to the development of entrepreneurial firms around the world. Venture capitalists not only support young entrepreneurial firms, they also provide their expertise and capital at different points in a firm's life cycle.

Definition of Venture Capital

Though its definition has evolved over the years, venture capital is generally defined as capital provided to private businesses aimed at accelerating a firm's development through access to capital and a wide range of business support services. The Webster's Dictionary defines "venture capital" as "a very risky investment." The Collins English Dictionary, defines venture capital as "capital for investment, which may easily be lost in risky projects, but also can provide high returns."

In examining the meaning of this type of investing, it is important to distinguish between industry terms that are used interchangeably, such as "venture capital" and "private equity." The European Private Equity and Venture Capital Association (EVCA) defines private equity as equity capital provided to firms not quoted on a stock exchange. This association further underlines that private equity can be used to develop new products and technologies, to support working capital needs, to make acquisitions, or to strengthen a company's balance sheet. It can also be used to deal with ownership and management issues. On the other hand, EVCA defines venture capital as capital co-invested alongside the entrepreneur for the purpose of providing capital and know-how to early-stage businesses (i.e., seed, start-up, or first stage of expansion). Venture capital is often regarded as a subset of private equity, referring more to investments made during the launch stages of a business.

The popularity of the term venture capital reflects the fact that in the early days of direct financial participation in private firms, early-stage firms received this type of financing. There are also geographical factors: North American investors used to prefer investing in early-stage firms (as confirmed by their investment into early-stage firms as a percentage of total investment); hence, their investments were increasingly regarded as venture capital. Comparatively, European investors historically pursued later-stage expansion deals; consequently, they preferred the term private equity.

To simplify matters, this book will use the term venture capital as its primary description of investing into private firms. Consequently, it will use the term "venture capitalist" (and not "private equity investor") to denote the manager of a venture capital or private equity firm who holds ultimate responsibility for the management of the fund's investments in specific firms and its portfolio of investee firms.

Venture capital can be most simply defined as risk-equity investing. It is an activity by which investors support firms with a combination of two important components—"know-how" and capital—in order to exploit market opportunities. Venture capitalists aim to achieve long-term, above-average returns.

Over the lifetime of a venture capital firm, venture capitalists aim to realize net returns on an entire portfolio of investee firms. These returns are expected to exceed the possible returns available from alternative investment possibilities (i.e., from the stock exchange). In fact, venture capitalists need to achieve above-average returns to justify the risks associated with young entrepreneurial firms, risky undertakings (i.e., new product development or expansion into an unknown geographic region), and the long periods of illiquidity inherent to venture capital investing. The strong returns expected by venture capitalists also need to cover the operating costs of the fund (from 1 to 2 percent of the value of the fund per annum, charged against the capital contributed by those institutions providing capital to the managers) and venture capitalists' own costs (which take the form of a carried interest). Since venture capitalists make long-term investments in the entrepreneurial firms they invest in, the aggregate value of their equity positions in these firms must significantly increase in order to provide net returns to limited partners (LPs). If a venture capitalist expects to achieve returns on an entire portfolio of firms in the range of 20–30 percent, any successes must also compensate for the underperforming firms and other additional costs. Each dollar invested in a portfolio of firms must multiply by 2.5 times in five years (the average holding period for venture capital firms) to achieve a compounded 20 percent rate of return, and by over 3.7 times to achieve a 30 percent compounded return. Table 1.1 presents a simple matrix describing the internal rate of return achievable under the assumption of the years spent holding the investment and the achieved cash-on-cash return.

Venture capitalists, who manage investments on behalf of LPs, have two constraints on their activities: time and money. To address the issue of an optimal allocation of time, venture capitalists generally attempt to focus their efforts on a specific industry, geographic region, or firms' stage of development. There are two investment models used. The first approach is based on the assumption that a careful evaluation of investment prospects (based on detailed deal negotiations, the preparation of comprehensive legal documents, countless revisions of the business plan, and the involvement of external experts) will result in fewer

Table 1.1 The internal rate of return (IRR) matrix expressed in percentages given the assumptions of the years holding the investment and the cash-on-cash return

Years	Cash-on-cash multiple								
	2x	2.5x	3x	3.5x	4x	5x	6x	8x	10x
2	41	58	73	87	100	124	145	183	216
3	26	36	44	52	59	71	82	100	115
4	19	26	32	37	41	50	57	68	78
5	15	20	25	28	32	38	43	52	58
6	12	16	20	23	26	31	35	41	47
7	10	14	17	20	22	26	29	35	39
8	09	12	15	17	19	22	25	30	33
9	08	11	13	15	17	20	22	26	29
10	07	10	12	13	15	17	20	23	26

investment mistakes and superior returns. Venture capital firms that subscribe to such an approach take their time and make fewer deals. On the other hand, there are venture capital firms that believe in the "laws of statistics," or the philosophy that certain deals will under-perform regardless of the amount of time spent on due diligence. Such firms also believe that writing comprehensive, all encompassing legal documents is counterproductive, as no legal documents will effectively save the deal if the investee firm proves unsuccessful. As a result, these venture capital firms complete more transactions. While there is no academic research to confirm which approach is superior, most venture capitalists appear to follow a "two-six-two" formula: two superior investments, six single-digit or no-return investments, and two write-offs.

Types of Financing for Firms

Firms generally rely upon two types of financing: internal and external. Internal sources of financing are limited, and can be generated by the firm itself. If the firm has been operating for some time and is profitable, it can support its own operations from internally generated cash flow. If the firm is unprofitable, it can manage its working capital in such a way that it is able to pay its liabilities on time. The firm can also invite its existing shareholders to contribute additional capital into the firm. In such a case, the existing shareholders would generally subscribe to new capital in proportion to their ownership stake in the firm (on a pro rata basis). The following section describes the most common types of financing.

First, firms can obtain financing by selling their shares in the stock exchange (through an initial public offering, an IPO, on the primary market, or through a subsequent offer of its shares in the secondary market). However, this is an option unavailable to most firms. Larger firms that have been operating for a few years and have a track record of growing sales and profits are ideal candidates for this type of financing. These firms are leaders in their respective marketplace seeking additional capital to expand their operations, acquire other firms in the sector, or develop new products. A founder's desire to realize profits (i.e., cash-out) or obtain high visibility in the marketplace through an IPO may also serve as a motivator to go public.

Second, firms can borrow capital from financial institutions (i.e., banks). Obtaining external finance from a bank is challenging—banks do not tolerate risk well. Contrary to general public opinion, banks may not be as friendly to business owners, particularly toward new firms that want to expand their products, build new facilities, or develop markets outside of their home market. The process of approving the loan is time consuming. In addition, banks require collateral that can exceed the value of the initial loan by two–three times. When firms get into financial troubles, banks are often quick to "pull the plug," or at best refer the troubled case to the bank's workout department (often located away from the local market, at the bank's headquarters), where the firm effectively becomes one of many nonperforming loans. From this pool of troubled loans, the bank tries to recover a certain percentage of funds, not necessarily being concerned about which firm the loan is recovered from. In many instances, the firm loses its relationship with a local banker, who initially approved the loan.

Third, equipment manufacturers and product suppliers may be willing to offer preferential payment terms to the firm. An extended payment term can effectively act as a substitute for a bank loan. While this is not a typical form of financing, many firms are able to manage their external relationships in such a way that they can effectively generate cash to support expansion. This facility may not be available to young firms.

Fourth, some firms operating in certain sectors of the economy can rely on preferential treatment from the government. This assistance may range from a direct payment to the firm to a reduction in taxes through preferential tax treatments (i.e., tax credits) or loans (often below a market rate). The nature of government-based programs, however, is that they are uncertain, limited, and politically driven; they are not sustainable for the government in the long term. In addition, it takes an extended period of time to apply for and subsequently receive the assistance.

Fifth, the firm can sell its shares to another firm (i.e., to a strategic investor from the same sector). While such a transaction does not create additional capital for the firm right away (since the acquirer only purchases an ownership stake in the firm), the new shareholder may be able to participate in subsequent capital increases. There is also the challenge of finding a new partner to assume an ownership stake in the business. Larger firms, for example, prefer to take a majority stake in a business, often leading to a lack of control for the founding entrepreneur.

Finally, there is venture capital.

The demand for these particular forms of financing depends on the firm's level of development, its profitability, the nature of the industry, investment programs, and the tolerance to risk shown by the providers of finance. While larger firms can generally take advantage of all financing options, smaller entrepreneurial firms have fewer opportunities. Table 1.2 summarizes the choices available to firms in various stages of development, and confirms that venture capital is perhaps the most flexible form of financing, though variations exist within different geographical markets.

Classic venture capital can be distinguished from other types of financing in several ways. Venture capital is equity oriented, which means that capital is usually provided in exchange for equity rather than debt. The most popular security held by venture capitalists is a convertible preferred share. A convertible preferred share is a hybrid security that combines the preferential protection of value offered by a preferred share with the upside potential offered by a common share. Venture capital is often subordinate to other types of financing and is not secured through any assets of the entrepreneurs or the investee firm. This means that venture capital has a lower priority of repayment in the event of problems. For example, if the investee firm becomes bankrupt, winds down its operations, is sold under distress, or experiences financial difficulties, venture capitalists may recover very little of or outright lose their entire investment.

Table 1.2   The possibility of financing through a variety of sources

	Early stages			Expansion stages		
	Seed	Start-up	First stage	Second stage	Third stage	Fourth stage
Demand for capital	Low	High	High	High/ medium	Medium	Low
Possibility of Financing by:						
Founder's capital	High	High	Medium	Low	Low	Low
Debt/bank loans	Low	Low	Low	Medium	High	High
Stock market	Low	Low	Medium	Medium	High	Low
Supplier/manufacturer credits	Low	Low	Low	Medium	High	Low
Government programs	High	High	High	Medium	Low	Low
Net profits	Low	Low	Low	High	High	High
Sale of shares/capital increase	Low	Low	Medium	High	High	High
Venture capital	Medium	High	High	High	High	Low

Venture capital is highly selective in its choice of investee firms. Traditionally, venture capitalists provide financing to one out of every one hundred business plans they review (venture capitalists need to review about five hundred business plans just to make five investments). This underscores a fundamental point that venture capitalists succeed by efficiently allocating the capital with which they have been entrusted among their investee firms. Consequently, it is not surprising that venture capitalists attempt to provide capital to firms that are highly profitable, have above-average future growth prospects, maintain a strong market share and significant competitive advantages over their rivals, and are led by a superior management team. On the other hand, venture capitalists tend to avoid firms requiring significant capital resources, competing in markets with dominant market players, and investing in small firms with commoditized products. The selective nature of venture capital investing aims to assure above-average returns while minimizing investment risk. To achieve this, venture capitalists methodically investigate each firm and its future prospects. The due diligence process takes weeks or months to complete and aims to address the risks associated with the business. Venture capital firms also make a medium to long-term commitment to their investee firms. Venture capitalists, on average, hold their investment for a period of three– five years, after which they seek to dispose of their shares. This holding period is normally synchronized with the firm's achievement of peak value and may be longer for young entrepreneurial firms that require more time to develop and grow.

Another important feature of venture capital is illiquidity. Venture capitalists participate in their investee firms, on average, for a period of three–five years. This time is dedicated to growing the business and achieving a suitable exit. The lack of liquidity is reflected in lower valuations of the businesses and a higher expected return to compensate venture capitalists for their inability to sell their holdings at just any point in the process (higher perceived risks mean higher discount rates applied when discounting the firm's stream of cash flows; higher discount rates translate into lower business valuations). A contractual agreement is drawn to assure a proper incubation period for the business, and the resulting illiquidity of the investment acts as a deterrent against venture capitalists' being opportunistic or having caprice to exit from an investment too early. Venture capitalists may be tempted to take such actions, especially during the fundraising period, when exit achievement is critical to raising new capital. The second motivator relates to how venture capital firms need capital to support their own operations and to be in a position to provide follow-on investments to existing portfolio firms. Some venture capital firms are precluded from using realized funds to put into other deals and support the cost of their current operations.

Venture capitalists make money from growth in the value of a business rather than through a pre-negotiated return with preset timing for the repayment of capital. Dividends are not normally paid out through the holding period and all profits are reinvested into the development of new products or services, the building of new production facilities, the acquisition of other businesses, or the strengthening of distribution capabilities. While normal return expectations in Western countries range from the high teens to low twenties over the holding period, these expectations double in emerging markets where the political, operational, and financial risks are higher. Venture capitalists normally try to achieve returns higher than those available in public markets to compensate for their high tolerance for risk and illiquidity.

Implicit in the definition of venture capital is a commitment to contribute more than capital to the process of working with a business. Venture capitalists have a degree of active involvement in the management of the firm, which receives capital. Some venture capitalists argue that they are in the "business of building businesses," and such hands-on support is the cornerstone of venture capitalist involvement in investee firms. Venture capital is the business of participating as an active partner in the management of a business through active involvement on the board of directors and, occasionally, as a manager of last resort (venture capitalists temporarily assume the roles of business managers, CEOs, CFOs, etc.). In interactions with investee firms, venture capitalists aim for high ethical standards (see box 1.1).

Box 1.1   Ethical considerations in venture capital: The European Venture Capital and Private Equity Association and the code of ethics

In 1983, the European Venture Capital and Private Equity Association (EVCA) issued its first set of guidelines with respect to the desired conduct of its members. These guidelines are captured in the form of the code of ethics. The EVCA prides itself in promoting the highest ethical and professional standards within the private equity industry. In order to continue to provide its members with a self-regulatory framework, the EVCA has issued a number of other guides related to corporate governance (EVCA Corporate Governance Guidelines), valuation (International Private Equity and Venture Capital Valuation Guidelines), fund operations (The Governing Principles), and financial reporting (EVCA Reporting Guidelines). The EVCA also developed the Placement Agents Supplementary Code of Conduct, which provides an outline of conduct for placement agents or intermediaries that have become important stakeholders in the private equity and venture capital industry in Europe.

In 2006, EVCA established its code of conduct with three major objectives in mind. First, it wanted to restate and update its principles from those issued in 1983. Venture capital and private equity have evolved over the years and the challenges faced by venture capitalists have changed. Membership in EVCA has also increased, and the organization now represents a more diverse base of firms and investment professionals than it once did. Second, EVCA wished to establish and assert a common set of guidelines for their members to use as directives in their daily interactions with limited partners, investee firms, and colleagues in the industry. It is important that all the stakeholders in the industry abide by a common set of business practices. Last, the code was established to form the basis for any disciplinary action taken toward members that chose to violate the professional conduct expected by EVCA.

The code is based on six principles related to integrity, keeping promises, conflicts of interest, fairness, confidentiality, and behavior friendly to the industry. The first principle relates to maintaining and acting with integrity and maintaining trust as a fundamental cornerstone of interpersonal relations between venture capitalists and entrepreneurs. Keeping promises is a further extension of trust. The venture capital industry often operates on verbal and written promises—these expectations begin early in the process when the two sides sign an informal letter of terms (called a terms sheet), which, although not legally binding, constitutes a strong moral agreement. Disclosing conflicts of interest is important in any business and especially in the venture capital industry. Venture capitalists expect this behavior from their investee firms and should abide themselves by the same disclosure standards. Acting in fairness means conducting oneself appropriately and with adherence to agreed-upon rules, mechanisms, and principles. This is very important, as the circumstances of limited partners, investee firms, and venture capitalists often change—all stakeholders need to expect that whatever issues or conflicts arise will be addressed in a fair manner. Since venture capitalists analyze many businesses (often in the same industry), they need be especially careful to maintain confidentiality over sensitive information they receive from investee firms and potential investment candidates. Last, venture capitalists are expected to exhibit friendly and non-harmful behavior toward their colleagues in the industry. The competitive nature of the venture capital industry and the pursuit of returns for limited partners should not cloud venture capitalists' judgment about the overall well-being of the venture capital and private equity industry.

The most important characteristic of venture capital is its focus on the disposal of shares at the end of a holding period. This is commonly described as an "exit." Venture capitalists must be reasonably certain that they can sell their shares. There are two preferred exit routes. First, venture capitalists may be able to sell their stake to a strategic investor (likely an international corporation looking to expand its production capabilities, acquire a business with a unique product or service offering, or access a desired client group). Second, venture capitalists can sell shares to the public by offering them on the stock exchange. Many venture capitalists spend a considerable amount of time and resources on this exit issue and may not choose to pursue an attractive business if the exit opportunity appears weak.

Venture capital is a cyclical business. This cycle usually begins with a small number of venture capital firms making successful investments and exits. At this stage, investment opportunities are easily generated and venture capitalists are able to acquire investee firms at discount valuations. Encouraged by the initial successes of these market participants, new venture capital firms are established and financial investors (who provide capital to venture capital firms for management) are willing to dedicate significant amounts of capital toward the market. Increased amounts of capital are made available for investment purposes and ultimately create more competition for attractive investment opportunities. The deals become more expensive, thereby putting downward pressure on potential returns. In effect, "too many dollars are chasing too few deals." Consequently, many venture capital firms either complete transactions at valuations that are too high (resulting in limited or no returns) or make investments into less attractive companies, risking operational problems, liquidation, and even bankruptcy. These unattractive prospects discourage venture capital firms and encourage them to leave the market. Over time, the amount of capital available in the market declines and a new cycle begins.

Venture capital cycles do not always coincide with economic cycles (measured by GDP movements), but movements in GDP drive firms' operational and strategic choices. Experienced venture capitalists realize that these cycles impact an entrepreneurial firm's financial performance and result in a positive or negative exit prospect.

Venture Capital and Stages of Financing

Venture capital can generally be divided into two major stages: the financing of young entrepreneurial firms and the expansion stages of the firm's development. The early-stage financing includes seed financing, start-up financing, and first-stage financing. The expansion stage includes subsequent stages of financing. In practice, venture capitalists are involved in a variety of different types of financing, including the provision of start-up finance, the provision of secondary and subsequent rounds of capital for later stages of the firm's expansion, and the financing of management buy-outs and buy-ins. These types of financing generally occur in cycles. For this reason, specific types of venture capital financing can be categorized with respect to the point in the firm's life cycle when the financing is provided. The key characteristics of each stage of venture capital financing are discussed in the following paragraphs. The distinguishing features of each stage may include the completeness of the management team, product development and maturity, operational risks, financial performance, and future prospects. Figure 1.1 presents a simplified landscape of the main forms of venture capital. The key criteria selected for mapping the different types of venture capital financing were the capital need of the firm and the "hands-on" managerial assistance requirement provided by venture capitalists to the firm. The oval around each stage in figure 1.1 represents the breadth of hands-on assistance and the need for capital.

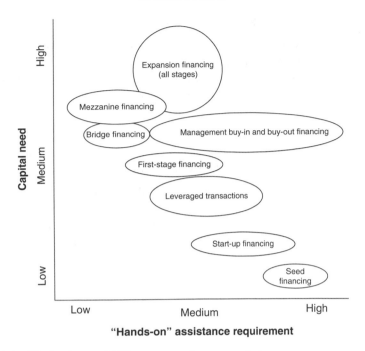

Figure 1.1 The landscape of different types of venture capital.

Seed financing is generally provided to firms that have not been able to convert their concept into a workable business plan. Capital is deployed to finance market research, a product feasibility study, or the development of a complete business plan. The firm may not have established its legal status at this stage. The financing in this stage is small (generally less than one hundred thousand dollars), with the firms generally focusing on technical issues over market orientation.

Start-up financing is provided to legally established firms that have been working on a product prototype and are ready to test its market potential. The total financing needs at this stage can be equal to a few hundred thousand dollars. If the product prototype test proves successful, the process of developing a management team begins. This process is a prerequisite for obtaining subsequent rounds of financing.

First-stage financing is provided to firms that have successfully passed the market test and are ready to commence production. At this stage, the entrepreneurial firm needs all the necessary business components to affect production and sales. This includes building production facilities, hiring necessary production staff and management personnel, developing distribution structures, engaging into marketing and promotional campaigns, and more. Later stage or *expansion financing* (and its phases two–four) is geared toward firms operating at different stages of development. These firms generate strong growth in sales, but may not yet be profitable. Capital at this stage is directed toward working capital (a significant increase in working capital is required when there is a rapid increase in revenue) or business expansion.

Mezzanine financing is capital provided to a firm in the form of a hybrid of debt and equity and is normally used to finance expansion projects (thus granting the financiers the right to convert to an equity interest). This type of financing is provided to the borrower very quickly with little due diligence on the part of venture capital firm and with limited collateral from the borrower. It is also aggressively priced and expensive to the borrower firm. The ultimate return for venture capitalists may come from structured interest payments and an upside potential from holding an equity stake in the business.

Bridge financing is directed at firms looking to go public. These firms require capital well before they can obtain listing on the stock exchange.

Venture capital is also used in other specific situations where the management is leading the purchase of shares. For example, *management buyouts* involve the provision of capital to enable the management of an existing business to acquire existing product lines or the entire business. Conversely, *management buy-ins* focus on capital provided by venture capitalists to a manager or a group of managers from outside of the firm to buy into it. Such buy-ins often occur in situations where larger multinational firms have decided to sell off parts of their business. *Leveraged transactions* generally involve a buy-out event where an existing or newly established firm's capital structure is based on the use of high level of debt secured against the firm's assets (or, sometimes, assets and shares).

Venture capitalists can commence their relationships with firms at any stage of their development. Some venture capitalists prefer to obtain exposure to firms in the early stages of development while others prefer to participate in subsequent rounds of financing when the firm's operational risks are mitigated or entirely removed.

This strategy and focus often reflects the initial strategy of venture capitalists established during the fundraising process. In many instances, venture capitalists provide follow-on investments that result from the firm's meeting its operational targets and financial milestones. In other situations, venture capitalists must make more difficult decisions, such as whether or not to provide an additional round of financing or allow the firm to go bankrupt.

Structure of a Typical Venture Capital Fund

Venture capital firms are commonly structured in the form of limited partnerships. In a limited partnership, there are two classes of partners: general and limited. The former actively participate in the management of the business. Limited partners usually contribute capital and share in the profits, but take no part in running the business—they are passive investors. As a result, general partners (GPs) usually contract for a more favorable allocation of ownership and profits than otherwise would be possible. They have unlimited liability for the partnership activities. Limited partners are only liable for the amounts they contribute into the partnership.

In the venture capital setting, managers and employees in the venture capital firm jointly serve as GPs and are responsible for day-to-day management of the fund. In a typical venture capital firm, LPs (i.e., financial institutions, multinational corporations, private individuals, university endowments, pension funds managers, etc.) contribute about 99 percent of the capital of the fund. They generally request that managers and employees (the GP) make a meaningful contribution to the venture capital firm, equal to about 1 percent of the fund's capital. As an example, for the size of a fund equal to five hundred million dollars, the GP has to contribute five million dollars at the outset—a large amount of capital, especially for managers new to the venture capital industry. The financial contribution of GPs to the partnership is based on the principle of "winning together and losing together." If the GPs did not make a financial contribution into the firm, only the LPs would be affected if the firm suffered problems. This financial contribution assures that GPs have some capital at risk.

The typical structure of a venture capital firm is presented in figure 1.2. As previously mentioned, the venture capital firm is established as a limited partnership, with LPs and the GP. There

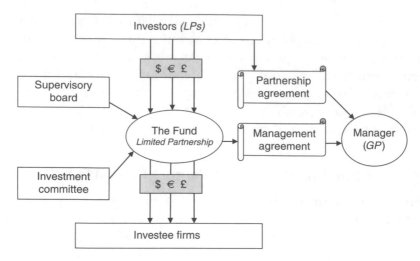

Figure 1.2   The typical structure of a venture capital firm.

are usually two agreements in place. The first one—the partnership agreement between the GP and the LPs—establishes the
broad terms of the GP's compensation structure. It also includes
various covenants that restrict a GP from engaging in certain
activities. The second agreement—the management agreement
between the limited partnership and the GP—describes the operational aspects of the cooperation between the two groups. This
outlines the roles and scope of duties for the investment committee and supervisory board (LPs tend to appoint their representatives to this monitoring function). The investment committee,
with the recommendation of the GP or fund managers, recom-
mends investments for completion. The investment committee
also raises critical issues for investigation. The supervisory board
usually meets quarterly and oversees the financial aspects of the
operation.

   Limited partners—the ultimate cash investors in the venture
capital firm—effectively purchase investment management service from the GP. By investing directly into the partnership and
indirectly into the partnership's investee firms, LPs delegate the
activities of selecting, structuring, monitoring, and exiting from
investee firms to realize the return. In turn, venture capitalists can
raise additional capital if they are able to consistently provide superior returns to the LPs. Limited partners do not contribute all of
their capital into the venture capital firm at once. Instead, these

contributions are staged to reflect the rate of investment completed by the fund.

In terms of the contractual and financial arrangements between LPs and GPs, LPs pay an annual management fee of 1–2.5 percent of the capital committed to the fund. If the venture capital firm raised five hundred million dollars and negotiated a fee structure of 2 percent, the fund manager—the GP—would receive ten million dollars in annual expenditure. Assuming that the venture capital firm is established for a period of ten years, the total chargeable expenses equal one hundred million dollars over the life of the fund. This means that the fund manager effectively has four hundred million dollars to commit to actual deals that need to produce a return. The GP, at minimum, has to make an annual compounded return of 2.5 percent over ten years on all of its investments just to be able to recover the initial value of the capital raised. Limited partners generally receive 80 percent of the profits of the fund, plus any amount above the initial value (i.e., five hundred million dollars), while GPs receive 20 percent of the profits (this is called *carried interest*)—a potentially lucrative arrangement if the venture capital firm performs well. This upside profit potential for a venture capital firm lies at the heart of a firm's motivational structure.

Another important component of the financial arrangements between LPs and venture capitalists is the hurdle rate: a rate of return that must be achieved by LPs on the initial capital (i.e., five hundred million dollars) before the GP is entitled to receive its carried interest allocation of 20 percent of proceeds upon the realization of the fund. The hurdle rate is commonly set at the level of risk-free rate of return (i.e., the rate of return offered on Treasury Bills). While first-time venture capital firms normally have a limited (1 or 2 percent) to no hurdle rate, an established fund's rate oscillates around 5 percent.

Let's briefly examine the impact of the hurdle rate upon the GP's financial performance and carried interest. Let's assume that we have three cases. In the first, the venture capital firm raised five hundred million dollars; there is no hurdle rate, and the venture capital fund's realized value is equal to six hundred million dollars after ten years of operations. In the second case, all other parameters stay the same while the GP expects a hurdle rate of 1 percent. In the third case, the hurdle rate has increased to 2 percent. Table 1.3 presents these calculations.

Table 1.3 The calculations of general partner's proceeds under different hurdle rate assumptions (in $ or as indicated otherwise)

	Case 1	Case 2	Case 3
Initial capital (Mn)	500	500	500
Realized value (Mn)	600	600	600
Hurdle rate (%)	0	1	2
Life of the venture capital firm (years)	10	10	10
Profit split between LPs and GP (%)	80/20	80/20	80/20
Profit to GP (Mn)	20.0	9.5	0.0
Profit to LPs (Mn)	80.0	90.5	100.0
LPs' implied proceeds from the hurdle rate (Mn)	0	52.3	100.0
LPs' profits upon 80/20 allocation (Mn)	80.0	38.2	0.0
Total proceeds to LPs above initial capital (Mn)	80.0	90.5	100.0

Note: For Case 2, the value of profit to the GP is calculated as follows: $500 million $\times (1 + 0.01)^{10}$ = $500 million $\times 1.1046$ = $552.3 million. $600 million − $552.3 million = $47.7 million. Allocation to the GP is equal to $47.7 million $\times 20\%$ = $9.5 million. Allocation to the LPs is equal to a combination of proceeds from the hurdle rate (i.e., $52.3 million) and proceeds from the 80 percent allocation of the fund's profits accrued to the LPs ($38.2 million). This amounts to a total of $90.5 million. To calculate GP's profits, equal to $9.5 million, simply deduct the allocation to the GP from the $100 million ($100 million less $90.5 million). For Case 3, the value of LPs' theoretical proceeds from the hurdle rate is equal to $109.5 million. However, since the total realized value of the fund is equal to $600 million ($100 million above the initial value), the LPs only receive $100 million from the hurdle rate.

The results demonstrate a simple point, namely that a small difference in the amount of the hurdle rate (even from 0 to 1 percent) can make a significant difference to the ultimate profits of the general manager. In the second case, the venture capitalists earn $9.5 million with a hurdle rate of only 1 percent. When that rate increases to 2 percent, venture capitalists receive no carried interest.

There are interesting industry trends relating to the establishment of financial arrangements between venture capitalists and LPs. First, there is a trend toward lowered management fees. Limited partners realize that the fees represent a significant portion of the committed capital; a significant size of the fee may alone constitute an attractive compensation scheme to venture capital fund managers, thereby reducing their appetite for risk. Second, LPs prefer to set the fees on a variable basis to reflect the actual amount of invested capital. This encourages GPs to invest capital as quickly as possible. Third, some LPs set fees to reflect the ongoing value of the fund. This represents additional incentive for venture capitalists to focus on the value creation process.

Fourth, the commitment of venture capitalists may vary during a venture capital firm's life cycle. Many LPs argue that the workload is front-loaded while the latter phases of the fund's life require less work due to monitoring and exiting activities; as a result, venture capitalists should be able to lower their fees at the end of the fund's life.

Entrepreneurs' Perceptions of Venture Capital

A firm receives venture capital financing in exchange for an equity stake in the firm. This capital comes in the form of convertible preferred shares, common shares, or other forms of security. It is always important for the firm seeking external financing to evaluate all possible financing alternatives (this is especially true with respect to debt instruments that do not dilute the founder's ownership position in the firm). Early-stage entrepreneurial firms often have no alternative to venture capital financing—they are not profitable, they have limited assets, and their business prospects are uncertain. The following sections explore some of the advantages and disadvantages of venture capital from the point of view of entrepreneurs.

Benefits of Venture Capital

Venture capital offers a number of tangible advantages for the firm and its founding entrepreneurs. First, venture capital financing is a permanent capital that does not require repayment; no regular interim payments are expected throughout the relationship with the venture capital firm. Second, additional capital increases the firm's creditworthiness by increasing its capital base, thereby improving its net asset value. This becomes important for the firm when seeking additional bank financing or leasing arrangements. Banks or other financial institutions often make increasing the firm's capital a prerequisite to receive bank financing. Third, venture capital financing often improves the firm's credibility with the firm's customers, material suppliers, distributors, banks, and other financial institutions. This credibility is based on the assumption that venture capitalists are highly selective in their choices and only invest in firms with strong potential for growth. The firm's stakeholders know that venture capitalists only benefit if the investee firm continues to be successful, and this serves as a credible endorsement for the firm. Fourth, the capital provided by venture capitalists does not require the firm to pay out dividends, ensuring that the founders can operate their business without operational constraints. Venture capitalists are only there to ensure that the pre-agreed business plan is achieved and any operational issues are addressed in a timely and effective manner. This premise of "founder independence" may be revisited in a circumstance where a firm is seen to under-perform. In such an instance, venture capitalists may invoke some of their rights allowing them to make corrective actions. A fifth and often unappreciated advantage to entrepreneurs is that venture capitalists do not provide personal guarantees or collateral from the founders. Consequently, the founders' personal assets remain intact. On occasion, venture capitalists may ask for a personal contribution in cash, meaningful to the founder; this may occur during seed or start-up financing and is unlikely to occur at later stages.

It is also important to discuss some of the "softer" contributions made by venture capitalists to the firm. These nonmonetary contributions have become increasingly important, especially for younger firms looking to reach their market potential and increase their value. Venture capitalists serve as invaluable external consultants to the founders and their firms, preventing firms—both younger and more mature—from making costly business mistakes. The nature of the due diligence process—which requires entrepreneurs to answer multiple questions, rethink their expansion plans, and to revise their financial forecasts—often forces entrepreneurs to consider potential business risks and draw back-up plans to avert them in the future. As a part of their daily interactions with investee firms, venture capitalists can provide investee firms with access to their networks of contacts. Networking is often regarded as one of the most valuable tools for use in "nourishing" firms. These business contacts may include an in-house network of technical specialists, accounting, taxation, and legal experts, and functional specialists (especially in the areas of marketing and promotions). Venture capitalists also have a wide range of industrial contacts. Strategic partnerships or alliances with larger multinational corporations, access to new technologies and know-how, and personnel support programs can all develop out of these contacts. Venture capitalists believe in developing a strong and committed management team with a long-term perspective and have an interest in building a market leader. Consequently, venture capitalists ensure that the firm employs the best available talent in functional areas and that there are no gaps in senior or middle management teams. These management teams are then given proper incentive through performance-based stock option programs and bonuses. In fact, venture capitalists often agree with the founders to establish a pool of shares dedicated solely to the management team.

Venture capitalists serve as valuable partners to firms and are interested in the long-term viability and success of the business well beyond the anticipated time horizon. While profit is the primary motivator for venture capitalists, they often display an interest in long-term business growth. Even if venture capitalists ultimately dispose of their ownership stake in a business, they need to ensure that there is sufficient upside potential in growth of revenues and profits for the new buyer or the public market to view the investment as attractive. The value placed on growth inherent to venture capital investing sits in contrast to other potential financial or non-financial investors interested in speculative investment opportunities and who often display short-term appetites for healthy returns (i.e., hedge funds).

Drawbacks of Venture Capital

The most pronounced and obvious disadvantage of accepting venture capital is the founders' dilution of ownership. During negotiations, venture capitalists determine the entry value of the business and assume an ownership stake on the basis of the capital provided to the firm. The founders provide venture capitalists with an opportunity to earn almost unlimited profit potential or return from their investment. This uncapped upside potential is what truly motivates venture capitalists and is the driving force behind their risk-taking behavior. Had the founders not accepted another partner (i.e., a venture capitalist) into their business, they themselves would be the ones to achieve the upside potential.

The second disadvantage of venture capital is inherently connected with the first, namely that in the moment of an ultimate sale of the business in the future, the acceptance of venture capital is more expensive than debt. To illustrate this point, let's assume that there are two firms: Firm A and Firm B. Firm A raises debt, while B accepts venture capital financing. We can assume that the two forms of financing (debt versus equity) provide the same amount of capital and assure the same growth potential for the firm. Venture capitalists take a 50 percent ownership stake in Firm B. If we assume that the terminal value of both firms is equal to one hundred million dollars, Firm A only pays the interest on the borrowed capital while Firm B eventually gives away fifty million dollars of value to venture capitalists. While this example is simplistic, it demonstrates that the ultimate cost of venture capital financing is well in excess of bank debt expenses. Venture capitalists would argue that Firm B is incapable of raising any other types of financing, so the achieved growth in the value of the firm cannot be realized. They would also argue that significant value is created from the hands-on assistance provided by venture capitalists. In the case of borrowing from banks, such assistance is virtually nonexistent.

The third disadvantage of equity investing comes from its long-term orientation and partnership-based nature. The contractual arrangement between venture capitalists and entrepreneurs tends not to anticipate a premature dissolution of the relationship prior to the achievement of the desired exit. Consequently, the partnership is irrevocable and definite. In the case of any disagreements, disputes, and differing points of view, the relationship must continue. While venture capitalists and entrepreneurs may have opportunities to resolve intolerable and unbearable situations through re-negotiations, the ultimate cost to the entrepreneur and venture capitalist alike is very high. For the entrepreneur it may mean an operational gridlock, missed market opportunities, and costly legal disputes; for venture capitalists, the result may be a partial write-off of or a total loss on the investment.

Another disadvantage relates to the nature of venture capital investing. In special circumstances, venture capitalists may assume partial or full control over a business. This can occur under two circumstances: material under-performance of the business or if the founder is engaging in criminal behavior. In such cases, venture capitalists either assume operational responsibility for the business or appoint external advisors to do so on their behalf. For example, under the terms of a "voting flip-over event"—a clause often introduced by venture capitalists into the legal agreement—venture capitalists can assume operational responsibility for a business if the firm misses achieving certain revenue or operating profit targets by a certain percentage (i.e., 50 percent under-performance).

The last and most often underestimated disadvantage of venture capital investment is the time commitment. A venture capital deal may take anywhere from six to nine months to complete. During this time, venture capitalists place high demands on the firm seeking financing: a variety of documents must be prepared during this period (i.e., a business plan, with multiple revisions of financial forecasts) and countless meetings must be conducted to discuss the prepared documents and negotiate the actual transaction. The added expense of hiring lawyers and business advisors results in additional financial pressure for the business seeking capital. The most commonly voiced complaint by entrepreneurs is that venture capitalists take their time away from running their business. While this may be a necessary investment on the part of entrepreneurs, there can be no assurance that a deal will ultimately be reached.

Questions to Consider

1. What are the key characteristics of venture capital? How does venture capital differ from private equity?
2. Compare venture capital to other types of financing available for firms. Is venture capital a more preferable option for financing younger or more mature firms?
3. Why is achieving an exit one of the most important aspects of venture capital?
4. Let's imagine that you worked for a venture capital fund in the last ten years. The fund started with a total value of ten million dollars and after ten years it is worth fifty-five million dollars. The investors' hurdle rate is 7 percent. The split of the carried interest between your investors and the management team is 80/20. You personally get 25 percent of the carried interest the team gets. How much will you make in carried interest?
5. Discuss the advantages and disadvantages of venture capital investing from the entrepreneurs' point of view.

The Carlyle Group

Key characteristics

Year founded:	1987
Founding partners:	William E. Conway, Jr., Daniel A. D'Aniello, and David M. Rubenstein
Number of limited partners:	~1,300 (68 countries; CalPERS, CalSTERS)
Geographic coverage:	North America (6 offices), Europe (9), Asia (7), Australia (1), Middle East/North Africa (4), Latin America (1)
Headquarter location:	Washington (USA)
Focus (if any):	Buyout and real estate
Funds under management:	$86.1 billion
Number of completed deals/IPO exits:	920 ($56.3 billion)/N/A
Private/public:	Private
Most publicly recognized deals:	Dunkin' Brands, Hertz, Moncler, United Defense Industries, HD Supply, Booz Allen Hamilton, Le Figaro,
Number of investment professionals:	~475

With more than $86 billion under management, the Carlyle Group is one of the world's largest investment firms. Founded in 1987, the Carlyle Group quickly established a global presence and now has over 28 offices across 20 countries. Carlyle has formed 64 investment and private equity funds and has executed about 920 deals by committing over $56 billion. It is also one of the first major private equity firms to establish offices in China.

Carlyle has diverse investment interests (the main ones being energy and power, aerospace and defense, and automotive and transportation) and geographic interests. These interests can be combined into four major investment themes: buyouts (68 percent of total commitment), leveraged finance (16 percent), real estate (12 percent), and growth finance (4 percent). The firm's strategy is executed by a sizeable pool of investment professionals (more than 475 people) from industrial, financial, and academic backgrounds. Carlyle's employees have committed more than $3.6 billion of their own capital into the venture.

Carlyle's global commitment to the investment industry has resulted in the firm receiving many prestigious awards, including Private Equity Firm of the Year in the United States (*Financial Times*—2008), Most Powerful Buyout Firm (*Fortune Magazine*—2008), and Turnaround of the Year (*Buyouts Magazine*—2007).

Source: www.carlyle.com; 2008 Annual Report.

Chapter 2

An Overview of the Venture Capital Investment Process

The completion of a successful venture capital deal requires the deal to progress through a multistage process. This process is no easy task, as venture capitalists face a number of unique challenges along the way. First, it is up to venture capitalists to educate the young entrepreneurs who often confuse venture capital with other types of financing. The initial interactions between the two sides are difficult, as venture capitalists must fill the dual role of educator and negotiator. Second, entrepreneurs are often not prepared to receive venture capital. They may not have any formal documentation describing their business, and may not have prepared business plans or financial forecasts—the cornerstones of venture capital evaluation. Third, the process of structuring and negotiating venture capital deals is inherently difficult—a fact that is especially true for first-time venture capital recipients.

Initial attempts to describe the venture capital investment process were made by academics in the mid-1990s. The first attempt involved developing a five-stage model of venture capital investing (deal origination, screening, evaluation, deal structuring, and post-investment activities). While this first definition was generally descriptive and simplistic, it consolidated the heterogeneity of the investment process across different venture capital firms. The model described the investment process and broadly highlighted key venture capital activities at each stage. The second attempt investigated the venture capitalist decision-making model in more detail. This attempt considered some of the internal workings of venture capital firms and the complexities of the internal decision-making process.

It further focused on venture capitalists' initial, pre-investment decisions to invest, as well as related decision-making criteria. This attempt proposed a six-stage model (origination, venture capital firm's specific screen, generic screen, first-phase evaluation, second-phase evaluation, and closing). It is unfortunate that such a detailed discussion did not extend beyond the deal closing stage of the venture capital process.

The Revised Model of the Venture Capital Investment Process

Before a more comprehensive view of the venture capital investment process is proposed, it is important to make a couple of general observations. Some venture capitalists do not rely on formal and structured investment processes. This is not to imply that no process guides the investment activities at such firms; instead, the venture capital process is "silent," as venture capitalists rely on tacit knowledge and transfer the art of venture capital investing from one employee to another through active interactions with entrepreneurs. Conversely, other venture capital firms have broken down the investment process to a near-science; details are laid out and investment process manuals are strictly adhered to by all employees of the firm. Employees of such firms know precisely what the steps are, what needs to be done to get to another level, when they are deviating from a "normal" course of the investment process, and the human resource commitment to every project.

This book proposes a more comprehensive view of the venture capital investment process. The mechanics of processing venture capital deals are more complex than initially suggested. The following eight-stage model aims to capture the essence of the venture capital investment process. The stages include: deal generation, initial screening, due diligence phase I and internal feedback, pre-approval completions, due diligence phase II and internal approvals, deal completion, monitoring, and exit. Figure 2.1 compares the proposed approach with the two most well-known models developed during the mid-1990s.

The proposed model has a number of unique features. First, it defines the various approval processes that venture capitalists must go through with their venture capital firms' approval

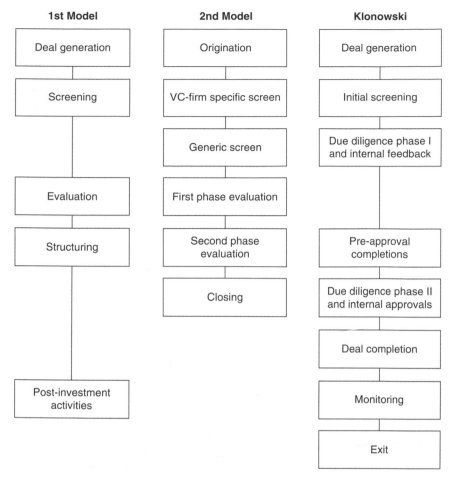

Figure 2.1 A comparison of various models of the venture capital investment process.

bodies (namely, the investment committee and supervisory board) in order to complete the deal and exit. Venture capitalists must effectively consult with these decision-making units during every step of the investment process. Second, the level of internal documentation needed throughout the life of any investment is high to ensure a careful approval process. Venture capitalists need to produce at least ten different pieces of documentation for review by internal team members or the investment committee and supervisory board. This fact undoubtedly highlights the extraordinary scrutiny that venture capital firms are subjected to by their capital providers (namely, limited partners) and reflects the high perceived level of risk that limited partners see in the marketplace. Third, the model provides a clearer definition of the differences between the specific stages that occur during the evaluation of investee firms. The initial screening stage, for example, is based on the original document or presentation provided by the potential investee firm. No extra costs are incurred at this stage by the venture capital firm. Due diligence phase I focuses on the due diligence program organized by venture capitalists based on more intense interactions with founders and entrepreneurs. No extra costs are incurred here, also. The third level of evaluation is generally driven by external consultants (i.e., accountants, lawyers, environmental and technical specialists, etc.) with limited involvement from venture capitalists. This represents the most expensive stage of the evaluation process.

The model also defines the venture capital process in terms of three basic channels of activity: document channel, information channel, and decision channel. The document channel involves the preparation of various documents by venture capitalists for internal use (i.e., call reports, investment memoranda, exit memoranda), for external communication with founders and entrepreneurs (i.e., term sheets, heads of terms, legal documents), and the venture capital firm's decision-making units (i.e., general partner's resolutions, custodian instruction letters). The information channel is the information related to the deal and the investee firm. Information is gathered through the review process and both phases of due diligence; any relevant information is then used by venture capitalists as source material for the preparation of various internal documents. The decision channel involves decision-making by various participants in the venture capital investment process (i.e., investment committees, supervisory boards, managing directors, investment officers). All channels are interrelated and required for the successful completion of a venture capital deal. The model of the venture capital process in figures 2.1–2.5 also shows areas where the transfers between document, information, and decision channels occur (a line documents these activities). The model also outlines the relevant organizational units (venture capitalists, investment committee, supervisory board, etc.) and mentions the key documents used during each stage.

The discussion that follows provides an overview of the key stages of the venture capital investment process.

Deal Generation

Access to information about high quality investment opportunities, or the deal flow, is crucial to a venture capital firm. Venture capital firms rely on their relationships with investment bankers, brokers, consultants, and lawyers to obtain leads on attractive investment prospects. They also count on referrals from firms they have successfully financed in the past. Venture capital firms also compete directly with other agents (i.e., investment advisory firms or brokerage houses) to locate suitable investment candidates.

Some of the most popular deal generating techniques include self-generation (where firms seeking capital identify venture capital players individually or through professional advisers) and direct marketing (where the venture capital firm's efforts are focused on identifying deals in the desired size range, industry, stage of development, etc.). When a business plan is received, the managing director or chief operating officer of the venture capital firm assigns the investment proposal to an investment officer in the firm; this person is then expected to meet with management or entrepreneurs to conduct initial discussions (see figure 2.2). Venture capitalists are responsible for registering any new deals into a deal log and for making initial assessments about the attractiveness of deals and their suitability to the venture capital firm (e.g., some venture capitalists have restrictions on investing into specific sectors, such as military equipment, alcohol, tobacco, etc.). Venture capitalists will generally attempt to visit potential investee firms unless it is immediately obvious that the deal is unlikely to occur. These company visits are especially useful for new employees learning to distinguish the difference between good and bad investment prospects.

Any meeting that is held between a venture capitalist and an entrepreneur that may result in a project, or turn into a prospective project, is recorded in an initial report (venture capitalists refer to this document as a "call report" or "meeting report"). This initial internal report is distributed to the venture capital firm's entire team prior to an internal meeting known as a "deal meeting" (these generally occur weekly or bi-monthly). A presentation by a venture capitalist to the rest of the investment officers at the venture capital firm may be followed by a brief discussion. The decision is then made on whether to continue with further steps or reject the project. If a decision to "proceed" is made, an agreement is reached among the firm's venture capitalists with respect to the next steps

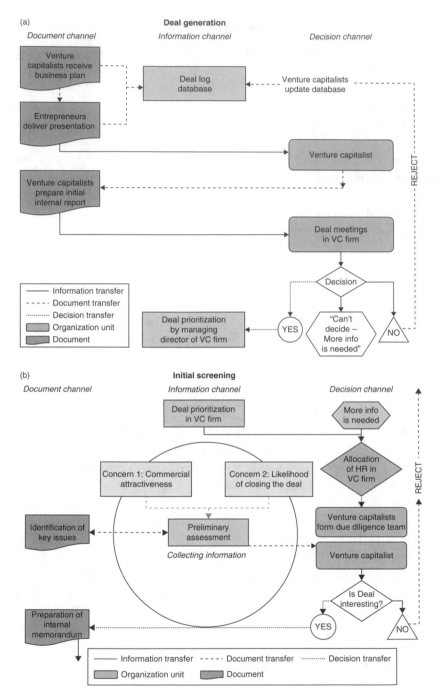

Figure 2.2 Deal generation and initial screening stages of the venture capital investment process.

to be implemented by the investment officer leading the deal. The participating venture capitalists list their issues and a preliminary list of critical commercial concerns to be further investigated is generated. The discussion is noted in the minutes of the deal meeting, and the minutes are distributed to team members shortly after the meeting. This document forms the basis for further analysis and due diligence. Conversely, if a decision to "reject" the deal is made, the venture capitalist sends a personalized rejection letter to the entrepreneurs or management clearly stating the reasons for rejecting the deal. In addition, these reasons are written into an internal database. This is an important step for venture capitalists, as rejected deals may become viable investment prospects if the reason for rejection can be rectified in the future.

Initial Screening

Venture capitalists commonly receive many business proposals, of which only less than 5 percent convert to actual investments. In order to filter out the majority of the received proposals, venture capitalists use a process known as screening. Venture capitalists generally reject proposals that are perceived to not meet the venture capital firm's internal criteria, have been previously unsuccessful in certain sectors, or seem unpromising.

The managing director or chief operating officer of the venture capital firm decides upon the composition of the team that will investigate the deal (see figure 2.2). In addition, a deal leader or "deal promoter" is appointed from a pool of the firm's senior venture capitalists. The managing director or chief operating officer also weighs in on the investment priorities for the firm so that appropriate resources can be allocated to the best investment opportunities. The managing director or chief operating officer briefly consults with venture capitalists in other countries (assuming that the venture capital firm has operations elsewhere) to determine whether a deal in the same or a similar sector has been achieved elsewhere. This is done to leverage the venture capital firm's experience in the sector. Generally, a two-person team—supervised by a senior partner in the firm—is formed to oversee each deal.

Two key aspects of this initial "screening" are aimed at locating potential "deal breakers" as quickly as possible in the investment process. First, venture capitalists investigate the attractiveness of the

underlying investee firm or its commercial proposition. A preliminary analysis is performed on all commercial areas of the business
(management, product, market, competition, finance) as quickly as
possible in the investment process. This preliminary assessment is
performed on the basis of available information (a business plan from
the investee firm, the initial presentation, the venture capital firm's
internal research, etc.) and the internal "knowledge base" of the
venture capital firm. The assessment is a relatively straightforward
exercise, as many of the venture capitalists appointed to the team
are likely to have relevant industry experience and are able to make
an informed assessment without dedicating a significant amount of
time to the process. If a business plan or financial model is available,
preliminary IRR calculations are made. Second, venture capitalists
attempt to ascertain the likelihood of closing the deal. A preliminary discussion is held with founders or entrepreneurs regarding
the basic terms the venture capitalists are likely to require in order
to complete the deal. This discussion is usually held early in the
investment process to assess the chances of closing the deal. Such
an exercise also helps to identify any potential deal breakers early on
in the investment process. The key areas of discussion relate to exit
provisions, corporate governance, and circumstances or events that
can lead to changes of control (i.e., "voting flip-over events"). This
is an important area of assessment for venture capitalists because the
probability of not closing a deal is above average.

The venture capitalists then prepare their first internal document,
which may be called a deal alert, an initial or preliminary memorandum, or a preliminary deal qualification memorandum. The
evaluation is focused on the following areas: quality and breadth
of the firm's management team; size and projected growth of the
firm's target markets; the ability of the firm to develop and maintain a competitive advantage in those markets; a potential for capital appreciation relative to overall risk; a preliminary assessment of
the firm's financial projections; and an ability to successfully liquidate the investment within three–five years.

There are two distinguishing features of the screening stage of
the analysis that sets this stage of the process apart from subsequent evaluations of the investee firm. First, there are no costs for
external expenses incurred at this stage by the venture capital firm.
Second, the venture capital firm holds a limited number of meetings with the candidate firm.

Due Diligence Phase I and Internal Feedback

The initial internal document is presented to the investment committee and/or the supervisory board of the venture capital firm for initial feedback (see figure 2.3). The investment committee is an internal decision-making body of the venture capital firm that formally approves deals and allows them to be moved forward to the next step (and ultimately to the deal completion stage). The supervisory board is comprised of representatives of limited partners in the venture capital firm. In some venture capital firms, the supervisory board is not a decision-making body; rather, it acts to provide guidance on some of the strategic issues faced by the firm (including proper cash management and draw-downs of capital from limited partners, realization and exits, sector focus, hiring key employees, approving employee allocations for the carried interest, etc.).

The investment committee does not generally focus on the details of the deal at this stage of the analysis; instead, the members of the committee present their views on the business concept and the sector or industry (at some venture capital firms, consultations with these decision-making bodies may not occur at this stage of the process). The members also list their concerns related to the deal. This list of commercial and deal issues is updated by venture capitalists. Once the members of the investment committee have been satisfied, venture capitalists commence a more intensive round of interactions with management and entrepreneurs. These interactions relate to two basic areas: financial forecasting and valuation. First, a thorough investigation of the firm's financial forecasts is implemented (this does not involve evaluations performed by external consultants). The purpose of venture capitalists' interaction with entrepreneurs is to understand all the commercial realities of the firm in the context of the financial forecasts. Venture capitalists' questions are prepared in written form and subsequently sent to management or entrepreneurs. Management or entrepreneurs are then expected to produce written material for meetings with venture capitalists, effectively providing a "defense" of their financial forecasts. Venture capitalists then continue their discussions on the terms of the transaction with the founders or entrepreneurs. This discussion occurs in the context of the firm's valuation. The major parts of due diligence phase I are the preparations of financial forecasting and business valuation—these topics are discussed

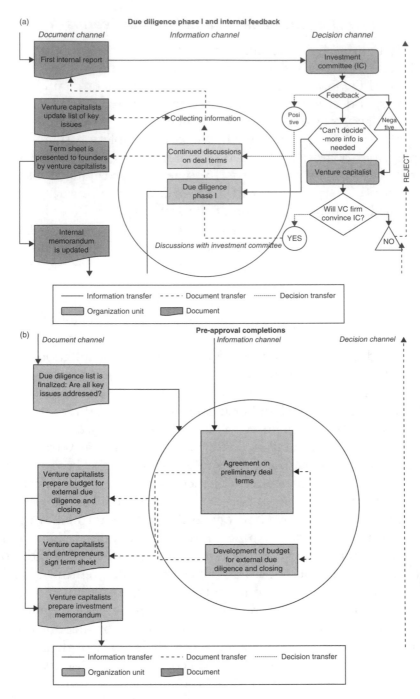

Figure 2.3 Due diligence phase I and internal feedback and pre-approval completions stages of the venture capital investment process.

in chapter five. It is important to note that during this stage, the venture capital firm has not incurred any additional costs.

During this stage, venture capitalists continue to redraft the list of key issues related to the deal. This list is refined throughout the due diligence process and after discussions with management or entrepreneurs. The list also forms the basis for the development of a more comprehensive due diligence plan implemented later in the process and informs the creation of key terms in the deal (or, the nature and type of protections likely required given what could go wrong with the business or deal). The generic "term sheet" or "heads of terms" developed internally by the venture capital firm are often used as a starting point or template for the formation of deal-specific terms and criteria.

Pre-Approval Completions

Having understood the issues related to financial forecasting and business valuation, venture capitalists proceed to conclude one of the most important steps in the early stage of the investment process—negotiation and finalization of the terms of the deal with entrepreneurs. This is a critical step to complete prior to obtaining internal approvals from the investment committee.

Deal structuring in venture capital is defined as the negotiation of deal pricing, various rights and provisions, and the formation of securities. Owing to a desire to optimize the tax structure of the venture capital fund and due to the significant imperfections of legal infrastructure in many markets around the world, venture capitalists must carefully consider how they structure deals. Whether utilizing local or foreign vehicles or some other combination, an optimal trade-off between risks and returns must be achieved to maximize the value of venture capitalists' investment.

Negotiations of the major terms of the deal are to have been completed and the term sheet is to have been signed before the deal is presented to the investment committee for formal approval. The term sheet allows venture capitalists to show to the investment committee that the deal, in principle, is signed and that the major areas of commercial investigation have been checked off.

The venture capitalists summarize the due diligence findings in a full internal memorandum, often called the investment memorandum, deal qualification memorandum, or deal memorandum (see figure 2.3). The format of these documents differs from one venture capital firm to another, but they generally address the same types of concerns.

Due Diligence Phase II and Internal Approvals

Once a favorable hearing has been obtained from the investment committee upon a thorough discussion of the investment memorandum, venture capitalists receive approval to conduct external due diligence (see figure 2.4). This constitutes "Due Diligence Phase II"—a generally expensive process. On average, venture capital firms spend between 1 and 2 percent of the invested capital on external due diligence. These costs are often reimbursed to the venture capital firm by the investee firm if and when the deal is consummated.

The minutes from the investment committee meeting confirm the approval to proceed with the deal and the approval of the due diligence budget. The minutes also outline any issues or concerns raised during the meeting and any timing issues to be addressed. The investment committee may approve the budget for partial due diligence if specific issues prove to be deal breakers in the project and need to be investigated before a full due diligence program is rolled out. These problem areas are then dealt with.

Venture capitalists commence external due diligence. The key areas of investigation are of an accounting, legal, and environmental nature. The accounting investigation focuses on the following areas: reviewing the investee firm's historical financial data and, if necessary, restating the financial data in international accounting standards (either GAAP or IAS); identifying off-balance sheet liabilities (i.e., tax matters, internal loans); and the adequacy of the accounting department's internal processes. The legal investigation is an audit of all legal matters in the investee firm related to the title to the assets, agreements with external parties (i.e., consumers, suppliers, and financial institutions), the proper constitution and proceedings of the investee firm, and related-party transactions. The environmental investigation generally focuses on waste management and disposal, as well as other environmental concerns important to the public. In addition, industry experts may be invited to participate in the due diligence process if the venture capital team lacks depth or experience in specific areas. On occasion, the

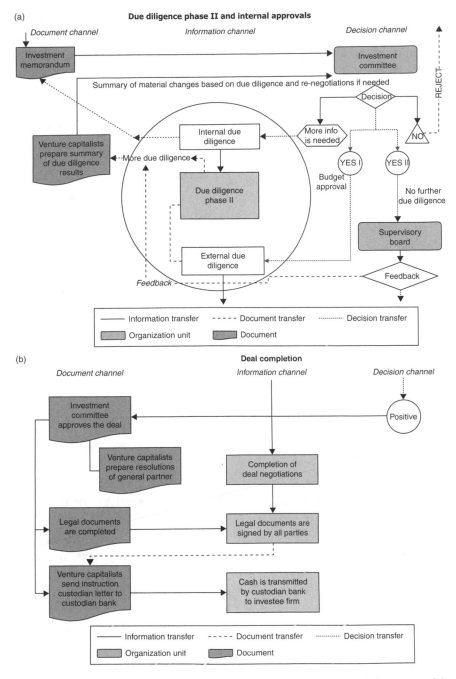

Figure 2.4 Due diligence phase II and internal approvals and deal completion stages of the venture capital investment process.

investment committee authorizes venture capitalists to conduct personal background checks on founders, entrepreneurs, and management. The aim of such investigation is to discover any past criminal behavior.

After conducting external due diligence, venture capitalists report the findings to the investment committee in a written document. In this document, venture capitalists make recommendations on whether the findings form the basis for any re-negotiation of terms of the initial deal agreed to by the parties and whether the due diligence accurately reflects the preliminary assessment of the potential investee firm made by the venture capital team. The investment committee then discusses the document and a decision is made on whether to proceed, reject, or re-negotiate. Following this decision, members of the supervisory board are also brought into the consultative process.

If further discussions are required, or if re-negotiations with founders or entrepreneurs are needed, venture capitalists proceed with such actions. Venture capitalists are expected to update the investment committee on their interactions with the entrepreneurs. In other cases, venture capitalists submit a budget for finalizing the transaction to the investment committee. This expense generally relates to the incurring of legal costs for the purpose of converting the initial term sheet into a set of binding legal documents.

Deal Completion

Deal completion involves concluding the negotiations of detailed documents of the transaction with entrepreneurs (see figure 2.4). Unanticipated legal issues often arise at this point in the process as the general terms of the deal captured in the term sheet are converted into detailed legal documents. If material issues arise during the drafting of these legal documents, venture capitalists once again need to obtain approval for the deal from the investment committee. At this stage, all legal documents (shareholders' agreements, articles of association or deeds, option agreements, subscription agreements, etc.) are in the final stages of completion. After the parties sign the legal documents, venture capitalists prepare an internal document called a custodian instruction letter. This document is the basis for settling the deal in cash terms and provides detailed instructions to the custodian bank of the venture capital firm and its administrator.

Monitoring

The active involvement of venture capitalists in their investee firms relates to an asymmetry of information (access to critical information varies among stakeholders) and an extended period of illiquidity. Differences in access to information may cause venture capitalists to misunderstand certain operational aspects of the business (i.e., agency risks) that may be otherwise addressed by closely monitoring the business and its external reviews (i.e., financial reports and audits). An extended period of illiquidity can result in challenges to exit prospects, undervaluation of the business, and, consequently, disappointing returns. Venture capitalists meet with their investee firms as changes in market conditions, business opportunities, and operational goals may occur, and these changes can lead to a review of certain aspects of the deal agreed upon at the outset of the partnership between entrepreneurs and venture capitalists.

The purpose of the deal monitoring stage is for venture capitalists and entrepreneurs to focus on specific operational and financial milestones (see figure 2.5). This serves as the basis for any decision-making conducted by shareholders. All decisions made at the supervisory board level of the investee firm are documented in formal minutes. The key question asked by venture capitalists during the monitoring phase is whether the investee firm is developing according to the initial budget. If the investment is performing in accordance with the initial investment premise, the venture capital firm presumes that the deal will progress toward a desired exit and no action will be required. If this is not the case, a revised budget is developed by the investee firm. This revised budget must be accepted by all shareholders. Budget revisions occur regularly, thus reflecting the dynamic nature of venture capital investing and the types of investee firms venture capital supports. If any deviations occur from the initial investment plan, venture capitalists need to update the investment committee and seek approval to continue (in some cases an update occurs). An internal memorandum is then developed and discussed with the investment committee. In situations where additional rounds of equity injection may

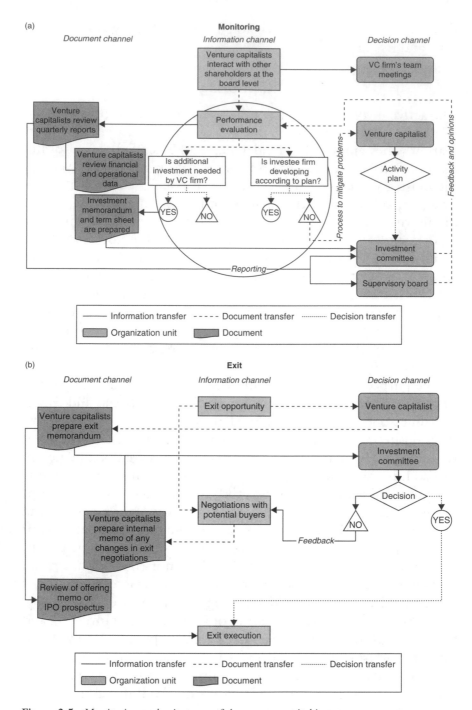

Figure 2.5 Monitoring and exit stages of the venture capital investment process.

be required, the existing venture capital firms are often expected to participate in the deal (even at a minimal level of cash exposure) to yield credibility to any new rounds of financing and to support business valuation at a particular level. Of course, this may not be possible if the existing venture capital deal has limited financial resources or has exceeded its allowable per-deal limit. New rounds of financing, if required, generally create the same types of internal obligations for venture capital firms making new investment decisions (including negotiating a term sheet, completing legal documentation, investigating exit opportunities, and making IRR calculations). These initial business assumptions are then revisited and the venture capitalists confirm that they still hold true under new circumstances. At this stage, many venture capital firms request an operational review by an external consultant; management issues are also addressed.

Venture capitalists receive two types of reports: monthly or quarterly and annual. The monthly reports generally include financial and operational updates. The key objective is to receive all financial statements, including the income statement, balance sheet, and cash flow. Written information on the firm's operations includes: a new customer list, any new product lines added, the new markets entered, changes in distribution channels, new competition entering the markets, the activities of competitors, any significant pricing changes, changes to operations, and changes to the middle and senior management teams. In addition, there may be numerous reporting requirements specified in the firm's constitutional documents (i.e., deeds or articles of association) and shareholders' agreements. Annual reports include similar information to that required on a monthly or quarterly basis. In addition, venture capitalists require audited financial statements and an annual business plan for the next fiscal year, including an operating budget and a capital expenditure program that is part of a rolling 3-year plan.

Exit

Achieving an exit, or divestment, is the most important part of the venture capital process. An exit is driven by venture capitalists' objective to return a profit to limited partners and earn carried interest. The final stage of the process can be achieved through two common avenues: a public offer (IPO) or a sale to a strategic investor. These exit routes have different consequences for venture capitalists.

Venture capitalists generally prefer a sale to a strategic investor, as this almost certainly ends the venture capitalists' involvement in the investee firm (venture capitalists receive a lump sum from a strategic investor). On occasion, a small amount of the final purchase consideration is retained in an escrow account, subject to any unforeseen liabilities emerging during the first few months after the acquisition of the business by the strategic investor. Investee firms, their managers, and their founders generally prefer a public offering because an IPO preserves the independence of the firm while the public market has continued access to finance. For venture capitalists, a public offering rarely concludes their relationship with the investee firm—the underwriters often prevent venture capitalists from disposing of their shares at the time of an IPO or for a post-IPO period of around 18 months. If venture capitalists sit on the board of directors of the publicly quoted investee firm, additional restrictions on the timing of their share disposals may apply.

During the period in which an exit opportunity is crystallized, venture capitalists prepare an exit memorandum that is then presented to the investment committee. This final internal memorandum summarizes the type of exit sought by venture capitalists, the buyer, the price for the business and IRR calculations, and any conditions attached to the sale (i.e., escrow arrangements). If the sale occurs through the IPO process, the venture capitalists attach the offering memorandum and discuss their timing for the disposal of the investee firm's shares. If the investment committee does not accept the proposed deal, the deal needs to be re-negotiated and venture capitalists are required to report back to the committee (see figure 2.5).

Deal Types and Completion Schedules

Given the human resource constraints, capital requirements, and costs involved, venture capitalists want to process attractive deals quickly. However, it is not surprising that venture capital deals take differing amounts of time to complete. The time needed to complete a deal depends on the collaborative effort of the two interested parties: the entrepreneur and the venture capitalist. On the entrepreneur's side, the key to a timely completion of the deal is preparation. This includes preparing an information memorandum or pertinent information about the business, the financial forecast or budgets, the ability to respond to venture capitalists' questions and inquiries, and, finally, experience and the readiness to negotiate. The process of negotiating a deal, especially for "first-time" entrepreneurs, can be time consuming. These types of entrepreneurs must learn financial and venture capital lingo, understand the specific nature of venture capital investing, and appreciate the specific terms required by venture capitalists—particularly the more draconian clauses such as exit clauses, change of control provisions, and approval requirements.

On the venture capitalists' side, the progression of the deal depends on the human resources dedicated to investigating the business, the monetary resources devoted to hiring external advisers, and the venture capital firm's own internal processes. In order to process a deal in a timely manner, venture capitalists must prepare a number of internal documents in a short period of time. In many instances, they are also expected to entirely redo or partially replicate the financial forecasts prepared by the firms seeking capital. While venture capitalists customarily use ready-made excel model templates and make incremental improvements to them to reflect the specific nature of the business being modeled, the exercise is often complex and requires significant input from the firm and external experts. The venture capital firm's internal process can be another hurdle. Investment committees often have certain expectations in terms of the quality of information they see represented within internal documentation. This means that deals cannot be presented to investment committees too early, as all critical information must be included within the internal documents (including financial forecasts, IRR calculations, valuation, etc.). In many venture capital firms, investment committees meet infrequently (i.e., bi-monthly); other firms prefer a more casual approach (i.e., convening a meeting whenever necessary). The proper overlap and coordination of these processes—run simultaneously on behalf of venture capitalists and entrepreneurs— ensures that deals are progressed in a timely manner.

Generally speaking, there are two types of deals: expansion and early-stage. These are deals where both entrepreneurs and venture capitalists can be proactive and effectively drive the deal completion timetable. A special category of venture capital transactions are privatization deals, which are effectively run as "tender processes" (the tender process is also used in some situations where a competitive tender is organized by the firms seeking capital; venture capitalists and strategic investors are then invited to participate). In the case of privatization deals, the state (i.e., ministry of trade, ministry of privatization) lays out the schedule of activities and venture capitalists are merely respondents to the external process. This deal category is described in box 2.1.

Box 2.1   International perspective on venture capital: privatization deals

Venture capital firms operating in emerging markets of Asia, Central and Eastern Europe, South America, and Africa have an opportunity to participate in a special category of deals called privatization transactions.

The privatization process generally begins with the government announcing "an invitation to tender" for all interested parties to participate in the privatization of a state-owned firm. This announcement briefly describes the privatized firm (a few short sentences), specifies the deadline for submitting the preliminary expressions of interest (the announcement generally gives interested parties four–six weeks to submit an initial offer), and requests that all interested parties outline their experience relative to the privatized firm.

Once the initial expression of interest is made and a confidentiality agreement is signed by the interested party, an information memorandum is made available with further, detailed instructions outlining the process. This document serves as the basis for making an initial, non-binding offer. The offers are generally evaluated on three criteria: the price of shares, the social package (i.e. including wage and employment guarantees), and the investment program. The government's key consideration is price, while the social package is critical for employees (their lack of support can effectively break the deal). Potential investors are also expected to present their proposals to management and the union (if present) to obtain their approval. The government determines who proceeds to the next round of offers, which are binding. Last, on the basis of a binding offer, the government chooses one candidate with which to negotiate the final deal.

A privatization process creates multiple challenges for venture capitalists. First, the window of opportunity to perform due diligence on the privatized firm is short and forces venture capitalists to have external advisers on stand-by. Second, the information is rudimentary and incomplete. Access to financial audits without access to back-up information is of little value. The financial projections are often unavailable, or available only in the later stages of the bidding process. No full business plan is provided. Third, the final consideration for the deal (as well as the number of shares) is not revealed by the government until the latter part of the process. Venture capitalists must also orchestrate their decision-making process to fit within the privatization schedule. This means the decisions made by the venture capitalists leading the deal, as well as those made by the investment committee, are based on incomplete information and situational assessment.

The discussion that follows is based on some fundamental assumptions. For one, it is assumed that the firms—whether in their expansion or early-stage phases—are actively looking for financing. This implies that the firm has a business plan, with accompanying financial forecasts for the future. If the business plan is not available, the process can be prolonged by six–eight weeks. While most firms seeking capital are able to prepare a comprehensive business plan on their own, some require assistance from external advisers. In rare instances when a deal appears very attractive, venture capitalists are willing to work with the firm to prepare the business plan. Through this exercise, venture capitalists effectively safeguard the deal from being shopped around to other competing venture capital firms. Second, entrepreneurs or founders have a rudimentary understanding of venture capital financing; they realize that there are specific clauses that aim to allow venture capitalists an active role in the business and assure liquidity of their investments at some future point in time. If no prior knowledge of venture capital exists, entrepreneurs will face a steep learning curve. Internalizing some of the required features of venture capital requires effort, acceptance, and time. In such cases, interactions between the two sides can be choppy and unstable; this has the potential to add three–four weeks to the process. Third, entrepreneurs have to be committed to spending regular time with venture capitalists. This is not easy task.

In terms of time, expansion deals can take longer to achieve than early-stage deals. This may be for a variety of reasons. Start-ups have no operating history and no investigation or audits of past performance (i.e., financial, technical, and environmental) are required to process the deal. Limited historical information forces the analytical focus to concentrate on the expected future performance of the business. In cases where products or services are not yet in existence, it may be difficult to estimate basic information relating to the market and competitive forces. As a result, simplified assumptions are made. In cases where the markets are easily identified, due diligence focuses on market growth rates and the potential behavior of existing market players and new entrants.

The general perception that early-stage deals take shorter periods of time to complete is easily defeated under certain circumstances. For example, if venture capitalists are unconvinced as to the market acceptance of a product or service, they may ask for an external expert to be brought in to make an assessment. Such an analysis can easily take six–eight weeks to complete. If venture capitalists, on the other hand, believe in the commercial attractiveness of the new business, they may want to wait for a few months until the new venture completes the pilot project, or better yet, secures clients with sales. In this case, venture capitalists would string the process forward for some time until their perception of risk changes.

Deal generation is perhaps the most undefined stage of the investment process with respect to time. The assumption is that the venture capital firm knows the sector in which it wants to place an investment and the general courtship phase takes about two weeks. In reality, this may take longer, depending on the effectiveness of the deal generation program.

It is important to note that the investment process used by a venture capital firm can be an important competitive advantage. This is especially true when multiple firms pursue the same prospect and the deal terms offered to the potential firm are broadly the same. Venture capital firms generally aim to address similar types of risks, albeit through different means. In such circumstances, the deal processing capability of the firm becomes critical.

Expansion-Stage Deals

There are perhaps three fundamental points of reference in processing the venture capital deal: feedback from the investment committee, internal deal approval by the investment committee, and deal completion. Venture capitalists aim to obtain preliminary feedback from the investment committee as quickly as possible to ensure that the deals they are working on are viewed favorably. The investment committee, along with the venture capitalists working on the deal, identifies three–five business risks be addressed throughout the process. The ability of the venture capitalists to address these concerns effectively determines whether the deal will receive final approval. The second major milestone in the process is getting the deal approved, in principle, by the investment committee. This approval is based on the assumption that the fundamentals of the deal have been agreed upon by the entrepreneurs, that the financial model has been rerun, that major due diligence issues have been addressed in a satisfactory manner, and that all previous accomplishments have been captured within an investment memorandum. Many venture capital firms aim to reach this point within six–eight weeks of their initial contact with the entrepreneurial firm. The final step is to sign the deal and achieve deal completion. Somewhere between the approval and completion of the deal, the attention of venture capitalists shifts away from due diligence and toward finalizing the deal. During this time, lawyers convert the letter of intent into final legal documents, and external advisers review the firm. Most venture capital firms aim to close deals in three–four months.

Since the average holding period is about three years post closing, the first two years are used to actively work with the firm and implement its expansion plans. Subsequent years are used to examine and explore exit opportunities. Figure 2.6 presents the hypothetical time schedule for processing deals in the expansion stage.

Early-Stage Deals

There are two general comments that apply to early-stage deals. Due to their development phases, early-stage deals inherently carry a high probability of failure. Consequently, venture capitalists either reject these deals due to the perceived high risk profile or attempt to close transactions quickly due to a perceived attractiveness. A similar dynamic can be noted in exit activities. For these reasons, Internet-related, high-tech, and bioscience firms are either able to achieve a significant market recognition in a very short period of time and, consequently, become viable acquisition targets for large multinationals or are effectively ahead of their market in terms of development and take a long time to flourish. If venture capitalists have the patience and financial resources, these firms can survive and ultimately succeed. If not, they end up back in the hands of management or in liquidation, resulting in smaller or larger write-offs for venture capitalists.

One advantage of early-stage deals is that they are less time consuming (see figure 2.6). Effectively, many deal pre-completion stages are performed in less time due to a limited operating history of the business (resulting in less information for venture

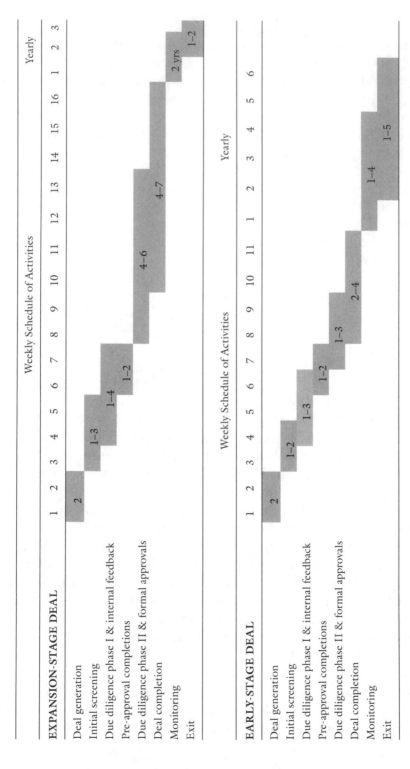

Figure 2.6 Deal processing schedules for expansion-stage and early-stage transactions.

capitalists to digest). Initial feedback from the investment committee arrives in about four weeks. Deals are approved in about eight weeks, with deal completion occurring in ten weeks. As these firms generally have no other options of financing at this stage of development, negotiations with venture capitalists take less time.

As previously mentioned, the most fascinating domain of the early-stage firm is the exit. Very short and financially rewarding exits or long and costly exits are the most common cases.

The Venture Capital Investment Process and a Typology of Venture Capital Firms

In any business, a competitive strategy is defined as a set of deliberate activities performed by a firm in order to achieve a targeted objective. This strategy is the management team's plan for competing successfully with its rivals in the marketplace. It is also a combination of actions to please customers by providing them with superior value that represents the most optimal combination of price, quality, services, and other important attributes. While there are countless variations of the competitive strategy that firms use, Michael Porter delineated two basic competitive strategies available to a firm: cost strategy and differentiation strategy. The basis for competitive advantage for effective cost strategy is the firm's ability to offer the lowest overall cost for a product or service. The differentiation strategy offers customers a unique product or services.

The venture capital industry is competitive and the venture capital firms competing in it vary from one to another. Venture capital firms compete on multiple fronts. Foremost, they compete to obtain preferential access to deals, which translates into strong exits and returns and, ultimately, a successful fundraising future for the firm. They also compete to recruit talented personnel. Venture capitalists' superior ability to assess entrepreneurial firms, anticipate business risks, and deal with unexpected challenges converts into a larger number of stellar performers and fewer write-offs for the firm. Venture capital firms also evolve. As they are in the industry longer, they achieve more success in their investment and fundraising activities. They also reconfirm their operational strengths and use them as a source of competitive strategy in the marketplace.

Figure 2.7 proposes a simplified matrix for analyzing the venture capital industry and the firms operating within the context of the venture capital investment process. The first descriptive characteristic of the proposed model is the venture capital firm's ability to process deals. Venture capital firms can either set up their internal processes to close deals in a timely manner (i.e., fast) or use a more protracted process. The fast firms use their ability to close deals quickly as a strong competitive tool. They are very efficient in focusing on the key issues of due diligence and address concerns quickly. They also write shorter internal documents (i.e., an investment memorandum of up to ten pages). Their internal decision-making functions are flexible and timely, recognizing that unexpected events occur and critical discoveries are made throughout the due diligence and negotiating process. Their interactions with entrepreneurial firms are based on the belief that they are not able to predict all of the risks in the firm and, consequently, negotiating and writing extensive legal documents to protect against such risks is counterproductive. These types of venture capital firms close deals quickly, invest in more firms, and end up with high numbers of winners *and* write-offs in their portfolios.

The slower-moving firms accept the opposite point of view. In terms of their deal philosophies, they believe that spending

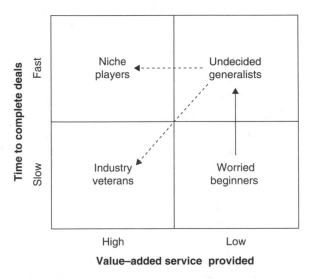

Figure 2.7   A typology of venture capital firms and their possible evolution.

significant amounts of time on every single identified issue is likely to address, reduce, or totally eliminate the risk associated with it. Their due diligence process is lengthy, and as a result can be frustrating to the entrepreneurial firm. Their negotiations are also lengthy, as extensive legal documents are often drafted. In terms of portfolio characteristics, they may close a smaller number of deals, may take longer to close a deal, and may end up with more mediocre deals, with no exceptional successes and fewer write-offs. These firms operate on the belief that a protracted process is likely to convert to better returns.

The second component of the proposed matrix refers to the ability of venture capital firms to provide value-added services to their investee firms, be they high or low. While academic studies have provided conflicting evidence to support that a venture capitalist's involvement in a portfolio firm results in the firm's superior performance, it is safe to assume that the good business advice and incremental value-added service provided to entrepreneurial firms by venture capitalists is better than the lack of advice they would otherwise receive. It can be further argued that sound business advice can translate into superior returns—notwithstanding the fact that venture capitalists are, on occasion, wrong in their assessments of their portfolio firms and their future prospects.

Figure 2.7 also presents a typology of venture capital firms based on two descriptive characteristics. The graph also presents the evolution of venture capital firms captured by these two descriptions. The *Worried Beginners* would be the first-time venture capital firms. The size of these firms would be relatively small ($50 million–200 million), with an average deal size of $3 million–5 million invested in expansions deals. These firms would be considered by the venture capital team to be "safe bets." In spite of their conservative investment philosophies and long due diligence periods, these firms would have a significant number of under-performers and write-offs in their portfolios. Many of the first-time firms would not provide any meaningful returns to limited partners (i.e., these firms would struggle to return the principal plus a single-digit return). In order to raise another fund, these firms would have to possess strong operational performers, good exits (both through an IPO and trade sales), a strong deal pipeline, and an established and tested team. The team would be limited to four–five professionals and support staff.

The successful Worried Beginners would generally transition to become *Undecided Generalists*. These firms would be larger in size compared to the Worried Beginners ($150 million–500 million). Their initial success (or a lack of disastrous failure) may motivate the general partners to expand geographically or to attempt different types of deals. They would also continue to pursue a wide variety of industrial sectors. The initial experience of having a previous venture capital firm or firms would allow them to become more efficient deal processors, as they would be more attuned to deal risks. However, while the experience of the team would allow for improvements to the provision of value-added service to investee firms, it would still be considered low when compared to the more experienced market players. As a result, syndicate partners are relied upon to drive deals and provide value-added services.

The Undecided Generalists follow two paths of development: they become sector-focused players, or continue to focus on a wide range of deals. Having been exposed to a number of deals, the Undecided Generalists may come to a clearer decision as to what deals are best for their firms and consequently become more focused in their approach. In such cases, they would become *Niche Players*. Niche Players focus on a specific sector or sectors of the economy. Exposure to preferential sectors leads them to become experts in specific fields and provide significant value to their investee firms as they become increasingly involved in their strategic and operational activities. Their deal processing ability is better than that of the Worried Beginners due to experience.

If an Undecided Generalist continues without any sector or industry specialization, but becomes very good at investing and supporting entrepreneurial firms, this firm becomes an *Industry Veteran*. These firms are successful in raising multiple venture capital firms, often operating them alongside each other and with billions of dollars under management. These firms are also high value added investors, which reflects their broad experience in the industry and wide industry contacts. Since such firms have strong reputations in the marketplace, they do not aggressively compete for deals; rather, deals come to them. As a result, the time needed to process deals is lessened.

Questions to Consider

1. What are the basic stages of the venture capital investment process?
2. Describe the role of an investment committee in the venture capital process.
3. What are the differences between due diligence Phase I and II?
4. What are the most important components of pre-approval completions?
5. Describe a common typology of venture capital firms.

Kleiner Perkins Caufield & Byers

Key characteristics

Year founded:	1972
Founding partners:	Eugene Kleiner, Tom Perkins, Frank J. Caufield, and Brook Byers
Number of limited partners:	N/A
Geographic coverage:	USA (1 location), Asia (2)
Headquarter location:	Menlo Park (USA)
Focus (if any):	Early stage science
Funds under management:	$10 billion (estimate)
Number of completed deals/ IPO exits:	~500/~150
Private/public:	Private
Most publicly recognized deals:	Amazon, Google, Genentech, Compaq, Segway, Sun Microsystems
Number of investment professionals:	~31

Kleiner Perkins Caufield & Byers (KPCB) is one of Silicon Valley's premier venture capital firms. KPCB predominantly focuses on early-stage, science-focused companies. The firm's high-profile investments include Google, Genentech, Sun Microsystems, and Amazon. Out of approximately 500 deals, KPCB has achieved a public listing for more than 150, and their other investee firms are frequently acquired by strategic investors. The firm's continued success and its high profile ability to successfully incubate early-stage firms have allowed it to raise 13 funds. While no public information exits indicating the amount of capital under management by KPCB, the amount is estimated to exceed $10 billion.

KPCB focuses on four major strategic areas of investment: information technology, life sciences, pandemic preparedness and bio-defense, and Apple collaboration initiatives. For its deal generation and incubation activities, the fund relies heavily on a proven network of scientists, executives, policy experts, and business managers. KPCB, strengthened by its industry-knowledgeable partners, is able to provide effective hands-on experience when developing investee firms.

KPCB is known to operate closely with its investee firms and within their respective areas of strategic investment. Industry experts comment that such a keiretsu-like approach to young enterprise development allows KPCB to develop new technologies, applications, and even build new industries quickly and effectively.

Source: www.kpcb.com.

Chapter 3

Deal Generation

Deal generation is a fundamental concept in venture capital financing. Some venture capitalists argue that it represents the most important function in the venture capital investment process. A strong pipeline of high quality deals almost always converts into superior returns for the venture capital firm. Deal generation, commonly called deal flow, is understood as the venture capital firm's ability to generate a stream of investment opportunities.

The importance of strong deal flow is understood in three ways. Venture capital firms generate hundreds of investment opportunities per year, but only invest in one or two firms out of every hundred. If the deal generation is weak or inconsistent, the venture capital firm reviews less investment proposals and, by default, invests in firms from a weaker pool of opportunities. Second, the venture capital industry is competitive. Getting to the most promising investment prospects first means lower competition for the deal. If no other competitor spots an attractive investment prospect, the venture capital firm that is "first at the door" has an opportunity to develop a sound relationship with the investee firm and its founders, to conduct due diligence in an orchestrated manner, and to negotiate a transaction with the most favorable terms possible (including deal pricing). Third, and most importantly, the continuation of a strong deal flow is pivotal to the long-term survival of any venture capital firm. If a venture capital firm (especially this that is first-time operator) faces a problem with deal flow, it almost certainly is not going to raise another fund. An ability to generate consistent, high quality deal flow is one of the most critical considerations made by potential investors.

Many venture capital firms argue that deal flow is about quality, not volume. These firms generally rely on a proprietary deal flow that stems from their long-term relations in the marketplace, reputation, and market experience.

Key Considerations to Deal Flow

Venture capital firms invest significant amounts of time into deciding which types of investment portfolios they wish to construct. There are numerous considerations to analyze. Venture capitalists must initially consider the amount of capital available for investment. This, in turn, is likely to drive the amount of human resources required to generate, process, monitor, and exit deals. The type of capital and amount of human resources used further influence the firm's deal orientation. A small deal team is unlikely to pursue and process a large number of deals within varying sectors, as it may not have sufficient expertise to cover a wide spectrum of sectors effectively. A small deal team is also unable to pursue deals where a significant amount of hands-on involvement is anticipated (i.e., early-stage deals). The following section focuses on the four main considerations of venture capital firms when crafting their investment strategies. These considerations include the amount of capital under management, deal orientation, sector or industry focus, and the competitive nature of the venture capital industry (as it applies geographically to the fund).

Before we discuss these considerations, let's review some key concepts in finance related to portfolio theory—namely, diversification and portfolio allocation. The concepts of diversification and risk moderation provide profound insights into the mechanics of portfolio construction. The total risk in a portfolio consisting of a number of assets (i.e., investee firms in the case of venture capital investing) is comprised of two types of risks: diversifiable and nondiversifiable. Diversifiable risk, also called unsystematic risk or controllable risk, relates to changes in the value of an asset (e.g., firm) that relate to the specific circumstances of that asset (e.g., a firm may lose business contracts or clients, get sued, or its employees may go on strike). This type of risk can be virtually eliminated from the portfolio by diversification, or investing into assets that behave differently. How successfully diversification reduces this type of risk depends on the degree of correlation between the behavior

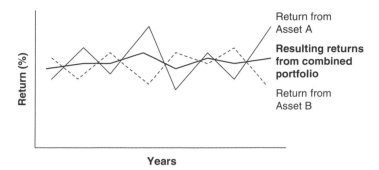

Figure 3.1   The effect of diversification when two assets are negatively correlated.

of the firms (correlation indicates the degree to which one variable is linearly related to another). Figure 3.1 presents a simple case where two assets or firms are negatively correlated with each other. It shows how returns from firms A and B vary over time. Notice that the fluctuations of each curve are such that gains in one firm almost completely offset losses in the other. The overall risk of the portfolio is small due to these offsetting effects. Non-diversifiable risk, also called systematic or market risk, is a characteristic of the overall market because it is produced by factors that are shared, to a greater or lesser degree, by most firms in the marketplace. These factors may include inflation, interest rates, exchange rates, credit crunch, natural disasters, and so on. These risks cannot be diversified away by adding new assets or firms into the portfolio. This risk may be common to an entire sector, asset class, or industry.

In a nutshell, if the portfolio of assets or firms is divided among greater numbers of assets or firms, the standard deviation (note that standard deviation in finance is denoted as a measure of risk) of the entire portfolio continues to fall as long as the newly added assets or firms have possible returns that are less than positively correlated with those of the existing portfolio. Figure 3.2 demonstrates that as each new asset or firm is added to the existing portfolio of firms, the diversification effect causes the standard deviation (i.e., the variability of returns) or risk of the entire portfolio to decrease. After about 20 assets or firms have been added, the effect of adding further firms to reduce the portfolio risk is slight. The remaining degree of risk is non-diversifiable risk.

Portfolio allocation is the process of dividing an investment portfolio into various classes of assets to preserve capital by protecting

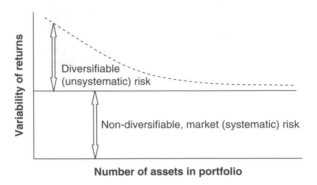

Figure 3.2   The reduction of risk through diversification.

against negative developments while taking advantage of positive ones. In other words, the concept underlines the importance of not placing all of your eggs in one basket, and choosing your baskets carefully. The approach is based on a Nobel prize winner's idea that a significant variation in returns is explained by the allocation of assets. If we extend this logic to venture capital, a sound decision toward appropriate allocation of venture capital to different types of securities, firms, industries, or sectors, and other considerations is likely to result in a strong financial performance for the portfolio. There are three basic approaches to asset allocation. The fixed-weightings approach is based on an asset allocation plan in which a fixed percentage of the portfolio is allocated to each asset category. The flexible-weightings approach refers to a method in which weights for each asset category are adjusted periodically based on market analysis. The tactical approach is based on using different investment vehicles (such as derivatives) to change a portfolio's asset allocation based on market behavior. These asset allocation concepts can be easily applied to the venture capital setting.

Capital under Management

The amount of capital the venture capital firm has under management is perhaps one of the most important considerations. The size of the fund drives the type of investment portfolio and, specifically, the number of investee businesses the venture capital firm should have. Capital also determines the resources available to manage the venture capital firm. The diversification concept in finance has simple implications for venture capitalists. If the optimal diversification is achieved by having approximately 20 assets or firms in the port-folio, venture capital firms aiming to achieve this effect should not have more than 20 firms in their portfolio in any given fund. This, in turn, affects the deal size the venture capital firm should target. For example, if the venture capital firm has one hundred million dollars under management, its average deal size should be around five million dollars.

A venture capital firm could also participate in a syndicated deal, where it supplies five million dollars to a larger pool of investment. Deal syndication is common in venture capital investing because it serves many important purposes. First, it allows participating ven-ture capital firms to spread the risk of investing into a business (especially when some risks are immediately apparent). Second, most venture capital firms have limits on the amount of capital they are able to deploy toward one firm (usually not more than 10 percent of total capital under management) or one sector of the economy (usually not more than 20 percent). Third, deal syndication fulfills an important reciprocity role in which venture capital firms aim to expand their portfolio by consciously limiting their exposure to a deal by allowing another fund or funds to participate. The hope, of course, is that other venture capital firms reciprocate at some future point with an equally attractive investment prospect.

Syndication possibilities are usually plentiful in the venture cap-ital business as investment officers move from firm-to-firm and young venture capital firms seek those with more experience in a particular situation or industry. Who leads the deal is also impor-tant. The leader is often credited with finding the deal, closing and negotiating it, and then monitoring it. Such a role has significant value. The lead investor is generally able to set the tone for how the firm achieves its goals and can decide whether or not they will have an active or passive role on the investee firm's board of directors.

Deal Orientation

The size of the deal has an immediate impact on the way venture capitalists view a potential universe of investment opportunities. If we assume that the venture capital firm wishes to accept a minority stake in an investee business, the firm must ideally target a busi-ness with a pre-money valuation of more than five million dollars. If we also assume that the venture capital firm wishes to hold a meaningful minority stake in several businesses (of not less than 25 percent), the range of possible business valuations ranges from five million dollars to fifteen million dollars.

Such a predefined valuation range provides insight into the types of hypothetical deals the venture capital firm is likely to target (assuming that the firm does not participate in deal syndication and wishes to negotiate a deal on its own). The firm is unlikely to aim for a later-stage expansion deal or privatization transaction where larger amounts of capital are necessary. Conversely, the firm will probably not be interested in seed or start-up situations where business valuations are often less than five million dollars (though many notable exceptions exist). It is likely that our hypothetical venture capital firm is eyeing young entrepreneurial firms with strong growth in sales and good operating or net profit levels. These firms, however, are usually in the early stages of development. They may also be mid-cap firms. Investee firms in this target zone likely have sales of ten million–fifty million dollars.

Sector or Industry Focus

As previously mentioned, asset allocation is one of the most important decisions a financial investor can make. For venture capitalists, this means allocation between different risk levels, types of firms, and industries or sectors. Considering that the risk related to the market, in which the firm operates, is one of the biggest enemies of entrepreneurial firms, selecting the right sector or industry is particularly important.

Many venture capital firms dedicate a significant amount of time to selecting sectors of future interest. Ideally, this exercise is performed well ahead of time, early in the process of constituting a new fund. Not all available human and capital resources may be available at the time of the new fund's formation—such analysis may only be done on a broad level, without the necessary analytical support. However, venture capitalists are mindful that sector characteristics may change over time, which, in turn, may necessitate the need to revisit initial assumptions about the attractiveness of various sectors of the economy. This may make such analysis early in the fund formation time-insensitive.

Venture capital firms generally adopt one of three approaches to defining their industrial interest. Some venture capital firms adopt a strategy of assuming a general yet undefined orientation toward sectors of the economy. They perform sector analysis sufficient enough to persuade limited partners to entrust them with capital. They assume that the "darling" sectors are likely to evolve in the future and their precise definition has limited value at the outset. They wish to remain flexible and not committed. They define their sector orientations in broad strokes as consumer, aging population, emerging markets, environmental, or "new discovery" sciences. Venture capital firms adopting such a strategy may be young, with limited experience in this exercise. Alternatively, the firm may be steered by industry veterans who have a proven track record based on historical returns. In this case, the limited partners have likely been generously rewarded in the past and will leave strategic sector decisions entirely in the hands of fund managers, without the need to know the sectors a priori. Second, some venture capital managers perform a fundamental analysis of all the major sectors of the economy with a view to identifying the most promising sectors in the long term. The idea is for venture capitalists to bet on certain sectors of the economy while ignoring others. Such analysis involves an evaluation of economic cycles, industrial sectors, demographic characteristics, social trends, government policies, and so on. This analysis may be done by the venture capital firm itself or subcontracted out to a consulting firm. The most successful venture capital firms always tend to rely on external feedback despite many successful years in venture capital investing. The most attractive sectors of the economy in the last few years have been those related to biotechnology, Internet technologies, and pharmaceuticals. Third, some venture capital firms use their previous successful experiences as a guide when selecting future investments. They believe that their historical experience is a strong indicator of future success. They also trust that their operational track record in specific sectors of the economy is likely to translate into strong returns. For example, if the venture capital firm closed deals and successfully exited from deals in certain sectors, they are likely to pursue similar sectors in the future in the same or different geographic markets.

The approaches to sectors described earlier are not mutually exclusive. The most successful firms are likely to use a combination of the three approaches. The influence of specific sector strategies upon the overall sector selection strategy is likely to differ depending on economic cycles, the fund's development stage, and the preferences of limited partners.

Once specific sectors of the economy are selected, the next step is to focus on specific firms in these sectors. While identifying sector leaders is an easy task for venture capitalists, establishing the need for capital for these firms is more difficult (especially if no prior knowledge of the sector exists within the venture capital firm). Personal contacts, sector expertise, and, most importantly, timing seem to be the key components. Specific marketing strategies for targeting firms in selected sectors are described in further sections of this chapter.

Competitive Dynamics in the Venture Capital Industry

Venture capital firms may conduct a detailed analysis of their internal deal amount specifications, perform a sector analysis and identify investment prospects, and decide on their deal orientation strategy. However, this analysis may not be sufficient and, ultimately, may prove unsuccessful for the venture capital firm. Venture capital firms need to consider the external forces and the competitive dynamics of the industry in which they plan to execute their business plan. Such analysis will determine whether their carefully crafted market strategy and marketing plan is likely to work. The implication is that if the venture capital firm chooses to focus on a competitive sector of the market where many venture capital firms with strong sector experience or deal orientation exist, the competitive dynamics may convert into higher valuations for investee firms, less optimal legal protections, and buyer's remorse. In such cases, an investment premise for the venture capital firm needs to be revised and a new, unique niche of the industry must be identified.

In most geographic markets around the globe, the venture capital industry has become quite competitive. Figure 3.3 represents an example of the competitive landscape of the 20 leading venture capital firms in one European country. The key criteria used to map the competitive spectrum are the deal size and the type of financing (seed, start-up, expansion, and other). The last category (i.e., other) includes any investment categories or activities such as management buy-outs, management buy-ins, privatizations, purchases of listed shares, restructuring and turnaround transactions, and the

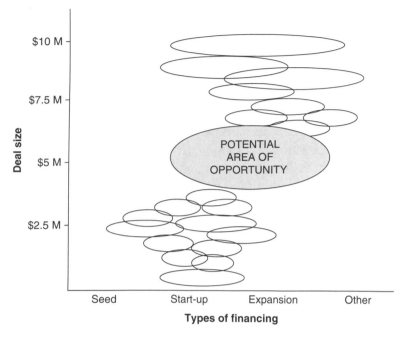

Figure 3.3 The competitive landscape of the 20 leading venture capital firms and financial institutions in one of the European countries.

refinancing of bank debt. The oval represents each venture capital firm and the breath of investment across various types of financing and transaction sizes.

Figure 3.3 shows that there are two distinctive clusters of venture capital firms. One cluster focuses on later-stage and other deals (i.e., MBO and leveraged buyouts), with the deal size between seven million and ten million dollars. The other focuses on early-stage opportunities with a deal size of around three million dollars. Clearly, a market opportunity exists for a venture capital firm that focuses on expansion deals with a deal size of around five million dollars.

The significance of the competitive section is to highlight the importance of competitive dynamics to venture capital firms when developing deal generation strategies. A careful strategy may translate into a short- or medium-term strategic window of opportunity for the venture capital firm, where the marketplace may be less crowded. Ultimately, if the strategy proves successful and exits yield handsome returns, the competitive window will be challenged and ultimately closed.

Other Considerations

Venture capital firms also face other considerations. Some firms may have a geographic preference to serve a specific part of their country, region, or continent. This preference is often related to time and costs of travel, language skills, knowledge of the market, business contacts, and so on. Investors generally prefer to make investments close to their home markets. Second, some venture capitalists prefer hands-on involvement in investee firms. Venture capitalists with industry career backgrounds are more likely to get involved in a firm's operations while those with consulting or financial backgrounds may have less practical experience and may not feel comfortable in such a role. Third, the behavior of venture capitalists may change during different stages of a fund's life. During the early stages, venture capital firms are generally occupied with deal generation and making new investments—they prefer less hands-on involvement. Fundraising for a new fund enables a venture capital firm to showcase its ability to exit from deals—and may drive its propensity to exit from investee firms.

Networking for Venture Capitalists

Relationships are a basic human need, and creating camaraderie and connections between others is instinctive to all individuals. One of the ways in which this is done is through social networking. Business opportunities are created through active interaction between people, whether by making contacts or by building strong relationships or partnerships. Such networks grow in size and deepen in strength. Over time, they yield other contacts, relationships, and opportunities. Networking is based on a mutual exchange of benefits and principles of reciprocity. It is the creation and cultivation of interpersonal relationships.

Networking is action-oriented. It involves sharing information, ideas, and contacts between one person and another. It may involve actions such as giving and receiving contacts and referrals, introducing people, making specific or general requests, sending notes and emails, exchanging business cards, and attending networking events. Networking requires constant action to maintain the regular flow of information. The regular exchange and accessing of information through an informal or formal network accomplishes this. A social network is a group of individuals with significant personal or business connections. It is an organized system in which information is exchanged; a multidimensional connection of individuals with common goals or purpose.

The value of a strong network of professional contacts is well recognized. Colloquial business sayings capture it best: "It's is not what you know, but who you know" or "It isn't who you know, but who knows you and knows what you know." Professional networking is often regarded as the lifeblood of strong careers and businesses. As traditional promotional tools become more expensive and ineffective on a smaller scale, professional business networking, done well, can be ten times more effective than traditional marketing mechanisms. Business networking also identifies hidden and unknown business opportunities that are likely to form the basis of a strong competitive advantage for firms. A strong professional network extends the sphere of the firm's opportunity beyond its direct business contacts.

Venture Capitalists and Networking

Venture capitalists are by nature active and dedicated networkers. They know that their professional business networks are critical to their success. The practical experience of many venture capitalists confirms that venture capital firms with sustainable business networks are able to convert them into strong returns, less operational problems, and more pronounced exits. These conclusions are intuitive to venture capitalists—more proprietary deals lead to higher quality deals. In their daily interactions, venture capitalists rely on a wide network of service providers: limited partners and their advisors, portfolio firms, investment bankers and deal brokers, commercial bankers, lawyers, accountants, recruitment specialists, various consultants, and so on. Venture capitalists also know that the best investment opportunities are not widely shopped around. The best deals are normally circulated among a circle of "friends-and-family," where strong prior professional and personal relationships exist. This is based on the fact that entrepreneurs most often start their search for capital from a point of comfort: the people they know or have done business with.

The following paragraphs describe the most common tools used by venture capitalists in developing professional business networks:

Contact Registry: Most venture capital firms maintain a searchable electronic registry of contacts or deal leads. Most venture capitalists review these lists, actively maintain them, and refresh the contacts on at least a semi-annual basis. Even a database of rejected deals, depending on the reason for rejection, may become a viable source of deal flow at some point in the future.

Professional Associations: Most venture capitalists belong to a venture capital association in their geographic district. Depending on their professional background, venture capitalists also belong to their respective professional associations (i.e., engineering, medical sciences, accounting, law). These associations are important portals in which to exchange information and contacts. Many venture capitalists are also in contact with organizations that aim to help small and medium sized businesses. These organizations include local chambers of commerce, regional small business administration offices, universities, business incubators, innovation centers, and so on.

Networking Sites: The use of the Internet to connect capital to entrepreneurial firms is one of fastest growing areas of entrepreneurial support. Most networking sites operate in a similar fashion. The website manager assumes responsibility for generating deals and prequalifies these deals before showing them to potential financiers (be they venture capital firms or angel investors). Entrepreneurial firms are asked to submit a brief business overview of the venture to the website, followed by a full business plan. The service can be free of charge or cost a nominal amount. Once financial providers have made a favorable assessment of interested candidates, personal contacts are made and the role of the website effectively ends.

Conferences: Venture capital firms and owners of young entrepreneurial firms are invited to a physical venue for live interaction. Essentially, entrepreneurial firms make short presentations to a wider group of venture capitalists and, subsequently, meet face-to-face to explore deals in more detail. These interactions are usually combined with a wide range of speakers in entrepreneurship and financing. Entrepreneurial firms often receive one-on-one coaching by conference organizers on presentation skills, preparation of documents, and the fundamentals of venture capital.

Trade Fairs: Exhibitions and trade fairs represent one of the most effective ways to generate new business, especially if venture capitalists are not familiar with a given industry. At these events, leading industry players present their products and services in an attempt to generate business. By walking from booth to booth, venture capitalists are able to quickly ascertain product and service quality, the level of interest from firm's potential clients, the firm's strategy in terms of product positioning in the marketplace, and other criteria.

Cold Calls: Most venture capital firms attest to the fact that a significant amount of deal flow comes from "cold calls." These are telephone calls placed by the venture capital firm to potential investment prospects. The leads to these unsolicited phone calls come from a variety of sources: publications and newspapers, Internet searches, entrepreneurial clubs and conferences, trade shows and trade associations, recruitment ads, and so on. Venture capital firms pursue various strategies with respect to cold calls. Some assign the job to junior staff, while in other circumstances associates prepare the background research and senior partners make direct contact with potential investee firms.

The Marketing Plan

The marketing plan for a venture capital firm usually consists of many different components. These include a brochure of the venture capital firm, a "pitch book," a website, and media presence (i.e., participation in public relations events, conferences, and newspaper articles). The first two components of the program (the fund's brochure and pitch book) are marketing materials used by the venture capital firm when it meets face-to-face with investment prospects. The latter two marketing tools (website and media presence) are used to promote the venture capital firm to a wider audience.

The brochure is a summary of basic information about the fund. It commonly includes the year founded, a list of limited partners, background information on key partners in the fund, a summary of deal characteristics sought by the fund, and a brief outline of its investment process. The brochure often includes a list of the fund's investee firms, which may be added to the brochure as leaflets. The firm's information is updated once per year and either a new brochure is printed or the updates are inserted as additional pages. Many venture capital firms also have a printed version of the document describing the key components of the business plan venture capitalists wish to see.

The pitch book is often used when the venture capital firm makes a face-to-face visit with the investee firm. Pitch books are used to outline general information about the fund, listing the key components as described earlier. Pitch books are often used in competitive situations where it is important to clearly lay out the differences between different venture capital firms seeking the attention of the potential investment prospect. In such cases, the pitch book outlines the sector expertise, the speed with which the fund is able to close the deal, the outline of key deal components, the description of the due diligence process, and other features. Venture capital firms generally have one general template of the pitch and tend to amend it to fit the specific circumstances of a situation.

The Internet website, on the other hand, has become an increasingly important tool for showcasing the activities of the venture capital firm. Websites become instruments for communication between employees, limited partners, and investee firms. Most websites include information similar to that found in the brochure or pitch book. While the Internet website rarely becomes a key factor in choosing the venture capital firm, it can easily create a negative perception if not done well. Ease of navigation through the website is considered an important feature.

Media presence can include a vast array of marketing techniques. Active venture capital firms regularly attend and present at conferences organized by local venture capital associations or entrepreneurial organizations and clubs. They also tend to write newspaper or magazine articles featuring new investments, exits, operational success stories, market analysis, and general business environment commentaries. These articles often include quotes from management or owners of investee firms. Such articles act as good advertising for the venture capital firm and its investee firms. Venture capital firms either perform this role internally by hiring a media specialist in the firm or by outsourcing this service to a specialized media relations firm.

Marketing Strategy

The marketing strategy for the venture capital firm involves deciding on the most effective use of its internal resources, both human and capital, to generate a desired stream of investment opportunities. Figure 3.4 presents a simplistic approach for depicting different

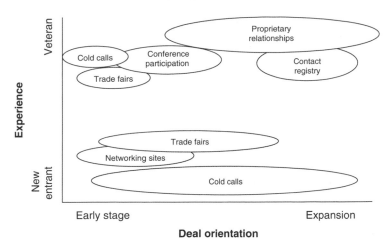

Figure 3.4 The effectiveness of various marketing tools used by venture capitalists when considering two criteria: the venture capital firm's experience in the market and its deal orientation.

marketing tactics and strategies within the context of the venture capital firm's experience in the industry (veteran versus new entrant) and its deal orientation (early-stage versus expansion deals).

Industry veterans normally rely on their past experience and a wide network of contacts to generate deals. They have excellent contacts with firms that have been in operation for some time as well as with new firms operated by serial entrepreneurs. Consequently, the most effective strategies for these firms involve the further nurturing of previous relationships. A careful review of deal contacts or the deal registry is also necessary. Veteran venture capital firms are usually invited to professional conferences as key speakers, moderators, and panel discussants. Their participation reflects their years of experience, knowledge of the industry, specific deal experience (both positive and negative), and reputation in the marketplace. Industry veterans also wish to maintain exposure to younger firms with which no prior relationships may exist. This is normally done through participation in trade fairs and cold calls.

New entrants into the venture capital industry generally have a difficult time generating deals. They must rely on "turning stones" by engaging in cold calling, attending trade fairs and exhibitions, and networking. For new venture capital firms, the experience of generating investment opportunities may be slightly different if the fund is founded by experienced venture capitalists with strong reputations and proprietary contacts in the industry.

Marketing Budget

The overall deal generation activities conducted by the venture capital firm can be expensive. These costs include human resources, printing, and travel and can add up to a substantial amount over a long period of time. However, many venture capital firms do not include expenses associated with deal generation activities when they are preparing to raise a new venture capital fund and do not budget for a specific amount when the fund is actually operating.

The importance of the budget to deal generation is threefold. First, it captures the amount of money actually committed to and used in deal generation activities. These amounts vary from year-to-year and the venture capital firm needs to track these amounts. The most active venture capital firms spend up to 5 percent of their management fee on deal generation, with the least active ones spending less than ten thousand dollars. Second, the budget forms the basis for an evaluation of which methods may be the most effective for deal generation within the firm. This is likely to differ from one firm to another and depends on the venture capital firm's operating region, the types of investment prospects sought, the size of the fund, travel requirements, and so on. Finally, the budget forces the venture capital firm to review deal generation activities on a regular basis. Some venture capital firms have a tendency to over-rely on proprietary deal flows; only when these end do they start paying attention to proactive deal generation activities.

The Entrepreneur's Pitch

A discussion on deal generation would not be complete without consideration to the type of "deal pitch" entrepreneurs should make to venture capitalists and, in turn, what types of presentations venture capitalists are likely to embrace. The sections that follow outline key areas that entrepreneurs should focus on and the biggest "turn-offs" for venture capitalists.

Sound Business Pitch

Numerous articles, blogs, books, and video presentations have been prepared on the art of pitching to venture capitalists. Some venture capitalists believe that the pitch should have a marketing orientation (it should be treated as a promotional presentation) while others believe that it should fulfill an educational role (to explain key concepts). In any case, there are critical points to remember when pitching to venture capitalists.

Most venture capitalists want the presentation kept to about ten slides (or less) and delivered in 20 minutes from start to finish. If it takes more than that to persuade the listeners, the pitch is unlikely to work. The slides are likely to include descriptions of the following items: firm's overview, team, problem, solution, customer value, competitive advantage, business model, market size, financial projections, financing needs, and operational milestones. The content of these slides is described in the following paragraphs.

Slide 1—Firm's overview: This is the foundational slide, which is explored in detail in later slides. This slide establishes the firm's credibility and focuses on the following components: the business, a unique value that addresses a particular market need (this could be unique technology or solutions), key business relationships (including any recognized brand names), and the firm's status (commencement date, current customers and order book, revenue, and funding needs).

Slide 2—The team: A brief summary of key personnel. This slide helps venture capitalists understand why a specific group of individuals is well suited to solve a market need or problem. The team's professional experience and track record is considered critical for achieving success. Venture capitalists look for a complete team rather than solo entrepreneurs. Some venture capitalists like to meet other members of the team in addition to the CEO or president.

Slide 3—The problem: This slide clearly identifies the market need that the entrepreneurs wish to address. This fundamental problem must be real rather than an inconvenience or a minor irritant to customers. This slide defines the extent of the problem, why it exists in the marketplace, and why it has not been corrected so far. The arguments need to be well grounded in market data, statistics, expert opinions, customer research, and so on—preferably this data is proprietary (gathered by the firm) rather than "generic."

Slide 4—Solution: The solution to the identified market problem is one of the most important points that venture capitalists must immediately understand. This is where many presentations fail. The slide must show how the venture solves the problem, why current solutions in the marketplace are inadequate or nonexistent, and what the product or service features and benefits are to customers. In other words, what is the magic solution?

Slide 5—Customer value: This slide provides the proof that the solution actually works in the marketplace. Venture capitalists want to know that a sound business idea has already been converted into orders or, better yet, actual sales—this proves that the concept is likely to work on a larger scale. This part of the presentation may include customer testimonials, an order book, a pricing strategy, and customer ROI.

Slide 6—Competitive advantage: This slide captures the competitive dynamics in the marketplace by describing direct competitors (both incumbents and new start-ups), key advantages of the business over them, and why these advantages are sustainable and defensible. It is important to outline real technological barriers and why other firms (with arguably larger wallets) are unlikely to pursue this same opportunity. Relevant intellectual property and know-how are important here, as well.

Slide 7—Business model: This slide focuses on how the various parts of the entrepreneurial firm may work together to make money for the firm and venture capitalists. This slide is about the economics of the business. It also includes a discussion of the firm's key relationships and partnerships. Venture capitalists prefer tested and proven business models rather than newly developed ones.

Slide 8: Market size: This section focuses on the size of the market, its growth, and its maturity. Market size is defined in terms of value and volume, based on verifiable data and analysis. Marketing and promotional strategies to capture the market are described. Market is regarded as the worst enemy of young entrepreneurial firms.

Slide 9—Financial projections: Key figures in the financial projections for the next three–five years include revenue growth, key profitability figures (EBIT or EBITDA), and cash flow. Key assumptions, milestones, and operating break-even points also need to be included. This slide also pinpoints metrics that drive revenue and cost structures.

Slide 10—Financial needs and operational milestones: This slide describes the rollout plan for the venture and its financial needs at key points in time. It includes an outline of how much the firm is looking to raise, what operational milestones can be reached, and how far venture capitalists' capital (ideally placed in tranches into the firm) lasts in conservative and pessimistic scenarios.

Entrepreneurs should also have additional slides "in reserve" describing other important points that may be introduced during the meeting. Issues that may arise for discussion include: proposed business valuation, exit strategy, detailed market analysis, full set of financial projections, and so on. Some venture capitalists also like opening and concluding slides.

Additional Hints for Effective Presentation

Venture capitalists want to see a clearly identified market need and a solution for it. They prefer basic business ideas rather than complex ones; they prefer easy-to-repeat stories that are easily recalled after the meeting has ended. Venture capitalists want to get the message quickly. This is why venture capitalists like it when the core concept of the presentation is distilled into a 30-second short statement, or "elevator pitch."

Venture capitalists prefer to hear a short and focused presentation instead of a boring and drawn-out presentation of all facts and figures. If they like the deal, they want to get into the value proposition quickly and the next steps right away. If they do not like the deal, no amount of additional persuasion is likely to change their minds. It is important for entrepreneurs to be in charge of the meeting and control the flow of the presentation. This also means that entrepreneurs must be flexible in their approach to the presentation (e.g., skipping a few slides) should venture capitalists want to inquire about other points (either included later in the presentation or not discussed in the slides). Entrepreneurs should be prepared to change their presentation midway through if the audience wants to hear more on a specific topic. Venture capitalists' body language and questions help entrepreneurs in this respect.

Venture capitalists like entrepreneurs to be passionate about their business idea and the firm. They like to see that entrepreneurs are committed to the success of the venture. The presentation should be upbeat, enthusiastic, interesting, and honest.

It is important for entrepreneurs to be selective in their approach to venture capital firms. Entrepreneurs need to investigate the specifics of the venture capital firm they are presenting to. They must obtain information on the venture capital firm's team members, the closed deals (including problem cases), areas of interest, philosophy, preferred mode of cooperation with investee firms, and so on. There is nothing worse than pitching to the "wrong" venture capital firm.

Turn-offs for Venture Capitalists

Table 3.1 presents a summary of key turn-offs for venture capitalists. The table also includes what venture capitalists would like to see in lieu of the specific turn-off. The turn-offs are classified into five major categories: business plan preparation, management, revenue model, unit economics, and personal contributions.

Table 3.1   A brief list of turn-offs for venture capitalists

Category	Turn-offs for venture capitalists	What venture capitalists would like to see
Business plan preparation	• Too polished, too slick • Prepared by consultants • Based on others' research	• Thought through business plan • Business plan resting on strong logic and own research
Management	• "First-time" entrepreneurs • Incomplete management team	• "Serial entrepreneurs" • Entrepreneurs and TEAM
Revenue model	• Sales: a "hockey stick" • High fixed asset base • High "cash burn"	• "Bottom-up" sales confirmation • High variable cost component • Low "cash burn" and break-even point
Unit economics	• Revenue model does not work for a single unit • Relying on "critical mass" to resolve problem above	• Concept works on a single unit basis • "Critical mass" increases firms' profitability
Personal contribution	• No financial commitment • Taking money out of firm	• Financial contribution meaningful to entrepreneurs • Limited or no money out

Questions to Consider

1. Suppose you are working for a newly created venture capital firm in your geographic region. The fund has $150 million under management and four employees so far. Prepare a brief marketing plan for your venture capital fund, including a basic budget.
2. Create a competitive landscape of venture capital firms operating in your geographic area. Use criteria used in this chapter to chart the competitive landscape or develop your own criteria (different criteria need to be evaluated to best map the competitive dynamics). Then, see if there is a market gap that a newly created venture capital firm could effectively fill.
3. How do marketing needs change as venture capital firms move from an early development stage to maturity?
4. Discuss the prerequisites of a successful venture capital pitch.
5. Discuss company specific and market risks and how these concepts may apply to venture capital.

Advent International

Key characteristics

Year founded:	1984
Founding partners:	Peter Brooke
Number of limited partners (example):	~200 (CPP, CalSTERS, Alpinvest)
Geographic coverage:	North America (1 location), Europe (10), Asia (1), Latin America (3)
Headquarter location:	Boston (USA)
Focus (if any):	Wide range
Funds under management:	$24.0 billion
Number of completed deals and IPO exits:	~500 deals/140 IPOs
Private/public:	Private
Most publicly recognized deals:	Lululemon, Dufry, Poundland, Hudson News, HMV
Number of investment professionals:	140

Advent International is regarded as one of the most traditional private equity firms and as one of the most regionally expansive private equity players. The firm manages over $24 billion, which is committed on behalf of more than 200 institutional limited partners (35 percent of the capital comes from public pension funds). This capital has been converted into more than 500 deals. The firm's strong exit orientation is confirmed by its achieving more than 140 IPO exits.

Advent's investment philosophy is based on global partnership, which includes collaboration between regional offices and strategic (operating) partnerships. Advent focuses on a wide range of sectors, including business and financial services, healthcare, industrial, retail, consumer goods, leisure, technology, media, and telecoms. Its buyout orientation is dedicated toward mid-market and upper-mid-market opportunities. Advent's disciplined approach to seeking out investment opportunities in these areas has allowed it to become an effective hands-on partner for growing an investee firms' value. This, in turn, has translated into many successful exits for the firm. Advent's expertise has been recognized through its being awarded many industry accolades, including Buyouts European Deal of the Year (2008) and Buyouts Emerging Market Deal of the Year (2007).

Advent's strategy is implemented by a pool of 140 investment professionals in 15 nations (Advent's network of affiliates extends its coverage by a further 8 countries). Advent prides itself on its close collaboration and communication with its different regional networks. A third of Advent's investment professionals have strong industrial, operational, or consulting backgrounds; others posses mostly financial expertise.

Source: *www.adventinternational.com.*

Chapter 4

Initial Screening

The process used by venture capitalists to make investment decisions lies at the heart of venture capital investing. Practitioners of venture capital regard the venture capital process as a combination of art and science. The science relates to the application of specific and concrete decision criteria to a detailed and technical investigation of the market or industry, competition, technical issues, the investee firm's financial performance, and its valuation. By relying on internal and external resources, venture capitalists are able to arrive at concrete, technical conclusions about a firm's future prospects and its past operational performance. There are, however, other aspects of the assessment that are more difficult to ascertain. The "art" of venturing relates to the "soft," unquantifiable, less tangible, non-concrete, and subtle evaluations embodied in the assessment of people, deal terms, negotiating tactics, and the "investment story." Sometimes referred to as "venture capitalist intuition," this assessment can be more appropriately categorized as an experience-based judgment call. Some academic researchers argue that the traditional approaches based on the concrete assessment of tangible criteria may be less reliable and relevant to venture capital decision-making today.

Extensive research has been conducted to examine the importance of the various decision-making criteria used by venture capitalists. The field can be separated into three broad areas: (1) studies assessing venture performance and returns; (2) research focusing on the venture capital process and the decision-making environment; and (3) literature focusing on the evaluation of venture capitalists' investment decision criteria.

Research investigating the decision criteria of venture capitalists has evolved over time, but has produced modestly consistent results. Three distinct phases can be identified. The earlier research conducted in the 1970s and 1980s focused on identifying the criteria used by venture capitalists in evaluating potential businesses and ascertaining their relative importance through the usage of descriptive statistics. The second wave of investigations focused on the use of linear statistical methods to condense the decision criteria into identifiable groups. Five groups or criteria reflecting five types of risks in venture capital investment were identified: management risk, investment risk, competitive risk, operational risk, and cash out risk. Others came up with similar decision criteria and identified the decision-making criteria focusing on the importance of management, market, product, external environment, and cash out. In an attempt to advance prior investigation (which had previously concentrated on the usage of a "laundry list" of decision criteria), other groupings of decision-making criteria were identified, including those related to product-market, strategic-competitive, financial, management-team, and management competence.

While considerable insight had been achieved by the middle of the 1980s, researchers still felt that the decision-making process of venture capitalists was not yet completely understood. One of the most distinguished academics in this area stated that prior research failed to capture and convey the richness, subtlety, and discernment embodied in the venture capitalist's decision process and criteria. Such a statement underscored the inability of researchers to fully quantify the complexities of the venture capital decision-making process. As a result, researchers in the 1990s and 2000s chose to focus on verbal protocol—a technique based on active interaction between researchers and respondents—to further expand their understanding of the decision criteria environment.

There are many factors that influence the final investment decisions made by venture capitalists. The initial screening process tends to be related to the assessment of two primary areas: the commercial attractiveness of the investment (the "commercial proposition") and project "do-ability." The key areas related to assessing a project's attractiveness are the entrepreneur and management (as well as their track record), market size, and growth (including market share). The second assessment area within the initial screening relates to the probability of the project being completed. In other words, this assessment relates to the venture capital firm's ability to successfully complete the deal on terms satisfactory to venture capitalists. This component generally relates to deal issues involving financial contracting, such as structuring, pricing (i.e., business valuation), and expected returns. Venture capitalists must be assured that, with significant rights and protections, they have negotiated the best deal. This assessment is especially important given the above-average risk of deal failure seen in venture capital industry.

The Analysis of the Commercial Proposition

The overall analysis of a business consists of a general assessment of the firm and a complete financial analysis. The two areas are interconnected and analysis in one area without a thorough understanding of the other would lead to an incomplete overall analysis and potentially inappropriate conclusions. For example, a proper investigation of the firm's financial standing cannot occur without a strong understanding of the firm's context (both internal strengths and external forces). On the other hand, the firm's general assessment cannot be properly done without reference to its financial standing, which often reflects the firm's strength in key business areas. A common ground of assessment for both key areas is the analysis of the firm's profitability (or its margins). This approach is presented in figure 4.1.

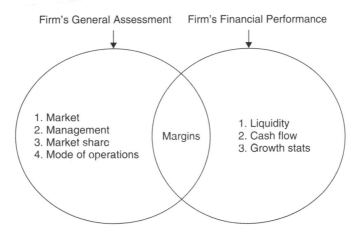

Figure 4.1 The two categories of the firm's analysis: its general assessment and the analysis of its financial performance.

Company General Assessment—5M Principles

This section focuses on the assessment of the attractiveness of the firm. This approach is based on "5M principle" analysis—a comprehensive methodology for analyzing firms. This framework can be applied not only toward the venture capital investment decision-making process, but also to firm self-assessment. The 5M-principle is based on the following components: market, market share, management, margins, and mode of business operations (i.e., the business model).

Market

A debate exists between venture capitalists as to whether or not the market or management is more important to a successful venture. Many venture capital firms hold the view that management is the key variable, while others believe that market potential ultimately drives the success of a firm. Careful observations and analysis from the business world suggest that many successful firms have been built with unproven management teams. On the other hand, even the most talented management teams will fail in the wrong markets. For this reason, a common sense approach suggests that the market criteria should be at the center of analysis. Venture capitalists can change, build, and develop inferior management teams; conversely, they cannot do anything about the market's conditions, its size, growth rates, customer perceptions, and so on. Consequently, venture capitalists regard market risks as their worst enemy (risks related to management, technology, operating, and financing are controllable to some extent). Venture capitalists will not pursue an investment if they have significant hesitations about the market and its future potential. A proper assessment of the market is regarded as the most strategic analysis undertaken by an entrepreneur. Consistent with the common saying "a rising tide raises all ships," venture capitalists prefer to invest in firms operating in markets that are sizeable, rapidly growing, have limited competition and no dominant players. Conversely, they avoid markets that are small, shrinking, competitive, and heavily regulated.

Defining customer interests, price sensitivities, loyalty, sales cycles, and other variables helps to forecast opportunities and enable the firms and venture capitalists to understand the driving forces of the market. The key components of market analysis are market size and growth rates. Firms need to know the size of the market in which they compete as defined in terms of value (expressed in dollars) and volume (in units). The size of the market determines the firm's potential level of sales, its existing competitive pressures, and its earning potential. Venture capitalists also focus on growth rates—both in the past and those projected for the future—for at least three subsequent years. This information determines the firm's market share and maximum growth rates without the need to take market share away from existing market competitors. What any business wants to avoid is participation in a market with declining demand. Many entrepreneurs argue that it is difficult to estimate market size and growth rates, especially in situations where market forecasts, industry reports, and expert opinions are not available.

Let's imagine that you are looking to start a business installing shingles in a town with a population of thirty thousand people, and that you are trying to estimate the market size. The city planning office confirms that there are five thousand houses in the city, of which about 25 percent are less than ten years old. The city planning office estimates that there are one hundred and fifty new houses built every year—this number has been going up by an average of 5 percent per year. There are about seven hundred buildings used for commercial purposes. We can further estimate that an average house needs approximately three thousand square feet of shingles. Each square foot of shingles costs one dollar. From this basic observation, we can estimate that if all the houses lost their shingles in a natural disaster—say, a tornado—the total cost to replace them would be equal to fifteen million dollars. Of course, this is not a realistic description of the market, but it outlines the maximum market potential at any one point in time. In the case of your shingling business, you would need to estimate how many new houses would need their shingles replaced every year. We can estimate this by obtaining from the city planning office a breakdown of ages of all the houses (they should have this information); otherwise, some guesswork would be required. Let's say that each house that is more than fifteen years old requires new shingles. Assuming that we know how old the houses are, we can estimate a current market that will see new additions to it every year. We can also estimate the percentage of people that will replace their shingles in the 16th year, 17th year, and so on. Once an estimate has been reached, we can add it to the estimated square footage of shingles used for new housing and obtain the total estimated square footage; from this, we can estimate the total market size.

Management

The presence of management is second only to the market as the most important variable for venture capitalists to consider. In order to succeed in business, management needs experience, education, values, a track record, capability in process management, and—most importantly—a clear vision (this is often supplied by the entrepreneur, who starts the business and pursues an opportunity-driven business action). A strong management team is also necessary, as venture capitalists tend to finance entrepreneurial teams rather than individual entrepreneurs.

One of the first decisions that entrepreneurs must face is whether to start the business on their own or build a management team. Academic research and business logic suggests that the firms with the most complete management teams have the highest chance of success in business. It is generally believed that a business started by a team has a distinct advantage over one started by an incomplete management team or a single entrepreneur. A team of individuals is a source of multiple talents, has more ideas, has access to a wider network of business contacts, and provides psychological support to one another. It is also important that members of the team have direct experience in the industry in which they plan to establish the business. This experience provides the team with an appreciation of the key success factors, business and profit drivers, competitive dynamics, and market growth opportunities that may affect them in the industry. In addition, access to an already developed business network is critical. Not surprisingly, relevant industry experience is also regarded as one of the key factors of business success. Ideally, entrepreneurs and management team members will possess a combination of relevant experience, prior entrepreneurial experience, university training, and a broad professional network.

The value of the management team rests on a number of assumptions. First, a team that has worked together in the past is perceived as more valuable than a group of individuals who have not. This underscores the need for strong team dynamics, trust in and personal appreciation for each others' skills and talents, and an ability to effectively address challenges and problems; in short, the team enjoys working together. A group of individuals untested in difficult circumstances may be less attractive to venture capitalists than a team that has weathered difficult situations in the past. Second, it is important that team members have a diverse range of business experience. Team members should not have talents, skills, and capabilities that are homogenous; rather, they should have complimentary skill sets. Differing backgrounds of team members ensures constructive debate, alternative points of view, and value-added conflict, which translates into better long-term decision-making for the business.

Market Share

Business strategy refers to the way a firm competes in a given industry. The business strategy must specify what resources are needed and how they will be obtained, as limited resources may be available. Without a strong business strategy to deal with important business issues, a business venture cannot grow and, therefore, will not survive.

A firm's competitive strategy focuses on improving the competitive position of the firm's products and services within its specific industry or market segment. Michael Porter provided a framework for analysis of the competitive dynamics in the marketplace (i.e., six forces—the threat of new entrants; rivalry among existing firms; the threat of substitute products or services; the bargaining power of buyers; the bargaining power of suppliers; and the relative power of shareholders). Porter argued in his book, *Competitive Strategy: Techniques for Analyzing Industries and Competitors,*[1] that the collective nature of these forces ultimately drives the industry's profit potential. Furthermore, he defined two basic competitive strategies available to firms. The cost leadership strategy relates to how firms seek a cost advantage over their competitors in their target market. Firms employing this strategy are extremely good at reducing the overall costs of their business. Examples include achieving economies of scale, going down the learning curve, reducing the cost of inputs, and revamping the value chain (i.e., by stripping away extra features or simplifying product design). This strategy is especially effective when price competition among market players is particularly vigorous, products offered in the marketplace are virtually identical, there are few ways of achieving product differentiation, and buyers are large and have significant bargaining power over suppliers. The differentiation strategy involves the creation of a product or service that is unique to the marketplace. Successful differentiators generally command premium pricing for their products and gain customer loyalty. This strategy is based on providing products and services with unique characteristics that are not easily imitated by rivals or that contain features competitors do not have. Product or service differentiation may come from different sources: multiple features, superior service, product reliability, technological leadership, and so on. These features may be the result of a product focus, superior supply chain activities, strong research and development, or superior marketing and promotional activities. The differentiation strategy works best when there are many avenues to differentiate a product and customers perceive these differentiators as having value, technological inventions are fast-paced, and customers have diverse preferences.

The key to being a successful competitor in the industry is achieving a sustainable competitive advantage. This relates to a firm's ability to use its internal knowledge (both explicit and tacit) to achieve a long-term superior market position over its competitors. The long-term sustainability of the competitive market position is defined by the firm's ability to maintain its capabilities, resources, and competencies (i.e., durability) and the rate at which these special attributes can be duplicated by competitors (i.e., imitability).

The essence of competitive dynamics in the marketplace and a firm's performance relative to other competitors can be captured by a single number—the market share. Market share defines the percentage of the total market that is captured by the firm's specific product or service and can be expressed in absolute or relative terms. When it is expressed in a percentile, it can be derived on the basis of value or unit sales volume. It most simply can be defined as a firm's sales or revenue divided by the total estimated market value (expressed in absolute terms). A market share expressed in relative terms would capture the firm's competitive position in relation to its competitors, expressed as a ratio.

Increasing market share is one of the most critical strategic objectives for any business. A growing market share indicates that the firm is offering a competitive product or service in the marketplace, that the firm has a loyal and supportive customer base, that the marketing is optimal, that the firm's distribution logistics work well, and that the firm has a sustainable competitive advantage. The most common reward for firms that grow their market share is an increase in profitability. A declining market share indicates the opposite—problems with the product or service offering, customer dissatisfaction, and distribution challenges. A continued period of declining market share quickly translates into declining profitability—a deadly combination for any business.

Margins

The margin or profitability analysis is normally a part of the firm's financial assessment. However, since a general assessment of the firm should also include a basic understanding of the firm's efficiency in generating sustainable levels of profitability at the most important parts of the income statement—namely EBITDA (earnings before interest, taxes, depreciation, and amortization) and EBIT (earnings before interest and taxes)—a discussion is warranted in this section. In other words, no proper assessment of the firm can be done without paying attention to an analysis of the firm's profitability.

Since the financial analysis section (which follows) discusses the firm's overall profitability, this section will focus on the profitability of the firm at the micro level. This process includes an analysis of profitability of individual products, services, contracts, projects, and clients. Venture capitalists need to see that a firm can operate its smaller units in a profitable manner and that all the micro parts of the business make a meaningful contribution to the overall profitability of the business. The objective of margin analysis is to gain an understanding of the most profitable parts of the business. This information is then used to maximize profitability and minimize the less profitable or money-losing units.

Additional discussion of this area is included in the "Financial Analysis of Business Plans" section.

The Mode of Operations or Business Model

A business model may be simply defined as a framework that a firm uses to create value. It is a formal description of the inner components or building blocks of the firm and their relationships to one another. In other words, a business model is an analysis of the structural and operational features of a firm, of how these components fit together, and how they ultimately convert into value for founding shareholders. These features include operating strategies, distribution channels, corporate structure, sources of competitive and sustainable competitive advantage, marketing and promotional procedures, value proposition, target customer base, customer relationships, and cost structure. In short, the business model outlines the way the business is operated.

Today, entrepreneurs and business owners can operate their businesses in a variety of ways. They can operate their firms on a full-time or part-time basis (while retaining their job), or start their business with limited financial contributions and center their operations on the virtual transfer of products through the use of Internet technologies. They can also develop their operations with know-how and capital assistance from nearby business incubators that temporarily house their operations.

While some approaches to business carry with them different risks, rewards, start-up and operating expenses, and abilities to generate revenue and profit, business owners have a wide variety of business models to choose from. The most popular approaches to business include: home-based models, "brick-and-mortar" (BAM) models, e-commerce models, franchising models, licensing models, and multilevel marketing (MLM) models. These business models are described in table 4.1, along with a description of their advantages and disadvantages. Some of the business models described in table 4.1 may be employed on a stand-alone basis, while others may be amalgamated into combinations or clusters. The most popular business combination clusters are home-based e-commerce and home-based licensing. Many successful Internet-based businesses have been started from garages or sheds and many successful software programs have been written in the home basement.

A successful, value-generating business model is tied directly to a proper understanding of value-creating activities. This framework of activities is generally described as a value chain. A typical value chain for a manufacturing firm includes raw material sourcing, manufacturing, distributing, and retailing. The critical point in such an analysis is to understand the firm's center of gravity in the value chain. This represents the area in which the firm has the most expertise and, therefore, a competitive advantage. The key point in value chain analysis is to investigate the value-creating activities of the firm that will result in the most profit potential for the business.

Table 4.1 Business models and their advantages/disadvantages to business owners

Business model	Brief description	Advantages	Disadvantages
Home-based	• Mainly focused on product resale • Run from a dedicated place	• Ability to test the market without incurring "normal" operational costs • Ease to scale and adjust • Ability to outsource products • Can sustain some growth in operations • Low-cost operation	• Customer traffic in residential area may not be welcomed by neighbors • Requires permits and zoning approvals • Product storage and distribution may be problematic • "Flight-by-night" perception of the business • Potential conflict between business and home life
Brick-and-mortar (BAM)	• A dedicated physical facility outside of home • Available facility for product storage, production, and distribution • Facility to house employees	• Customers' perception of a "real business" • Physical presence of the business may induce customer traffic and increase revenues	• Higher start-up costs • Wind-up costs if business does not perform • Requires a longer-term financial commitment • May not be scalable
E-commerce	• Internet-based business • Customer traffic mainly related to Internet activities • Maybe operated from home	• Lower risk and lower start-ups costs • Maybe be operated on a part-time basis • Scalable • Ability to develop nationally or internationally • Opportunity for a rapid business expansion	• Limited face-to-face interaction with customers • Limited physical space may limit operations • Web development costs may be substantial • High competition on the web may make products difficult to spot by customers

Continued

Table 4.1 Continued

Business model	Brief description	Advantages	Disadvantages
Franchising	• Based on a long-term agreement with the franchisor • Operating an already proven concept • Variety of business opportunities available	• Lower operational risk by using proven business processes • Hands-on assistance from a franchisor • Recognized and established brand • Lower business failure risk possibility • Availability of new products or services	• Upfront licensing fees and high royalty fees (about 2–4 percent of revenue) • Franchise guidelines can restrict operational freedom and limit creativity in developing business opportunities
Licensing	• Based on a product that is already developed • Based on providing rights to sell products by another business	• Ability to test a new product • Other businesses assume market risk for introducing and selling the product • Lower start-up costs of the business	• Finding the right partner may take time • Seller may require product development • Low earning potential (profit based on royalties)
Multilevel marketing (MLM)	• Effectively a multilayer distribution structure • Based on a network of individuals	• Limited start-up costs • Maybe operated from home on a part-time basis • Variety of products may be sold	• Finding the right people • Management of complex structure • Business credibility

Financial Analysis of Business Plans

Venture capitalists may be tempted to search for a quick-and-easy yardstick to assess the historical financial performance of a company. A common question is whether there are any methods that can be used to determine the financial performance of a firm at a glance. The answer is "no," and for a number of reasons. First, there are different types of firms with fundamentally different business models. For example, firms in the telecommunications industry and natural gas or energy sectors (often referred to as utilities) have large amounts of fixed assets and are highly leveraged. They also have steady cash flows from a large and stable customer base, and their profits are consistent and less influenced by business cycles. Industrial firms have the opposite characteristic—they manufacture products for consumption by end-users or as input by other firms or delivery services. Firms in these sectors often present more potential for growth and appreciation in value. Second, businesses go through cycles where financial performance deteriorates or improves with no immediate implication for the viability of the business. This implies that performance measures are needed for both good and bad times.

Venture capitalists use ratio analysis to interpret the raw numbers on financial statements. A financial ratio is a number that expresses the value of one financial variable relative to another. Ratios are also comparative measures. Since ratios present relative value, they allow for a comparison of information not found in raw data. Ratios may be used to compare the firm's past performance to management's goals or the firm's forecast performance. However, the most important analysis is the comparative analysis—a comparison of the firm's financial performance with other firms in the industry.

A typical financial analysis of a firm would include an investigation of each historical financial statement (income statement, balance sheet, cash flow, and retained earnings statement) of the business from the last three–five years. This process involves scrutinizing the financial statements and calculating changes that occur in the individual categories of these statements from one year to the next. Traditional ratio analysis focuses on the application of a number of ratios to financial statements. Most applied ratios are designed to focus on certain financial statements such as an income statement or a balance sheet. The most common ratios include liquidity ratios, profitability ratios, asset activity ratios, leverage ratios, and market valuation ratios. These ratios are often applied on a laundry-list basis to any business without attention to their relative importance.

The analysis of the financial statements given later focuses on a hierarchical progression of the financial analysis. The proposed analysis centers on four steps and tests the following aspects of the firm's financial performance: liquidity, cash generating ability, profitability, and growth dynamics. Each step in the analysis represents a decision to continue with further financial investigation.

The first step of the investigation (liquidity) represents a fundamental health check for the business. For example, if the firm has fundamental problems with liquidity (represented by its inability to pay suppliers, employees, banks, etc.), further analysis may not be necessary. Liquidity assures the firm's survival today, next week, and next month. The next step in the analysis is cash generating ability. This area of analysis centers on business valuation concerns, as discounted cash flows form the basis for business valuation. If the firm has strong, stable, or improving cash flows, it has a strong opportunity to grow in value in the future. The most popular method of business valuation—the discounted cash flow method—is based on the strength of cash flows. In the discounted cash flow method, cash flows for each year's financial projections are discounted to present and additional adjustments are made to arrive at the value of the shareholders' equity. In simple terms, the stronger the cash flow, the higher the valuation of the business. Alternatively, firms with weak and unstable cash flows are unlikely to generate the returns expected by venture capitalists. The first two ratios are "must haves" for venture capitalists.

Once the initial financial analysis has been completed, the overall effectiveness of the firm's management in converting sales into profits—namely, the firm's profitability—must be examined. The most fundamental areas of investigation are the EBITDA and EBIT lines of the income statement, expressed as a percentage of sales. Net profits—while important to the firm in deciding the level of potential dividends to be paid—are rarely a key area of focus for venture capitalists. Firms in different jurisdictions or geographical regions pay different percentages of taxes on taxable income and taxation incentives may also be available (i.e., investment tax credits). As a result, using net profit for comparative reasons can prove difficult.

The next step in the proposed financial analysis is an investigation of the business's sales growth dynamics, which can then be compared with the actual growth of the market in which the firm competes. A high growth rate is achieved through organic growth (by internally developing products or services), acquisitions, or some combination of the two strategies. The firm's sales growth rate is especially meaningful for venture capitalists when compared to the actual market growth rate. If the firm's growth rate in sales exceeds the market growth rate, the firm almost certainly has managed to take market share away from other competitors in the marketplace.

Liquidity

A firm must stay in business. Liquidity is generally concerned with working capital or the management of short-term assets and liabilities. The liquidity ratios indicate how quickly and easily the firm can obtain cash for its needs. The ratios measure the firm's ability to meet its short-term obligations. This section focuses on the three ratios that best outline the firm's liquidity position: current ratio, quick ratio, and times interest earned (see equations 4.1–4.3).

The current ratio compares all the current assets of the firm (cash and other assets that can be easily converted into cash) with all the firm's current liabilities. The quick ratio, often referred as the acid-test ratio, is similar to the current ratio, but is a more rigorous measure of liquidity because it excludes inventory (which is often hard to liquidate) from current assets. Times interest earned ratio is often used to assess the firm's ability to service the interest on its debt with operating income (i.e., EBIT).

$$\text{Current Ratio} = \frac{Current\ Assets}{Current\ Liabilities} > 2x \tag{4.1}$$

$$\text{Quick Ratio} = \frac{Current\ Assets - Inventory}{Current\ Liabilities} > 1x \tag{4.2}$$

$$\text{Times Interest Earned} = \frac{Operating\ Income\,(EBIT)}{Interest\ Paid} > 3x \tag{4.3}$$

Cash Generating Ability

The lack of operating cash flow is often regarded as the primary cause of business failure for many small and large businesses. Business owners often admit that cash flow issues "keep them up at night." It is unfortunate that even experienced business owners only learn about the importance of cash flow the hard way—during a period of problems with liquidity. Starting firms require cash and larger firms require even more of it for working capital, facilities and equipment, and operating expenses. The key challenge is to strike the right balance between consuming and generating cash. Strong financial management is critical to the success of any business, small or large. Cash flow can most simply be defined as the movement of capital in and out of a firm over a specific period of time. The cash flow statement not only presents what cash is left at the end of the period, but also the amounts that left and entered the business. Furthermore, it demonstrates whether, over time, the firm is adding to its cash reserves or slowly eroding them.

If the primary goal of the firm is to maximize market value for shareholders (including venture capitalists), the firm's cash generating ability is the most important component of this value creation process. A strong cash flow provides security against business failure and acts as a guarantor of the firm's future sustainable growth. It reflects a strong focus on generating profits, managing working capital, and investing in long-term assets. As such, the cash flow is perhaps the most comprehensive measure of the management team's caliber. Superior management teams are able to strike an optimal balance between sustaining the ongoing financial viability of the business and working toward future growth.

Profitability, working capital management, and capital intensity prove to be the most important drivers of cash flow. The first component of the firm's cash flow, its net income, outlines the operating efficiency of the business. However, even if net profits show a business to be healthy, it may not translate into an ability to have sufficient cash on hand to pay suppliers, rent, salaries, and loans. These expenses cannot be paid from net profits; rather, they are settled with cash. Working capital management deals with operating the most important items in the firm (namely inventory, accounts receivable and accounts payable). The capital intensity of the firm generally refers to the firm's need to maintain its current capacity and to improve its production capacity to take advantage of opportunities available in the marketplace. It is important to note that cash flow from financing activities is normally not included in the free cash flow or not considered as an indicator of the firm's cash generating ability. This is for two reasons. First, financial costs and leverage should not influence the assessment of a firm's cash generating ability since leverage represents an allocation of cash flow between creditors and shareholders; hence, its change does not indicate a change in cash generating ability. Second, decisions related to financing represent another type of managerial risk that may exist outside of the firm's control. When this business is valued, this risk is generally reflected in the discount rate.

A firm's ability to settle its short-term obligations in a timely manner is important because failure to do so can lead to bankruptcy. On the other hand, the firm needs to minimize its working capital. Minimizing working capital is accomplished through the speedy collection of cash from sale, increasing the rotation of the inventory, and slowing down the disbursement of cash to pay for the firm's obligations. Such an analysis is generally known as the cash conversion cycle or the liquidity gap analysis, and represents the sum of days of outstanding sales (i.e., the average collection period) and the days of sales in inventory less days of payables outstanding. Days of sales outstanding indicate the age, in days, of the firm's accounts receivable. This indicates how many days the firm's clients take to pay the firm (days accounts receivable = [accounts receivable*365]/sales). One of the most common cash traps is uncollected sales. Selling on credit is necessary for firms to compete in the marketplace. Most firms cannot effectively compete with their competitors unless they provide good credit terms to buyers. However, too often the firm's clients treat periods of extended credit as interest-free or perpetual loans. A firm with strong sales but lagging receivables may experience problems. Days inventory ratio estimates the average amount of days that inventory stays with the firm before it is sold (days inventory = [inventory*365]/cost of goods sold). This can be defined as the average age of the firm's inventory. Days payable indicates the age of the firm's accounts payable or simply how many days it takes to pay suppliers (days payable = [accounts payable*365]/ cost of goods sold). Adding days receivable to days inventory is indicative of how long it takes from the initiation of production to receive final receipt of payment from a customer. Days payable indicates how long suppliers have to wait to be paid for their inputs to production. In short, the financing gap can be defined as days receivable + days inventory—days payable. The desired number should be negative, meaning that the days payable are higher than the sum of the days receivable and the days inventory. Such a situation assures that any increases in sales (given that the efficiency of the working capital items stays the same) will not convert into additional working capital requirements.

Let's illustrate the liquidity gap through an example. Let's imagine that a firm called ABC carries inventory for only 5 days, on average, followed by extending its credits to customers for 20 days. So, in total, ABC ties up its capital in short-term working capital on the assets side for 25 days from the time inventory is bought to when cash is collected. However, ABC does not have to pay for its inventory for 29 days. As a result, ABC collects its sales 4 days $(5 + 20 - 29 = -4)$ before it is required to pay its creditors. ABC has a negative conversion cycle or liquidity gap of 4 days, which indicates that working capital management is efficient and that the firm is liquid.

Consistent growth is perhaps the best way to ensure limited pressure on the cash flow. This means that it is necessary to expand and strengthen the business during strong economic conditions by reinvesting into machinery. Often, during strong economic times, there is an easing up on payroll management, marketing and promotional expenditures are reduced, cash is spent on marginally profitable projects, and money is taken from the business in the form of dividends. In slower economic cycles, cash reserves can be quickly depleted by the operational pressures of the marketplace (i.e., clients requiring better payment terms).

Profitability

Profitability ratios measure how much of the firm's revenue is consumed by its expenses, or how much the firm earns relative to the sales it generates. The EBITDA margin is perhaps the most widely used measure of profitability by venture capitalists. It is calculated by taking operating income (EBIT) and adding back depreciation and amortization expenses and dividing the sum by net sales. EBITDA is important for at least three reasons. First, the EBITDA line is often used as the approximation of the internally generated cash flow. If the cash flow statement is not available, or if there is need for an approximation of the cash flow, the EBITDA line can indicate the strength of the cash flow. Second, EBITDA is used for comparison of the firm's financial performance relative to its competitors and the entire industry. Because EBITDA eliminates the impact of financing and accounting decisions, it provides a proper basis for comparison between firms in a particular industry. Third, since EBITDA approximates cash flow, it is often used to value the business (this will be discussed further in the following chapter).

Equations 4.4 and 4.5 present the two most common profitability measures calculated by venture capitalists: the EBITDA and EBIT margins. The EBITDA and EBIT lines from an income statement are only meaningful when they are expressed in relation to sales. The only difference between the two ratios is that EBITDA provides an assessment of a firm's profitability before depreciation and amortization expenses. This can be important, especially when comparing firms. For example, in the personal computer industry, IBM owns its own facilities (indicating a high level of depreciation expense) while Dell is effectively an outsourcer or assembler that owns limited fixed assets. A comparison between the two business models would not be meaningful if only the EAT (earnings after tax) lines of the income statement were assessed.

$$EBITDA\% = \frac{EBITDA}{Sales} \tag{4.4}$$

$$EBIT\% = \frac{EBIT}{Sales} \tag{4.5}$$

Business Growth Dynamics

Business growth is inherent to a firm's survival. Growth is also necessary to improve a firm's competitive position in the marketplace. In simple terms, in today's competitive environment, a business must continually grow or it will lose its market position or be overtaken by competitors. If a firm's revenues grow faster than those of its market, it is assumed that the firm is taking market share away from other competitors (even though it may not be known who the less fortunate competitors are). If the opposite occurs, the firm will almost certainly lose its competitive position in the marketplace. A firm's growth is easy to measure and is captured by a rate of increases in its revenues. A firm's growth in profits in dollar value is also of interest.

The essence of growing a business lies in a firm's ability to recognize and act upon opportunities in the market. Firms need to engage in a systematic investigation of their market opportunities to uncover new sales opportunities where market demand is greater than market supply. Through market gap analysis, a firm can make strategic decisions based on market demand. However, identifying market opportunities and inventing new products or services to fill market niches are only the beginning of the long road to achieving market acceptance; the firm needs to decide on the price and characteristics of its products and services and choose the appropriate model of delivering them to the marketplace.

The growth of a firm generally occurs in a pre-orchestrated manner. Corporate directional strategies deal with the firm's general orientation toward growth. A firm can grow internally (i.e., grow organically) by expanding its operations nationally or internationally or externally by way of mergers, partnerships, acquisitions, or strategic alliances. The most desired corporate directional strategies are those that convert to growing sales and profits. The most profitable growth generally occurs in instances where the firm effectively focuses the expansion around its core business and discovers new ways to outgrow its rivals by implementing an expansion model that is repeatable or predictable. The two most popular growth strategies are based in concentration (where a firm develops new product lines in its industry) and diversification (where the firm expands into new product lines in new industries). The two basic concentration strategies relate to vertical and horizontal growth. Vertical growth involves assuming a function previously provided by a supplier (backward integration) or a function previously provided by a distributor (forward integration). Horizontal growth involves offering a firm's existing product portfolio to new geographical regions. Diversification strategies deal with expanding the business into related or unrelated industries.

Venture Captial Deal "Do-Ability"

One of the key tasks for venture capitalists is to ascertain the likelihood of closing the deal. A preliminary discussion is held with founders or entrepreneurs about the basic philosophies or approaches with respect to cooperation between the two sides in the future. This discussion is usually held early in the investment process in order to assess whether the business philosophies and approaches of each can coincide. This gives venture capitalists an opportunity to assess the chances of closing the deal (assuming that the subsequent due diligence process proves positive). Such a discussion also helps to identify any potential "deal breakers" early on. The key areas of discussion relate to exit provisions, corporate governance, and circumstances or events that can lead to changes of control.

Many venture capital firms base their initial discussions with entrepreneurs or business owners around their approach to investment or operating philosophies. If the business owner or entrepreneur responds positively, there is a good chance that the two sides will be able to agree to and sign a preliminary agreement (i.e., the term sheet or heads of terms) and eventually close the deal. If the expectations of venture capitalists are seen to be challenging, the chances of closing the deal are limited or nil. In these initial discussions, venture capitalists generally focus on five aspects of future cooperation: long-term partnership, the alignment of financial rewards, investment in and development of management, fiduciary responsibilities to the venture capital firm's limited partners, and exit.

Long-term Partnership

Venture capitalists aim to agree upon the overall vision of the businesses they invest in and to understand the management team's long-term perspectives. They also believe that unless there is agreement on the "final destination" a firm is to reach, there is no point in starting a relationship with a management team or founders. An agreement on a vision for the business means reaching a consensus on a detailed business plan and budget. Such a document generally includes the timetable and key operational milestones for achieving this long-term vision.

Cooperation between venture capitalists and their investee firms is based on regular meetings with management. In these meetings, venture capitalists, owners, and business managers jointly review the progress of the firm as it compares to the agreed-upon timetable and key operational milestones. They will also change these plans and forecasts as needed and discuss the financial performance and future financing needs of the firm. In order to make these meetings concrete and valuable to both parties, venture capitalists expect that a brief monthly progress report, a summary of financial results, and an agenda will be circulated in advance of these meetings.

Venture capitalists expect that in these early collaborative interactions, meetings will be held monthly (and then, later, less frequently). They also make clear to business owners and managers that running the business is the management's responsibility. Venture capitalists have insufficient time to be involved in the day-to-day operations of their investee firms—they are only involved in the business so much as they can provide value. Venture capitalists believe that monthly or quarterly meetings are of great value to both parties, and are the most effective ways in which they can stay close to the business and make their expertise available without being overly intrusive.

Venture capitalists generally expect no dividends to be paid throughout the life of investment; their objective is to grow the value of the business over the long-term. Reinvesting profits is an integral part of this strategy. Having the long-term view of the business in mind, venture capitalists often turn a blind eye to the possibility of short-term financial gains. It is for this reason that venture capitalists insist that all shares be made nontransferable in the early years of the partnership (or at least until such a time that the long-term objectives are met).

Alignment of Financial Rewards

Once they have established the potential for a long-term successful partnership, venture capitalists must structure the deal so that the interests and financial rewards are aligned for both themselves and the business owners. While circumstances change and business plans almost never go according to plan, venture capitalists must establish that, in any situation, business owners and venture capitalists win-together and lose-together. Such an arrangement is seen by venture capitalists as the only way to limit the possibility of future conflict between the two sides.

Venture capitalists believe that there is a difference between losing and "not winning." If venture capitalists provide capital and their business partners earn equity solely through their "effort contribution" to the business, then, if the business fails, venture capitalists lose something whereas business owners simply "do not win." Therefore, venture capitalists expect that their business partners have something to lose should the business venture fail. In general terms, venture capitalists expect business owners to invest their own capital into the venture. It is not expected that the capital contribution of business owners match that of the venture capitalists; however, it should be of meaningful value.

Consistent with this distinction between losing and not winning, venture capitalists structure deals to ensure that all partners get their risk contributions back before other types of contributions are recognized. Venture capitalists call this the cash priority. The cash priority operates in such a manner that if the firms performs poorly or fails, all those who invested cash in the firm will get their money back (plus some nominal return) before noncash contributions are recognized. In the event the firm does well, proceeds are shared in proportion to shareholding, thus fully recognizing the role of the noncash contributions in the success of the firm.

Investment in Management

Many venture capitalists believe that management is by far the most important asset of any business. Sometimes outstanding people make a success of a mediocre idea, but rarely do mediocre people achieve success in the long-term with a great idea. Anyone can prepare a business plan, but circumstances change and the winning firms are the ones with management teams that can predict change and adapt.

Venture capitalists believe that long-term value is reflected in the equity value of a firm. For this reason, they insist that management have a substantial equity interest in the firm. The potential value of this ownership interest should have the potential to significantly exceed any form of compensation that management might receive. If the management team does not already own a substantial stake in the firm, venture capitalists can provide shares to management through a share ownership scheme, funded through shares that the venture capital firm acquires. Venture capitalists may set aside up to 5 percent of the firm's shareholding for management. In addition, since venture capitalists want to provide incentives to management to stay with the business in the long term, they may agree to provide a portion of their own shares to the management team through a share ownership scheme. To keep the management team involved in the business, a "vesting schedule" provides shares to management over time.

Venture capitalists generally do not consider investments where their partners and managers work part-time or are pursuing other business interests. Venture capitalists believe that if management has other interests, their commitment is likely to shift in favor of these interests when the firm may need them most. Venture capitalists, therefore, require management to be 100 percent committed to any business in which they invest.

As management is seen by venture capitalists as the core asset of any business, a manager's premature departure from a firm will be perceived as a reduction in value. For this reason, many venture capitalists believe that management should not only forego future vested shares, but also actually lose some. Thus, if management already owns a significant shareholding in the firm, venture capitalists can secure the right to buy a portion of their shares at a nominal price if management leaves prior to achieving the long-term objectives of the firm.

Fiduciary Responsibility to Limited Partners

Venture capitalists do not invest their own capital—cash for investment purposes comes from limited partners. These limited partners can be corporations, financial institutions, insurance companies, or pension funds. Venture capital firms have both legal and ethical obligations to these groups. It is therefore important that the venture capital firm takes all reasonable measures to secure the value of the capital provided by these limited partners.

Some venture capital firms believe that the best way to protect their interests is to take a majority position in their investments. This may not change the venture capital firm's philosophy that management is entirely responsible for the operations of the business, but it does ensure that the venture capital firm has control over certain key decisions and can exercise its rights should problems arise.

Other venture capital firms are indifferent to their ownership stake in the business. If they are minority partners, however, they may attempt to ensure that their relationships with business owners are based upon a balanced partnership. This means that venture capitalists may wish to secure additional minority rights. This means at least three things. First, venture capitalists would want to be party to certain key decisions or actions. It is important to note that venture capitalists do not seek to make decisions unilaterally. The following types of decisions would typically require the consent of venture capitalists: major changes to the business plan; decisions to hire or remove key management; increases in capital; sale of shares or significant assets; liquidation of the firm; and entering into long-term commitments or contracts. Second, venture capitalists require firms to commit to employing prudent business practices. These conditions aim to avoid damage to the firm in the event of extraordinary circumstances and benefit all shareholders alike. Examples include compliance with applicable laws and authorities; dual signing authority on high-value contacts; regulations governing conflicts of interest; and responsible policies toward environment and worker safety. Third, venture capitalists have a duty to protect themselves against being misled, misinformed, or only partially informed about the situation of a firm during the investment process. Venture capitalists therefore require standard representations and warranties from the firm's owners and management before signing the investment agreement.

Exit Orientation

Venture capital firms are normally set up for a period of ten years. Limited partners commit cash to the fund and expect that during these ten years, the venture capital firm will return a larger amount of cash to them. The investment is a failure if the venture capital firm fails to return cash to its investors. In other words, venture capital firms must secure ways to sell their shares within the target investment holding period.

Venture capitalists' partners may have different perspectives on holding than those of business owners or entrepreneurs. For example, they may be attracted by a future dividend stream, the ability to wait for a "preferred" buyer, or simply the ability to retain control of the firm and the status and self-fulfillment that goes with it. The difference in the perceived value of "unsold shares" means that the exit issue is often the one in which the interests of venture capitalists and business owners may diverge most.

The most important step that can be taken by a venture capitalist looking to secure their ability to sell is to agree to an acceptable and realistic exit strategy with their partners upfront. Venture capitalists believe that it is always best to have at least two desired exit routes. Commonly, these would include flotation on the stock exchange, trade sales to a strategic or financial investor, or the repurchase of shares by business owners. Venture capitalists know that if business owners have different views on how to achieve exit, the partnership will not work.

If, after an agreed-upon period, the desired exit has not been achieved, any restrictions on the sale of venture capitalists' shares will likely be removed and the venture capital firm will be free to sell them to any third party. If the possible exit route is flotation on the stock exchange, the venture capital firm would have the right to require the firm to file for registration.

Reading the Business Plan

An objective of business screening is to make an effective initial decision on the attractiveness of the received proposals or business plans. Some venture capital firms have an established process of reviewing business plans while others review them on a case-by-case basis. Regardless of the process involved, the objective is to assess the risks associated with the proposal, turn down the "misfits" quickly, and focus on the most promising investment opportunities.

A review of business plans or business concepts is an active process that requires at least two readings. The first reading should focus on a "macro" review of the major goals of the plan and identify the key risks associated with the business. The second reading should be detail-oriented. This second reading involves analysis of every assumption, table, chart, graph, and financial statement (including financial forecasts). Venture capitalists can be forgiving of typos, presentation style, recycled paper, and so on, but should be rigorous when investigating the underlying logic of the analysis.

An effective review of a business plan requires venture capitalists to focus on the substance found within the most critical areas of the plan (outlined in this chapter) rather than on form. Later stage firms are easier to analyze as they have an operational and financial track record, but the process may take longer given the amount of information available. Early stage firms—as a result of the limited information pertaining to their trading history—may need to be personally visited before an initial decision can be made and subsequent financial analysis can proceed.

The red flags of an initial screening include an insistence by management on participating in due diligence phone calls, difficulty in obtaining a business reference, an inability by the company to answer questions that might arise during discussion of the business plan, and the involvement of external consultants in the preparation of the business plan. Another strong "turn-off" for venture capitalists is excessive salary levels for the management team.

Any analysis of a business plan is incomplete until venture capitalists supplement their reading with other materials. These materials may include analyst reports, newsletters or newsfeeds, and information from the Internet. Most successful, long-standing venture capital firms have access to internal resources or libraries on key sectors of the economy.

Questions to Consider

1. Describe the most important aspects of "5M Principles."
2. Why is the market regarded as the worst enemy for an entrepreneurial firm?
3. What are the basic models of operating an entrepreneurial firm?
4. Name the advantages of using an EBITDA and an EBITDA margin in the financial analysis.
5. What are the key aspects of cooperation that are important to venture capitalists?

Note

1. Michael J. Porter (1998). *Competitive Strategy: Techniques for Analyzing Industries and Competitors.* New York: Free Press.

Enterprise Investors

Key characteristics

Year founded:	1990
Founding partners:	John Birkelund and Robert Faris
Number of limited partners:	N/A
Geographic coverage:	Central and Eastern Europe (3 locations)
Headquarter location:	Warsaw (Poland)
Focus (if any):	Regional (Central and Eastern Europe)
Funds under management:	$1.7 billion
Number of completed deals/ IPO exits:	~100/25
Private/public:	Private
Most publicly recognized deals:	Bulgaria Telecom, Orange Slovakia, Lukas, Magellan, Polfa Kutno, Sfinks
Number of investment professionals:	~30

Enterprise Investors (EI) is the premier private equity firm in Central and Eastern Europe (CEE). With over 100 completed deals, 25 IPOs, and numerous trade sales behind it, EI is an undisputed market leader in the CEE region. The success of EI is reflected in its ability to have raised six private equity funds and one venture capital fund focusing on small and medium-sized enterprises. Its sixth fund was two times oversubscribed and closed within three months. Enterprise Investors has been able to consistently achieve nearly three times cash-on-cash return for its limited partners.

The initial strategy of EI focused on the privatization of state-owned enterprises (in which it has developed strong expertise) and expansion deals. In subsequent years, EI moved more toward supporting expanding entrepreneurial firms in the CEE region. Today, the firm's strategy focuses on four major types of deals: founder buy-outs, equity increases combined with an IPO, leveraged buy-outs, and management buy-outs and buy-ins. The firm has achieved notable success in each of these categories.

Enterprise Investors implements its regional investment strategy through a network of offices across the CEE region (Poland, Romania, and Slovakia). The firm employs about 30 investment professionals (EI's 5 managing partners have been with the firm for more than 15 years). The firm's consistent market performance has earned it 17 awards, with "Best Private Equity Firm in Central and Eastern Europe" already captured by it five times (the award is granted by the readers of *International Private Equity*).

Source: www.ei.com.pl.

Chapter 5

Due Diligence Phase I and Internal Feedback

The investment committee, the internal decision-making body operating in the venture capital firm, initially provides venture capitalists with preliminary feedback on potential investee firms. Once the members of the investment committee have been satisfied with the preliminary analysis performed by venture capitalists, venture capitalists commence a more intensive round of interactions with the management and entrepreneurs of potential investee firms. These interactions relate to two basic areas: financial forecasting and business valuation.

Financial Forecasting

Venture capitalists are concerned with a firm's future performance rather than its past performance, as the firm's future achievements ultimately determine the return they obtain. The historical financial performance, however, is not to be totally discounted. Analyzing the past provides insight into the firm's strategy, its successes in the marketplace, its ability to embrace and implement innovation, and its internal ability to attract and retain talented personnel. Past trends in key performance parameters can also be used to help develop forecasts for the future. The simplest forecasts assume that the future mirrors the past. Venture capitalists using this approach anticipate that the firm's financial performance is likely to continue to be the same as it has been in the past.

A venture capitalist's ability to interpret financial forecasts depends on many factors. By their nature, financial forecasts are highly subjective. A proper interpretation of financial forecasts depends on the venture capitalist's skills in analyzing and understanding the firm's current strategy and anticipating its future performance in the context of historical achievements. It is also based on proper judgment of the external forces and environments that are likely to affect the firm's future market and earning potential. A proper assessment also reflects familiarity with the spreadsheet program, previous exposure to the marketplace the firm operates in, the time given to complete the financial model, and other circumstances. Precise financial forecasts are rooted in proper assumptions that relate to key operational parameters, the firm's competitive situation, its market share, and its market growth rate. Put simply, assumptions focus on the "5M Principles." These assumptions are the cornerstone of the financial forecasting process. The general rule is that the more precise the assumptions, the better the forecast. However, this is not to imply that focusing on every minute aspect of a business's operations is likely to translate into a better set of financial forecasts. Overextended financial forecasts may suffer from poor precision and quality, as overly complex models treat nearly all risks the same (venture capitalists, e.g., know that market risk is one of the most profound risks for any business). Such models also do not make sufficient distinctions with respect to business drivers, which are responsible for creating value.

Financial projections are a critical tool for venture capitalists for a variety of reasons. First, they serve as the basis for venture capitalists' analysis of the fortunes of the business as anticipated by management. Venture capitalists will scrutinize forecasts to a greater extent than they will the past financial performance. Second, the financial forecasts often become part of the legal documentation negotiated between venture capitalists and entrepreneurs. Many legal clauses (e.g., share-adjustment mechanisms, change of management clauses, budget monitoring clauses, and various approval clauses) are grounded in financial forecasts. Most importantly, the financial forecasts form the basis for the valuation of the business at the moment of venture capitalists' entry into the business and their exit. They are the input data on the basis of which venture capitalists' returns are calculated. Not surprisingly, venture capitalists want to see realistic and achievable financial forecasts.

There are two methods of financial forecasting: the cash basis and the accrual basis. While cash budgeting represents an intuitive method of forecasting business activities for many young entrepreneurs, especially those in emerging markets (see box 5.1), it is not sufficient for venture capitalists. Venture capitalists need to rely on a full set of financial projections. These financial statements need to be based on assumptions supported by market research (industry data, information clippings from newspapers,

---

Box 5.1 International perspective on venture capital: cash budgeting in emerging markets

Many young and mature businesses operating in emerging markets operate informally. They do not prepare a full set of financial forecasts, but rely on a much simpler forecasting tool—a cash budget.

So, what is a cash budget? A cash budget is a financial tool that focuses on cash receipts, cash disbursements, and their timing. This information is placed in a single schedule to effectively forecast cash shortages or excessive cash balances within a period of time. The cash budget consists of three parts: cash receipts, cash disbursements, and financing. In the cash receipts or cash collections section, it must be determined what percentage of sales will occur as cash sales (i.e., cash received the moment the sale is made) and what sales are likely to be collected in the future. The percentage of cash received immediately and in later periods can be estimated based on the past collection record. For example, a small restaurant owner knows that about 80 percent of sales are made on a cash basis, while 20 percent are made on credit (e.g., sales made from hosting a corporate event). The owner estimates that he receives payment for hosting events within ten business days from the date of the event. Estimating the amount of cash disbursements is an exercise in the opposite—the restaurant owner attempts to estimate how quickly he would need to pay his bills (raw materials, wages, utilities, etc.) and settle tax payments. More importantly, the owner does not need to remember to account for items such as amortization that do not require a cash outlay. By putting together a schedule of cash receipts and cash disbursements, the business owner is able to forecast his cash position for some time into the future. Depending on the outcome of such an exercise, the business may or may not need external cash. If a need for further cash arises, the business owner would be able to address this in the financing section of the cash budget.

The cash budget is very popular for a number of reasons. First, it is simple to prepare. The business owner does not need to prepare a full set of financial statements that include the income statement, balance sheet, cash flow, and the retained earnings statement. Instead, the owner prepares one statement that captures the essence of the business—proper accounting for revenues, cost, and their appropriate timing. Second, the cash balance is highly intuitive. Preparing the cash balance does not require any education or background in finance or accounting. In many respects, the cash balance is similar to the balance in a personal chequebook; both consist of credits and debits.

magazines, or the Internet), strong logic, and industry-grounded business judgment.

Firms seeking finance prepare their financial projections in different ways. Some firms seek assistance from external consultants to prepare their business plan and the accompanying financial projections. Other firms prepare their own business plans and financial numbers. Venture capitalists strongly prefer firms seeking finance to prepare their own business plans and financial projections. They argue that if external consultants are involved in the preparation of the business plan, entrepreneurs and managers will not effectively "own" the plan and may be less committed to achieving its key operational and financial milestones. Venture capitalists also believe that the time and resources a firm commits to preparing a business plan and their financial forecasts are well spent. The mere act of preparing and revising financial forecasts allows the firm's management to revisit, review, and rethink operational and strategic issues related to the business. The entire process creates an opportunity to refresh management's internal knowledge of their competitors, to elaborate on the external forces and environments influencing the firm, to identify product or service growth opportunities and potential acquisition targets, and to decide upon the human resources necessary to affect these desired outcomes. This is not to imply that businesses do not undertake these activities on their own on a regular basis. Preparing a business plan forces firms into a more systematic and structured process. The business owners get a chance to decide upon their involvement in the business, to crystallize their views on value creation, and to determine their willingness to financially support the firm.

A critical decision that venture capitalists must make is whether to rely on the financial projections supplied by the firm seeking capital (and request subsequent revisions of the business plan if necessary) or prepare their own set of financial statements (a sort of an interpretation of the financial forecasts prepared by the firm's managers). The process of recreating financial projections can be counterintuitive, but it generally fulfills two basic functions for venture capitalists: the due diligence function (i.e., understanding the key commercial issues of the firm) and the confirmatory function (i.e., is the financial model actually prepared correctly?). It also forces venture capitalists to carefully consider the firm's key commercial risks. A correct understanding of these risks can prevent many future business problems and even business failures.

If venture capitalists choose to recreate the firm's financial forecast, they follow their own methodology of preparing them. Some venture capital firms rely on preexisting spreadsheet template models that require that they only fill assumption sheets and the financial forecast is then mechanically prepared. The benefits of such an approach are that the process requires less time, less expertise and skill, and less understanding of the business; the drawbacks are that the process is quite mechanical, it does not require a thorough understanding of the underlying firm, and all commercial risks are treated as equal. Other venture capital firms build a financial model from scratch. This requires considerable time and effort. The advantages are that venture capitalists can focus on key business considerations, gain a thorough understanding of the business, verify the basic mechanics of the financial model prepared by the firm, and avoid imposition when running different scenarios of business performance (i.e., sensitivity analysis).

There may be five steps in preparing a full set of financial statements. The priority is the development of the income statement, which is the most time consuming aspect of financial forecasting (step 1). The income statement captures the essence of the firm's operational performance after considering the market success of its products, its investment in operational areas, its commitment to building a solid management team, its investment activities and expansion plans, and the financing structure of the business. The firm's income statement and, specifically, EBITDA performance are the key drivers of its valuation. The income statement is based on multiple assumptions, some of which are ultimately decided upon during the final fine-tuning of the financial model. Next, interim calculations are prepared (step 2); this allows putting together the cash flow statement (step 3). The balance sheet is then prepared (step 4), a rather mechanical function based on steps 1–3. The final step represents the verification process and centers on ratio analysis (step 5). During this phase, venture capitalists check whether the obtained output (in the form of financial ratios) produces an acceptable and realistic set of financial parameters. If the final result is not satisfactory and some financial ratios are found to be questionable, the process is repeated until the desired outcome is achieved.

The preparation of financial projections is an iterative process, where changes in assumptions in one area have an immediate effect in another. For example, a projected increase in sales in the marketplace often results in an additional investment in working capital and production capability, which, in turn, necessitates additional financing. Extra capital might change the projected interest expense if the expansion is financed by debt; net income would then suffer. Alternatively, the ownership structure may change if capital was brought in the form of additional equity. Venture capitalists must continue to revise their financial model until such time that the financial forecasts reflect their assessment of the business and the financial parameters fall within an acceptable range when compared to the firm's historical data and industry trends. This is accomplished through the benchmarking process. Steps 1–5 of this process are outlined later in the chapter.

The five-step benchmarking process will be discussed in the context of Blue Velvet (BV). The history of this firm dates back to World War II. The business was founded in 1947 by two entrepreneurs, pastry and ice-cream specialists who began small-scale handmade production of ice cream. They started production in a small, green wooden booth, but upon achieving initial success, they moved into a larger facility and progressively improved upon their original recipes, introducing new flavors. Mike Smith acquired the business in 1994. Smith invested his own money in the physical expansion of the operations, buying neighboring shops and production equipment. He also introduced new products. The staff grew to 20 people. For the next decade, the output of the one-shop operation grew steadily and by early 2000, the products had developed a strong reputation for quality. Blue Velvet became one of the most popular ice-cream parlors in its region. The initial success of the venture inspired the owner to expand beyond his original market. He built a small production facility outside of his local area on twelve hundred squared meters of land and began to build a more organized distribution system. Market demand drove BV's growth. In 2004, the firm acquired and leased additional production lines, bought more land and warehouse facilities, hired more people, and broadened its product range and distribution structure. By 2010, total sales revenue reached $14.0 million and the firm employed 300 people. The capital equipment purchases and the working capital throughout the expansion process were financed from internally generated cash flow.

In 2010, BV found itself at a crossroads. The firm suffered from capacity constraints at its existing premises. The business was nicely profitable and cash generative. The owners could continue to operate the business without major investment (or expansion) and enjoy a very high standard of living for the foreseeable future. However, the owner knew that true success would only come with expansion. His ambition was to maintain BV as the leading ice-cream producer in a broader geographic market and to achieve annual sales of $50 million. This would place the business amongst the five largest producers and distributors of its kind in the region. In order to achieve this level of sales, BV needed to invest about $13 million in new product range and develop its distribution network.

Table 5.1 presents BV's income statement, which includes both historical figures (2007–2010) and financial forecasts (2011–2015). These financial forecasts were prepared by BV's management team.

A brief analysis of the historical and projected income statement leads to some interesting observations about BV. First, the anticipated sales growth appears strong, but somewhat erratic. The firm estimates to grow sales by 22 percent in 2011, 38 percent in 2012, 41 percent in 2013, and 26 percent in 2014. Second, the profitability of the firm at different points in the income statement seems to skyrocket. Gross margins are estimated to increase from about 56 percent in 2011 to 65 in 2015. The EBITDA percentage almost doubles between 2010 and 2015, reaching 45 percent in 2015 (from 24.3 percent in 2010). A similar trend occurs at the net profitability level. Many venture capitalists would suggest that it is extremely difficult to increase margins; this generally stems from competitive pressures in the marketplace. Third, while not shown in table 5.1, BV has assumed that current favorable trends in working capital are likely to continue. This means that BV may be underestimating its financial needs. Business experience suggests that competitive pressures often force businesses to adjust their terms of payment. Similar pressures can also affect relationships with suppliers.

Step 1: Sales and Expense Forecasting

Sales Forecasting

Developing a forecast of sales is a complex matter. A sales forecast must reflect the competitive dynamics of the marketplace, new

Table 5.1 Blue Velvet's historical financial performance between 2007 and 2010 and financial projections for the years between 2011 and 2015 prepared by BV's management team

	Historical numbers				Forecast numbers				
	2007	2008	2009	2010	2011	2012	2013	2014	2015
Net sales	767	3,210	7,342	14,025	17,150	23,587	33,148	41,655	49,371
Growth (%)	*245*	*319*	*129*	*91*	*22*	*38*	*41*	*26*	*19*
Cost of goods sold	325	1,361	2,937	5,883	7,474	9,386	12,569	14,864	16,953
Gross margin	**442**	**1,849**	**4,405**	**8,142**	**9,676**	**14,201**	**20,579**	**26,791**	**32,418**
% Margin	*57.68%*	*57.59%*	*60.00%*	*58.05%*	*56.42%*	*60.21%*	*62.08%*	*64.32%*	*65.66%*
Energy	18	48	81	118	242	284	335	380	418
Salaries	115	417	881	1,640	1,715	2,358	3,314	4,165	4,937
Management	250	350	430	530	530	530	605	665	732
Transportation	19	87	227	505	601	780	920	1,010	1,201
Business travel	23	64	73	155	171	235	331	416	493
Maintenance	15	64	147	214	219	296	402	510	610
Other services	150	181	213	261	178	179	181	183	185
Marketing	76	122	156	453	850	850	850	850	850
Leasing costs	214	214	214	214	214	214	214	214	214

Other costs	598	592	587	581	575	645	330	109	31
EBITDA	**22,180**	**17,806**	**12,840**	**7,894**	**4,381**	**3,407**	**1,653**	**192**	**-469**
% Margin	*44.93%*	*42.75%*	*38.74%*	*33.47%*	*25.55%*	*24.29%*	*22.51%*	*5.98%*	*-61.10%*
Depreciation	1,700	1,700	1,600	1,500	1,200	800	400	250	180
Operating income (EBIT)	20,480	16,206	11,340	6,694	3,581	3,007	1,403	12	-649
% Margin	*41.48%*	*38.91%*	*34.21%*	*28.38%*	*20.88%*	*21.44%*	*19.10%*	*0.37%*	*-84.57%*
Interest expense	300	300	300	300	250	190	180	180	90
Earnings before taxes (EBT)	20,180	15,906	11,040	6,394	3,331	2,817	1,222	-169	-739
Taxes @ 40%	8,072	6,362	4,416	2,558	1,332	1,127	489	0	0
Earnings after tax (EAT)	**12,108**	**9,544**	**6,624**	**3,836**	**1,999**	**1,690**	**733**	**-169**	**-739**
% Margin	*24.52%*	*22.91%*	*19.98%*	*16.26%*	*11.65%*	*12.05%*	*9.99%*	*-5.25%*	*-96.33%*

product introductions and product innovation, customer sensitivity to product stimuli (i.e., price, quality), market responsiveness to promotional techniques, and customer loyalty. A sales forecast requires input from managers from different functional departments of the firm. Sales and marketing personnel usually provide an assessment of demand and competition. Production personnel usually provide estimates of manufacturing capacity, production constraints, timing, and costs. Top management makes strategic decisions affecting the firm as a whole. Financial managers coordinate, collect, and analyze the information. They also provide valuable input on whether financial resources are available to finance the firm's plans or whether additional financing needs to be secured in the form of debt or equity.

For venture capitalists engaged in the process of estimating the firm's financial forecasts, understanding the historical sales growth trends (expressed in the form of current average growth rates or CAGR) is key. The growth rates demonstrate where in its life cycle the firm is. The marketing and management literature breaks the firm's or product's life cycle into five stages (introduction, development, growth, maturity, and decline). If the firm or product is in the early stages of its life cycle (i.e., in the introductory and development stages), sales growth is rapid. A strong growth phase is characterized by growth rates increasing from year to year. In other words, the previous year's growth rate (in terms of percentage increases) is lower than that of the current year. The length of the rapid growth period varies from industry to industry, but it generally ranges from three to five years. In the case of Blue Velvet, the percentage sales growth increased from 245 percent in 2007 to 319 in 2008. If the firm were beyond an early stage of development, the sales curve would flatten and eventually decline should it not renew its product offering or find new markets. It is also important to note that sales by any firm have their natural plateau level, or a point of market saturation determined by the size of the market and the number of consumers within it. For example, the number of loafs of bread in any town is ultimately determined by the number of people eating bread and the frequency of purchase. Beyond a certain point, there would not be any incremental demand in the marketplace for bread (even if the price were to drop to zero). It is difficult for a firm to grow sales beyond its natural sales plateau.

Mainstream management literature treats each of the five stages of a firm's life cycle as more or less equal in terms of timing. This is far from true. For example, for firms in the pharmaceutical industry, the initial stages can be as long as 10–15 years (due to research, drug discovery and testing). Firms in this industry also enjoy a period of patent protection (for about 10 years) where no generic drugs made of similar chemical compositions are allowed to sell in the marketplace. For this reason, it can take some time for a pharmaceutical firm to become profitable. Firms in the Internet industry (i.e., Google) can enjoy rapid expansion during the early stages of their development and quick profitability. On the other hand, traditional product distributors (i.e., Home Depot) enjoy long, stable periods of growth. The key point here is that firms operating in different industries may experience different life cycles and the periods of time in each stage are likely to differ. The best way for venture capitalists to understand the curvature of the sales growth and the profitability potential of a business is to study different firms in the industry, understand their life cycles, and then superimpose these life cycles onto a similar firm in question.

If there is nothing extraordinary expected in terms of new products, competitors, or technologies entering into the marketplace, the sales trend will likely be a continuation of the historical growth trends. In other words, the estimates of future sales may be arrived at by extending the trend of past sales. If new product introductions are expected, the curvature of the sales forecast will change to reflect the timing of these new product introductions.

There are two basic methods of forecasting the level of sales growth for a business: top-down and bottom-up. The top-down approach centers around using the market forecast rates (i.e., industry expert predictions) and adding or deducting percentage growth rates for the firm based on its historical sales growth vis-à-vis the market growth. For example, if the market grew by 10 percent per annum (p.a.) in the past few years while the firm maintained a 15 percent growth rate per annum over the same time period, it can be anticipated that a similar difference of growth within the firm and the markets (equal to 5 percent p.a.) is likely to persist into the foreseeable future. If the market is expected to grow by 7 percent p.a. in the next five years, the firm's revenue growth may be estimated at 12 percent p.a. This method is intuitive and quick, but not always accurate. The top-down approach may be based on market comparative data. Let's assume, continuing with the ice-cream industry, that the actual consumption of ice cream for BV equals 4 kilograms per capita while the national average in the country equals 11 kilograms per capita. It is not unreasonable to assume that at a certain period in time, the consumption in BV's local market will equate to the national average. The only question relates to the period of time it will take for this to occur. The time period can be easily established by looking at other regions of the country and determining the time it took for them to "catch up" to the national average. It may also be possible to find another region of the country with similar demographics, consumption patterns, and competitive statistics to check its growth pattern and trajectory. Other countries or geographic regions can serve as useful base-line models. If it is determined that it is likely to take five years to reach the national average, the remaining calculations are straight forward. One can use present value (PV) calculations on a financial calculator: PV $= -4$, FV $= 11$, $n = 5$, PMT $= 0$, Find Y/I $= ?$ In this case, the projected annual growth rate would be equal to 22.4 percent. Of course, the growth rate would need to be adjusted depending on the firm's life cycle. If the firm is in its early stages, the growth rates may be front-loaded: higher at the beginning and lower in the latter years. If the firm is more mature in its development, the growth rates will likely be relatively similar.

The bottom-up approach is more complex. It effectively involves breaking up the region the firm serves into a number of discrete marketplaces and attempting to predict market demand in each small geographic region. This analysis would be substantially easier if the firm has access to market research reports, which ordinarily report market data in certain geographic regions in terms of sales shares (sales made to consumers expressed in standard units), average unit price (the average price per standard unit of weight), stock shares (the actual amount of total stock held by retailers), and numeric net distribution (the percentage of the number of shops that had stock at the time of the closing stock visit). The ice-cream business can break down its competitive market into smaller regional centers, with major cities identified in each, and predict the growth rates in each region. The firm would effectively ask: what is the market share achievable in each region; what is the pricing strategy that would allow for the achievement of a certain market share; is it possible to take market share away from other competitors and under what conditions; what is the volume of sales; what is the predicted market demand for certain products and product groups, and so on. The basic idea is to continue to break down the data into smaller and smaller data sets that are easier to forecast. The sum of total predictions in each market segment would equal the predicted firm's revenue and revenue growth for the entire region.

Cost Forecasting

The cost structure of a firm can also be determined through a structured process. The most critical part of this process is establishing the relationship between revenues and cost, or whether the relationship between the two components is fixed, variable, or somewhere in between (called a vertical analysis). Another aspect may be to discover the underlying trend, expressed as a formula, that would capture the relationship between costs in the same cost category from one year to another (called a horizontal analysis). This is where historical investigation and comparison to market growth rates become critical. The historical trends in costs may vary from year-to-year, but changes in the financial forecasts need to be investigated, confirmed, and deemed reasonable as well as logical. For example, a firm may claim that it aims to reduce the cost of raw materials. If this is the case, the firm should specifically outline which raw material costs are likely to change, how much the new cost will be, what a specific cost represents as a percentage of total raw material costs, and so on. If management does not provide a detailed explanation of the movement in cost items, the future material cost structure should be treated as an approximation of historical trends in the future.

Let's see how this analysis would specifically apply to the case of BV. The first component of the historical cost investigation would be to discover the underlying relationships between growth rates in cost items and in revenue and to understand the percentage increases in certain cost items on a year-to-year basis. A detailed investigation yields the results presented in table 5.2. Energy costs were observed to move in relation to sales volume, but the percentage increase was related to about half of the increase in sales growth. Percentage increases in salaries, business travel, maintenance, and other costs appeared related to volume and were set at 12, 2, 2, and 4, respectively, of sales in the financial projections.

Table 5.2 The historical relationships between sales and cost items and percentage increases in costs items on a year-to-year basis

A. *Costs items expressed as a percentage of sales*

Cost items	2007	2008	2009	2010	Range/average	Observation	Assumptions
Energy	2.3	1.5	1.1	0.8	1.1–2.3/1.4	Sales volume related	See below
Salaries	15.0	13.0	12.0	11.7	11.7–15.0/12.9	Sales volume related	12 percent of sales volume
Management	32.6	10.9	5.9	3.8	3.8–32.6/13.3	Unrelated	Decided upon actual needs
Transportation						Sales volume related	See below
Business travel	3.0	2.0	1.0	1.1	1.0–3.0/1.8	Sales volume related	2 percent of sales volume
Maintenance	2.0	2.0	2.0	1.5	1.5–2.0/1.9	Sales volume related	2 percent of sales volume
Other services	19.6	5.6	2.9	1.9	1.9–19.6/7.5	Unrelated	See below
Marketing	9.9	3.8	2.1	3.2	2.1–9.9/4.8	Unrelated	See below
Leasing costs	27.9	6.7	2.9	1.5	1.5–27.9/9.8	Unrelated	Fixed number based on contract
Other costs	4.0	3.4	4.5	4.6	3.4–4.6/4.1	Sales volume related	4 percent of sales volume

B. *Percentage increases in costs items from year-to-year*

Cost items	2007	2008	2009	2010	Observation	Assumptions
Energy	N/A	166.7	68.8	45.7	Increase by 50 percent slower than volume increases	$Energy_{n+1} = Energy_n \times (1 + sales\ increase/2)$
Salaries	N/A	262.7	111.1	86.1	Unrelated	See earlier
Management	N/A	40.0	22.9	23.3	Unrelated	Decided upon actual needs
Transportation	N/A	357.9	160.9	122.5	Increases by 30 percent more than volume	$Transportation_{n+1} = Transportation_n \times (1 + sales\ increase + 30\%)$
Business travel	N/A	179.0	14.4	111.1	Unrelated	See earlier
Maintenance	N/A	318.5	128.7	45.7	Somewhat related	See earlier
Other services	N/A	20.7	17.7	22.5	Increase by about 20 percent year-on-year	$Other\ services_{n+1} = Other\ services_n \times (1 + 20\%)$
Marketing	N/A	60.5	27.9	190.4	6–8 percent in benchmarking with competitors	Assumed 7 percent in 2011–2014 and 8 percent in 2015
Leasing costs	N/A	0.0	0.0	0.0	The same number	Fixed number based on contract
Other costs	N/A	255.7	202.7	95.2	Unrelated	See earlier
Sales growth	421.4	318.5	128.7	91.0		

Management costs were assumed to reflect the firm's financial projections and were treated as the basis for some adjustment. For example, $150,000 per year was added to anticipate the hiring of a CFO. An additional $100,000 per year was earmarked for other expansion-related management expenses (i.e., hiring middle managers). Other services grew by about 20 percent from year to year; this percentage was expected to hold true for the future. The marketing costs were judged to be unrealistically low on the absolute basis and as a percentage of sales. Other competitors in the marketplace assumed marketing expenditures of around 8 percent as a percentage of sales; hence, a progression of growth in marketing costs as a percentage of sales was assumed around this trajectory, starting at 7 percent of sales in 2011 and ending at 8 percent in 2015. Leasing costs were based on a long-term contract and assumed at a fixed figure. Transportation costs were related to volume growth and grew by about 30 percent faster compared to volume growth.

There are three expense categories that are not covered in the earlier discussion: depreciation expenses, interest expenses, and taxes. The depreciation expenses were calculated on a straight-line method, with assets depreciating at 10 percent per annum and reflecting the historical application of depreciation charges and the level of capital expenditure (i.e., CAPEX) needed to manufacture the desired volume of products. Generally, the lower the sales, the lower the CAPEX expenditures. The interest expenses were assumed to reflect the level of short- and long-term borrowing the firm may do. While the level of borrowing can be assumed at any level at the outset of financial forecasting (i.e., at the historical level of borrowing), the precise amount borrowed ultimately depends on the desired financing, the ratio analysis, and an investigation of the firm's ability to borrow in the marketplace. Tax rates were assumed to be equal to 40 percent of taxable income.

All the calculations given earlier and the assumptions included in table 5.2 permit completion of the revised projected income statement for the firm for the years 2011–2015. This is presented in table 5.3. The key results of the adjustments are as follows. First, BV's sales growth drops from 40 percent in 2011 to 15 percent in 2015. Second, margins decline at the EBITDA level, reflecting the fact that the firm appears to be under-spending in some key expense categories

Table 5.3   The full set of revised financial projections for Blue Velvet as prepared by venture capitalists

	2010	2011	2012	2013	2014	2015
Step 1: Assumptions and P&L						
Long-term debt	2,000	4,000	4,000	4,000	4,000	4,000
Investments		4,000	4,000	3,000	1,000	1,000
Fixed assets, gross	4,000	8,000	12,000	15,000	16,000	17,000
Depreciation @ 10 percent	400	800	1,200	1,500	1,600	1,700
Less: accumulated depreciation	1,010	1,810	3,010	4,510	6,110	7,810
Fixed assets, net	2,990	6,190	8,990	10,490	9,890	9,190
Common stock	1,000	3,000	4,000	4,000	4,000	4,000
Net sales	14,025	19,635	25,526	31,907	38,288	44,031
% Growth	*91*	*40*	*30*	*25*	*20*	*15*
Cost of goods sold	5,883	8,247	10,465	13,082	15,315	17,613
Gross margin	8,142	11,388	15,060	18,825	22,973	26,419
% Margin	*58.05*	*60.00*	*60.00*	*60.00*	*60.00*	*60.00*
Energy	118	142	163	183	202	217
Salaries	1,640	2,356	3,063	3,829	4,595	5,284
Management	530	780	780	855	915	992
Transportation	505	859	1,374	2,129	3,194	4,631
Business travel	155	295	383	479	574	660
Maintenance	214	393	511	638	766	881
Other services	261	313	376	451	541	649
Marketing	453	1,374	1,787	2,233	2,680	3,523
Leasing costs	214	214	214	214	214	214
Other costs	645	785	1,021	1,276	1,532	1,761
EBITDA	**3,407**	**3,878**	**5,390**	**6,537**	**7,761**	**7,607**
% Margin	*24.29*	*19.75*	*21.11*	*20.49*	*20.27*	*17.28*
Depreciation	400	800	1,200	1,500	1,600	1,700
Operating income (EBIT)	**3,007**	**3,078**	**4,190**	**5,037**	**6,161**	**5,907**
Interest expense	190	300	400	400	400	400
Earnings before taxes (EBIT)	2,817	2,778	3,790	4,637	5,761	5,507
Taxes	1,127	1,111	1,516	1,855	2,304	2,203
Earnings after tax (EAT)	**1,690**	**1,667**	**2,274**	**2,782**	**3,457**	**3,304**
% Margin	*12.05*	*8.49*	*8.91*	*8.72*	*9.03*	*7.50*

such as management and advertising. Higher costs assumed for some expense categories represent the venture capitalists' conservative approach to financial modeling. Third, the working capital assumptions are more realistic in terms of days A/R, inventory, and A/P. These adjustments reflect the competitive pressures that exist in the marketplace. Fourth, BV requires more cash than anticipated by its managerial team. In summary, if venture capitalists were to have simply relied on management's projections, they may have been forced to provide an additional and unexpected round of financing to the firm. Venture capitalists do not appreciate such surprises.

Step 2: Interim Calculations

One of the most frustrating problems encountered when preparing financial forecasts is that forecast balance sheets rarely balance. This may be due to a number of reasons, including errors in formula or logic, wrong assumptions, mathematical or data entry problems, or a lack of basic knowledge about the process. A good way to develop the balance sheet is to perform simple interim calculations based on assumptions related to working capital items.

Interim calculations make it easier to build the cash flow statement. Since the income statement already provides the net income figure as well as the depreciation expense (established in a preliminary manner at the beginning of the forecasting process), the key activity is calculating changes in working capital items—namely accounts receivable, inventory, and accounts payable—to arrive at cash from operating activities. To complete this analysis, it is important to begin with a historical analysis of trends in days receivable (A/R), days inventory, and days payable (A/P). A historical review of these components provides the following information: A/R = 42 days, inventory = 109 days, and A/P = 136 days. Management assumes that it will be easier to collect cash from the firm's clients in the future; consequently, A/R days are reduced from 37 in 2010 to 30 days in 2015. It further anticipates that other assumptions related to working capital management are not expected to be different from the data found in previous years.

Venture capitalists may disagree with some of these working capital assumptions. First, knowing the competitive nature of the ice-cream industry, venture capitalists may assume that customer credit extension may be an important competitive advantage, especially when the firm is attempting to develop markets beyond those core regions where the firm's brand recognition is strong. Venture capitalists could assume that BV needs to further extend its credit term to 60 days or more. The management of inventory at 109 days appears quite inefficient, but also reflects the cyclical nature of the industry and the firm's wide product offering. A more efficient management of working capital may be possible; if the competition has around 60 days of inventory, the same target of days is assumed to be reachable for BV. The supplier contracts, especially to new customers (like BV) in less geographically developed areas, may be favorable for some period of time. Over time, however, the suppliers may offer 70 days credit and propose volume discounts on raw material prices in exchange—a typical trade-off suppliers of raw materials are willing to accept. For example, the overall calculation of the liquidity gap for 2011 confirms that the gap is positive (45 + 100–90 = 55)—this means that any anticipated increases in sales would require an increase in investment in working capital.

The objective of interim calculations is to calculate the end balances of accounts receivables, inventory, and payables given assumptions made for days A/R, days inventory, and days A/P. For example, if we know that the formula for calculating days A/R is equal to accounts receivable divided by sales multiplied by 365 days, it is easy to adjust this formula to calculate the ending balance of A/R in dollars, given that days A/R are assumed (A/R ending balance in dollars = days A/R x Sales/365). In 2011, for example, this calculation would be equal to (45 x $19,635,000)/365 = $2,421,000. The remaining balances for inventory and accounts payable may be calculated in the same manner. Please note that the formulas for days inventory and days A/P use COGS, not sales, as the basis for the calculation. Table 5.4 shows the calculations of ending balances for working capital items.

There may be other aspects of working capital that need to be addressed: marketable securities, prepaid expense, notes, accrued expenses, and so on. The general rule for forecasting these items is that unless there is some fundamental reason to believe that these items will change, it is appropriate to leave them at their existing levels. This, of course, means that these items have no impact on the firm's cash flow.

Table 5.4 Working capital assumptions and ending balances in accounts receivable, inventory, and accounts payable

	Historical (2010)	Financial projections				
		2011	2012	2013	2014	2015
Step 2: Interim calculations						
Assumed days						
Accounts receivable (days)	42	45	45	50	60	60
Inventory (days)	109	100	90	80	70	60
Accounts payable (days)	136	90	80	70	70	70
Ending balances in $ '000						
Accounts receivable (days)	1,620	2,421	3,147	4,371	6,294	7,238
Inventory (days)	1,760	2,259	2,581	2,867	2,937	2,895
Accounts payable (days)	2,197	2,033	2,294	2,509	2,937	3,378

It is important to make realistic assumptions about working capital items. A loss of liquidity and poor management of working capital can lead to business failure. It is important to use benchmarking whenever possible. Over the long term, venture capitalists know that operational and financial efficiencies in working capital are limited by what is possible to accomplish in the marketplace. In other words, in the medium and long run, components of working capital management are likely to gravitate toward the industry average even if some temporary anomalies are experienced in the meantime. This is especially true for firms that are competing on a regional scale with limited exposure to national or international market forces.

Step 3: Cash Flow Statement Forecasting

A standard cash flow statement is made up of three main components: cash from operating activities, from investing activities, and from financing activities. Interim calculations and the calculations and assumptions made during the creation of the income statement comprise a significant part of the cash flow statement creation process. At this point, the cash flow statement must gather information from different parts of the income statement and gather the interim calculations. For example, both net income and depreciation expense come from the income statement, and the changes in working capital items come from interim calculations. The investment program reflects the level of anticipated sales and is prepared during initial calculations. The financing section is an area where an iterative process ultimately produces a final outcome. The financial section of the cash flow statement consists of the capital provided by external parties (i.e., venture capitalists) and debt providers. The financial model prepared by venture capitalists requires three million dollars of equity and an additional two million dollars of debt. This allows the firm to finance its expansion program, to invest into marketing and promotions, and to satisfy its working capital requirements.

The net result is that BV generates moderate amounts of cumulative internal cash flow in its initial years and a significant amount of cash in its later years. The cash flow reflects the firm's growth (and the initial expenses associated with such growth), its investment needs, and the additional working capital required. The cash flow statement is presented in table 5.5.

Step 4: Balance Sheet Forecasting

Once the income and the cash flow statements are prepared, the mechanics of preparing a balance sheet become relatively straight-forward. The previous discussions dealt with all parts of the balance sheet with the exception of the retained earnings section. The formula for calculating retained earnings is as follows: Retained Earnings $_{n+1}$ = Retained Earnings $_n$ + Net Income $_{n+1}$ − Dividends $_{n+1}$. Given that the closing balance sheet for the year 2010 is available, and that this also represents the opening balance sheet for the year 2011, it is easy to calculate the end balances of retained earnings in any specific year using the formula given earlier. An alternative is to develop a combined statement of income and retained earnings, where the value of "An Additional to Retained Earnings" represents the amount that needs to be added to the previous year's retained earnings balance to arrive at a new closing figure for the balance sheet. The balance sheet statement is presented in table 5.5.

Table 5.5 The full set of revised financial projections for Blue Velvet as prepared by venture capitalists (continued from tables 5.3 and 5.4)

		2011	2012	2013	2014	2015
Step 3: CF development						
Net income		1,667	2,274	2,782	3,457	3,304
Depreciation		800	1,200	1,500	1,600	1,700
Decrease (increase) in A/R		−801	−726	−1,224	−1,923	−944
Decrease (increase) in Inventory		−499	−321	−287	−70	42
Increase (decrease) in A/P		−164	260	215	428	441
Total cash from operating activities		**1,003**	**2,687**	**2,987**	**3,492**	**4,543**
Investments in fixed assets		−4,000	−4,000	−3,000	−1,000	−1,000
Total cash to investing activities		**−4,000**	**−4,000**	**−3,000**	**−1,000**	**−1,000**
Proceeds from L-T debt issue		2,000	0	0	0	0
Proceeds from issue of com-mon stock		2,000	1,000	0	0	0
Total cash from financing activities		**4,000**	**1,000**	**0**	**0**	**0**
Total change in cash flow		**1,003**	**−313**	**−13**	**2,492**	**3,543**
Step 4: BS development	2010	2011	2012	2013	2014	2015
Cash	343	1,346	1,033	1,020	3,512	7,054
Accounts receivable	1,620	2,421	3,147	4,371	6,294	7,238
Inventory	1,760	2,259	2,581	2,867	2,937	2,895

Continued

Table 5.5   Continued

	2010	2011	2012	2013	2014	2015
Fixed assets, gross	4,000	8,000	12,000	15,000	16,000	17,000
Accumulated depreciation	1,010	1,810	3,010	4,510	6,110	7,810
Fixed assets, net	2,990	6,190	8,990	10,490	9,890	9,190
Total assets	**6,713**	**12,216**	**15,750**	**18,748**	**22,633**	**26,378**
Accounts payable	2,197	2,033	2,294	2,509	2,937	3,378
Long-term debt	2,000	4,000	4,000	4,000	4,000	4,000
Total liabilities	**4,197**	**6,033**	**6,294**	**6,509**	**6,937**	**7,378**
Common stock	1,000	3,000	4,000	4,000	4,000	4,000
Retained earnings	1,516	3,183	5,456	8,239	11,696	15,000
Total shareholders' equity	**2,516**	**6,183**	**9,456**	**12,239**	**15,696**	**19,000**
Total liabilities and equity	**6,713**	**12,216**	**15,750**	**18,748**	**22,633**	**26,378**
Step 5: Ratio confirmation						
Gross profit margin (%)	58.05	58.00	59.00	59.00	60.00	60.00
Operating profit margin (%)	21.44	15.67	16.41	15.79	16.09	13.42
Net profit margin (%)	12.05	8.49	8.91	8.72	9.03	7.50
EBITDA margin (%)	24.29	19.75	21.11	20.49	20.27	17.28
Return on assets (%)	25.18	13.64	14.44	14.84	15.27	12.53
Return on equity (%)	67.17	26.96	24.04	22.73	22.02	17.39
Current ratio	1.69	2.96	2.95	3.29	4.34	5.09
Quick ratio	0.89	1.85	1.82	2.15	3.34	4.23
Debt/equity (%)	166.81	97.59	66.56	53.18	44.20	38.83
Debt/total assets (%)	62.52	49.39	39.96	34.72	30.65	27.97
Times interest earned	15.8	10.3	10.5	12.6	15.4	14.8

Step 5: Verification of Financial Ratios

The financial ratio analysis represents the last step in the process of building financial forecasts (see table 5.5). It is also the most important step, as it identifies major red flags on a stand-alone and comparative bases. A review of the financial ratios provides an opportunity to compare the obtained results with reference information (i.e., industry data). An analysis of the firm's internal trends is first performed. Key questions may include: Are any of the ratios based on financial forecasts that are in major conflict with historical data? Are these numbers consistent with historical trends? What areas of analysis show improvements and which show deterioration? The second area of investigation is to compare the resulting ratios with external sources of industry information. The key questions asked here are: Is the firm's revenue growth too aggressive given the anticipated market growth? Are margins comparable with those commonly found in the industry and what are the key reasons for over- or underachievement? Are working capital requirements correctly estimated? Is the firm able to obtain external financing as anticipated in the business plan? If the comparable analysis of ratios is found to be unfavorable, the iterative process continues until venture capitalists are content with the outcome.

In the case of Blue Velvet, the ratios show a reasonable outcome. For example, profitability ratios at the EBITDA level conservatively show a level below historical trends, as venture capitalists believe that some cost trends and items were underestimated. The level of EBITDA margins is estimated by venture capitalists to be at 18–21 percent. Return on equity is estimated in the low twenties. The liquidity and debt ratios seem steady. Asset activity ratios seem realistic given the competitive forces found in the marketplace.

Closing Remarks on Financial Forecasting

The preparation of financial forecasts is both a science and an art. The process is scientific in that it requires error-free development of the financial model through the creation of the spreadsheet. The art comes from using creativity, logic, and good judgment to develop key assumptions based on an understanding of the business and its historical performance.

The act of preparing a financial forecast is not about creating the most sophisticated spreadsheet model; it is about the proper assessment of risk. Venture capitalists believe that their ability to identify business risks allows them the basis to develop the most realistic set of financial projections for a firm. Venture capitalists are assisted with this process by their colleagues in the firm, members of the investment committee, and external experts (accountants, lawyers, technical experts, environmental specialists, etc.).

Venture capitalists know that the financial forecast of the business prepared prior to deal closing only represents the beginning of the business plan revision process, which is very likely to come at some point in venture development. There are numerous moments during the life of the investment where financial projections are revised to reflect new circumstances within the firm as well as in external environments. Venture capitalists often claim that the original business plans prepared by investee firms are almost never fulfilled. The most fundamental reason for this is that venture capitalists estimate that over half of all successful investments owe their success to products or services that were either not in the original business plan or were considered to be a minor part of the firm's business.

Business Valuation

Most commonly, business valuations measure the value of the business. Business valuations are performed ahead of the firm receiving additional capital, performing a merger, or engaging into an acquisition. The main objective of business valuation is to develop a valuation spectrum (the science) for the business, which best describes where the value of the firm may be. The science is based on a combination of mechanical functions on the spreadsheet coupled with assumptions about the future prospects of the business. This valuation spectrum proposes a range of values that will narrow the possible wide range of valuation numbers expected by entrepreneurs and venture capitalists. Ultimately, a final value of the business is established through negotiations (the art) reflecting basic market forces of supply and demand that determine the value of any asset.

The valuation spectrum or range is established on the basis of the application of different business valuation methodologies. Venture capitalists generally perform business valuation using at least two methods: the discounted cash flow (DCF) method and EBITDA-multiple method. In special circumstances, venture capitalists may rely on other methods; these include the replacement value, liquidation value, or net asset value methods.

Discounted Cash Flow Method

The DCF method represents a special application of time and value of money principles. The method generally involves projecting the firm's financial forecasts for a period of three–five years into the future and then subsequently discounting the firm's cash flows to the present with a discounted rate that represents the venture capital firm's expected rate of return. Special adjustments are made at the end of this process to arrive at the firm's net market value of common equity. Let's see how this procedure would work in the case of Blue Velvet.

The first step in the DCF method includes calculating the free cash flow (FCF) for each year's financial forecasts. The FCF is a sum of inflows and outflows, namely net income plus depreciation minus capital expenditure (CAPEX) plus changes in working capital items (these changes in working capital items may have a positive or negative impact on the FCF of the firm). Please note that the financial costs are excluded from this calculation since the costs of capital are generally captured in the discount rate. In the case of BV, the free cash flows for the projected five-year period would be equal to -\$3.0 million in 2011, -\$1.3 million in 2012, \$0.0 million in 2013, \$2.5 million in 2014, and \$3.5 million in 2015. The next step is to discount these values to the present by using the desired discount rate. The general formula for discounting future values to the present is shown here. The calculations can be done as given in equation 5.1, using the financial calculator or the spreadsheet. The total sum of all discounted values is equal to -\$0.8 million (see table 5.6).

$$\text{PV of FCF} = \frac{\text{FCF}}{(1+k)^n} \tag{5.1}$$

The discounted cash flows are calculated on the basis of the free cash flows anticipated to occur between the years 2011 and 2015 (a five-year period). This five-year period of time is the norm in which venture capitalists are comfortable projecting the fortunes for any business; it is extremely difficult to make financial projections beyond this point. However, BV does not plan to cease operations at the end of 2015. The methodology that allows venture capitalists to capture the value of a firm beyond a five-year period is related to terminal value (TV) calculations. Terminal value is calculated on the basis of the FCF in the last year (t) of the financial projections (i.e., 2015) adjusted by the anticipated growth rate in cash flow (g) and discounted by the adjusted discount rate (k). The formula for calculating TV is given in equation 5.2.

$$\text{TV} = \frac{\text{FCF}_t (1+g)}{k-g} \tag{5.2}$$

The anticipated growth rate in the FCF is generally set at low levels (zero to a maximum of 5 percent), as the formula reflects a perpetual growth of cash flow. It is unlikely that the FCF will grow at a rate consistent with historical data. The growth rate for BV was assumed at 2 percent. Additionally, it is not realistic to assume that a significant value of the firm can come from a cash flow that is projected at some future point in time. When preparing financial forecasts, some venture capitalists do not allow the present value of TV to exceed one-third or one-fourth of the sum of all present values from operations. This is based on the assumption that uncertain events in the future should not have such a significant influence on the ultimate value of the firm's operations—we do not make this adjustment here. In addition, the growth rate in the denominator in equation 5.2 acts to reduce the risk of the venture, thereby reducing the influence of the discount rate on the value of the firm. An additional step is to discount TV to the present, as TV captures the value of the business each year to the end of 2015. Using the desired rate of return, the discounted value of TV equals $8.1 million.

The sum of all FCFs discounted to the present and the present value of TV represents the operational value of the firm. In order to calculate the firm's net market value of common equity, the total discounted cash flow needs to be adjusted to reflect existing short-term assets and liabilities. As a consequence, current assets are added to the present value of FCFs while current liabilities, long-term debts, and preferred share capital are deducted from the sum. The total value of BV's common equity is equal to $6.8 million. The complete calculation of the DCF is presented in table 5.6.

Another area of the analysis that requires further discussion is the origin of the discount rate. The discount rate represents perceived risk in the venture. The higher the perceived risk, the lower the value venture capitalists are willing to assign to the business. In most venture capital firms, the discount rate or the desired internal rate of return (i.e., IRR) sought by venture capitalists is given

Table 5.6 Discounted cash flow method and calculation for Blue Velvet (in $ '000)

	2010	2011	2012	2013	2014	2015
Free cash flow		−2,997	−1,313	−13	2,492	3,543
PV of CF	−792					
TV						20,076
PV of TV	8,068					
Total PV of CF	7,277					
Plus current assets	3,723					
Less current liabilities	2,197					
Less LT debt	2,000					
Market value of equity for Blue Velvet	**6,803**					

Abbreviations: CF, cash flow; LT, long-term; PV, present value; TV, terminal value.

or decided upon by the venture capital firm's management team. Given the assumption of a certain return, venture capital firms do not make deals unless the rate of return "on paper" (based on projected or revised financial forecasts prepared by venture capitalists) exceeds their minimum requirement. This desired rate of return, or discount rate, can be increased if the business appears more risky than the average firm the venture capital firm is willing to finance. In Western countries, the minimum rate of return is set above the rate of return achieved from the public market. This higher expectation reflects the illiquidity risk venture capitalists assume. This risk premium is generally around 10–15 percent. In Western countries, the minimum IRR expectations range from 20 to 30 percent, while in emerging markets, these rates generally exceed 30 or 40 percent. This is not to say that these are the rates achieved by venture capitalists in these markets. Venture capitalists simply need to see the desired return on paper before proceeding with the deal.

In the absence of given return expectations, venture capitalists or analysts can rely on the capital asset pricing model (CAPM). The CAPM calculates the appropriate required rate of return for an investment project given its degree of risk as measured by beta (β). It also represents a project's degree of risk relative to the overall stock market. The formula for CAPM is given in equation 5.3. The three components of CAPM include the risk-free rate of return (k_{rf}), the market risk premium (k_m-k_{rf}), and the project's beta (this refers to the beta of the firm's competitive industry), which may be obtained from financial analysts' reports or calculated by running a regression analysis using the historical returns from stocks in the relevant industry and the market returns—a complex procedure. The risk-free rate is the rate of return that investors demand from a project or an investment that contains no risk. The risk-free rate is normally denoted by the rate of return obtained from 60 or 90-day Treasury bills. Risk-averse managers and owners always demand at least this rate of return from any investment project. The required rate of return on the overall market minus the risk-free rate (k_m-k_{rf}) represents the additional return demanded by investors for taking on the risk of investing in the market itself. For venture capitalists, additional compensation can come through investing into a firm that is private with shares not freely sellable at any point in time—this may be called the illiquidity premium (IP). The value of IP is generally believed to be around 10–15 percent.

$$k = k_{rf} + \beta(k_m - k_{rf}) + IP \tag{5.3}$$

Let's take an example from the world of Internet search engines. Imagine that we are starting a new search engine in the United States believed to be a formidable competitor to existing market players such as Google or Yahoo. We find that Google has a beta of 2 while other firms (both domestic and international) have betas larger than 1 (Yahoo—1.22; Sohu—2.57; Baidu—2.59). The average beta for these firms would equal 2.1. If the return on the stock market is 17 percent and the risk-free rate is equal to 5, then the required rate of return from this investment would be at least 45 percent (5% + 2.1 x [17%–5%] + 15 = 45.2%). This number provides a benchmark figure to venture capitalists that can be adjusted up or down based on other perceived risk factors.

EBITDA Multiple Method

Enterprise value (EV) represents the entire economic value of the firm from the point of view of the aggregate of all the financing sources. It is regarded as one of the most fundamental and comprehensive metrics used in business valuation and is a measure of a theoretical takeover price that an investor would need to pay to acquire a firm, free and clear of all financial obligations. Enterprise value is regarded as a more accurate estimate of a firm's value than market capitalization (calculated by multiplying the number of outstanding shares by the current share price), as it takes into consideration a number of important factors beyond the firm's common equity (such as preferred stock, debt, cash and cash equivalents, and other components). Enterprise value considers that a buyer must also bear the burden of the debt and other liabilities that the target firm has on its balance—these may include debt obligations, unfunded deficit in the firm's pension fund, unpaid bonuses to management, executive stock options, environmental provisions and related financial obligations, abandonment provisions, and so on. In addition, it takes into consideration the fact that the acquirer also receives the target firm's cash and cash equivalents (i.e., marketable securities the firm has on its balance sheet). Enterprise value is regarded as a capital structure-neutral measure as it is used to compare firms with diverse capital structures.

Enterprise value is calculated as a total of the firm's common stock equity (E_c) plus market value of debt and other liabilities (D) plus any minority interests outsiders hold in the subsidiary firm of the parent firm (MI) plus preferred stock (E_p) less cash and cash equivalents (C) see equation 5.4.

$$EV = E_c + E_p + MI + D - C \qquad\qquad (5.4)$$

Preferred stock is added to the net value of common stock. In its most classic form, preferred stock represents the firm's debt obligation (as it must be redeemed at a certain date for a certain price). It also carries a fixed divided requirement. The value of minority interest (minority interest is considered as the interest outsiders have in the subsidiary firm, owned by the parent firm, assuming venture capitalists seek to invest in the parent firm) is added because it reflects the claim on assets outside parties have on the assets of the parent firm. Debt and other liabilities are added because the acquirer would need to pay these obligations (this effectively increases the acquisition price) while cash and cash equivalents are subtracted because they reduce the net cost to the purchaser. Assuming that many firms financed by venture capital do not have minority interests in other firms and do not have preferred shares, the formula can be reduced to the following: $EV = E_c + D - C$. Since cash and cash equivalents act to reduce the firm's debt obligations, the formula can be further reduced to net debt (nD), net debt off cash, and cash equivalents. The final equation may be established as follows: $EV = E_c + nD$ (consequently, $E_c = EV - nD$).

The objective of the discounted cash flow method is to determine the value of the business given its cash flows, growth, and market value of assets and liabilities. The objective of the EBITDA multiple method is to value firms based on how firms in the same industry are currently priced in the marketplace. Therefore, this method effectively compares the values of businesses operating in the same industry. One of the most intuitive ways to measure the value of a firm is to think of the business as a multiple of the earnings the firm generates. For the purpose of this method, the EBITDA line of the firm's income statement is chosen to represent earnings.

In order to use this method, it is important to obtain comparable EVs. Publicly quoted firms' valuations are generally defined in terms of EV/EBITDA multiples. The EV/EBITDA figures of these firms are easy to find, as they appear in financial statements filed with security commissions on a quarterly basis. The multiples of nonpublic firms are obtained from private sector transactions. These data are more difficult to obtain, but are available in reports produced by research firms (these may have to be purchased by the venture capital firm). For the ice-cream business, the average EV/EBITDA multiple is estimated at 6—this is based on the multiples of other firms in the industry (e.g., Nestle, Unilever, Cadbury, Baskin-Robins, Danone). The EV/EBITDA-multiple method can be easily applied to the case of Blue Velvet. However, venture capitalists would normally discount the calculation by 25–50 percent from the level of publicly held firms. This is done for at least two reasons. Publicly quoted firms have to adhere to strict financial regulations and legal disclosures; therefore, venture capitalists would see their earnings as more stable and of higher quality. Second, the stock of the public firm is liquid, so additional discounts must be applied to a nonliquid entity in the industry.

In order to calculate the EV for Blue Velvet, venture capitalists would apply the EV/EBITDA multiple to historic or prospective (the current year's data) EBITDA. The application of EV/EBITDA multiples to historical data, verified by a financial audit, represents a preferred, more conservative approach to business valuation for venture capitalists. The average EV/EBITDA multiple for the sector is estimated at 6 (this may be relatively low compared to other industries). Once the multiple for the industry is determined, EV can be estimated as the average EBITDA multiple (i.e., the multiple is reduced by a reduction factor of 50 percent, equal to 3) multiplied by the firm's EBITDA from the income statement for the relevant year. The firm's enterprise value is equal to $10.2 million, based on the historic $EBITDA_{2010}$ ($3.4 million x 6 x [1—50%] = $10.2 million) and equal to $11.7 million based on the perspective $EBITDA_{2011}$ ($3.9 million x 3 = $11.7 million). The value of common stock equity can be estimated at $8.5 million based on historical data ($E = EV - nD$; $10.2 million − [$2.0 million—$0.3 million] = $8.5 million) and $9.0 million based on perspective data.

It is important to note that it may not be possible to obtain EV/EBITDA multiples for certain businesses. In the example given earlier from the ice-cream industry, all the major market players are involved in other food processing activities besides ice-cream. Realistically, no two firms will have exactly the same profile of business characteristics. The objective is to find benchmark cases that best compare to the business.

The valuation range for BV based on DCF and EBITDA multiple method would be equal to between $6.8 million and $9.0 million.

Other Business Valuation Methods

Other valuation techniques provide additional information in order to develop a valuation range. Additional valuation techniques can either mark the floor price for the business (i.e., net book value or liquidation value) or the ceiling price (i.e., replacement value). The valuation also reflects what transactions occur in the marketplace.

One of the simplest ways to value equity is to subtract the value of the firm's liabilities and preferred shares (if any) as recorded on the balance sheet from the value of its assets. The result is the net book value or net worth (book value of common equity = total assets—total liabilities—preferred share equity). However, the net book value has severe limitations. The asset values recorded on the firm's balance sheet usually reflect what the owners originally paid for the assets, not the current market value of the assets themselves. Due to these and other limitations, the net book value is used sparingly to estimate the market value of common equity.

The liquidation and net book valuation methods are similar, except that the liquidation method uses the market value of the assets and liabilities. The market values of the assets are the amounts the assets would earn on the open market if they were sold or liquidated. The market values of the liabilities are the amounts of money it would take to pay off the liabilities. Consequently, the liquidation value is the amount common shareholders would receive if the firm closed, sold all its assets, paid off all liabilities and preferred shares, and distributed the net proceeds to common shareholders. Although more reliable than the net book value method, liquidation value represents a worst-case valuation assessment. The firm's common shares should be worth at least the amount generated at liquidation. Because liquidation value does not consider the earnings and cash flows the firm is likely to generate in the future, it may provide misleading results for firms that have significant future earnings potential. This method is useful if the acquirer intends to sell the assets of the acquired firm. It may also be used to determine the fair book value of under- and overvalued assets. This valuation method often defines the floor price of the firm.

The replacement value of assets method is similar to the liquidation valuation. According to the concept underlying this method, the market value of a complete business cannot exceed the amount it would take to buy all of the firm's assets on the open market. Although it is simple in concept, the replacement value of assets method is not often applied to business valuations for at least two reasons. First, it is very difficult for similar assets to sell locally on the open market. Second, some of the firm's assets are difficult to define and quantify. Although it is difficult to use the replacement method to value a business, the method can be quite useful for estimating the value of individual assets in a business. For example, the value of a firm's nonproprietary software can be estimated by listing the various programs in use and then noting the prices of those programs in retail stores, catalogues, and on the Internet. Individual asset valuations of this type are most often employed when one business buys another and it is necessary to allocate the purchase price among the assets purchased. In such cases, the fair market value of the individual assets is estimated (using the replacement value of assets method, the discounted cash flow method, or some other method) and any remaining amounts are assigned to goodwill.

Questions to Consider

1. Differentiate between the main methods of business valuation. When is it most appropriate to use these methods?
2. Given the spreadsheet discussed in this chapter, "mechanize" the financial model by recreating all the financial statements in Excel.
3. Discuss the importance of the terminal value concept used in the DCF method.
4. What are the main steps in preparing financial forecasts? Can the order of these steps be changed?
5. How are interim calculations important to the process of preparing the financial model suggested in this chapter?

Apax Partners

Key characteristics

Year founded:	1969*
Founding partners:	Alan Particof
Number of limited partners:	N/A (Dutch ABP, PFZW, AlpInvest, GIC)
Geographic coverage:	North America (1), Europe (6), Asia (3)
Headquarter location:	London (UK)/New York (USA)
Focus (if any):	Five sectors
Funds under management:	$37 billion
Number of completed deals/IPO exits:	~350/N/A
Private/public:	Private
Most publicly recognized deals:	Emap, Tommy Hilfiger, HIT Entertainment, Trader Media (AutoTrader), Travelex, New Look, Apollo Hospitals
Number of investment professionals:	~300

Apax was founded through the combining of three entities (Patricof & Co., Multinational Management Group, MMG, and Saunders Karp & Megrue).

Apax Partners is one of the world's oldest private equity houses. It has about $37 billion under management, and it is largely based in the United States (40 percent of total raised funds) and Europe (38 percent). The most visible signature deals completed by Apax include: Tommy Hilfiger, Trader Media, New Look, and Travellex.

Apax focuses on five global growth sectors: media (25 percent of total portfolio), retail and consumer (21 percent), financial and business services (20 percent), healthcare (17 percent), and technology and telecommunications (13 percent); other sectors account for the remaining 4 percent. Apax invests in industry leaders or those with a strong market presence and exceptional expansion potential, and typically in firms valued between $1.5 billion and $7 billion.

Apax has traditionally maintained a strong presence in North America and Europe. However, it has recently opened offices in China (2005 and 2008) and India (2006). In total, Apax operates ten offices worldwide. The firm employs about three hundred investment professionals. The teams are organized along the major investment categories. Apax is also among the industry leaders in promoting social entrepreneurship (e.g., Ashoka, Bridges Social Entrepreneurs Fund, and Emmaus) and has been involved with numerous charity initiatives. The firm has also received numerous industry awards.

Source: www.apax.com.

Chapter 6

Pre-Approval Completions

Having understood the issues related to financial forecasting and business valuation, venture capitalists proceed to conclude one of the most important steps in the early stage of the investment process—negotiation and finalization of the terms of the deal with entrepreneurs. Negotiations of the major terms of the deal are to have been completed and the term sheet is to have been signed before the deal is presented to the investment committee for formal approval. The term sheet allows venture capitalists to show to the investment committee that the deal, in principle, is signed and that the major areas of commercial investigation have been checked off. This is a critical step to complete prior to obtaining any internal approvals and is the focal point of this chapter.

Deal structuring in venture capital is defined as the negotiation of deal pricing, various rights and provisions, and the formation of securities. Owing to a desire to optimize the tax structure of the venture capital fund and due to the significant imperfections of legal infrastructure in many markets around the world, venture capitalists must carefully consider how they structure deals. Whether utilizing local or foreign vehicles or some other combination, an optimal trade-off between risks and returns must be achieved to maximize the value of venture capitalists' investment.

Term Sheet Development

If due diligence does not identify any major issues of concern, venture capitalists proceed to negotiate a deal. The initial negotiations are captured in the form of a letter of intent, term sheet, or heads of terms.[1] This "milestone" document outlines an understanding between venture capitalists and entrepreneurs in which the two sides express their willingness to interact on a "best-effort" basis to develop a deal. The document is intended to provide each side with a reasonable degree of comfort as to the intentions of and commitment to each partner. Even though most of the terms included in this document are not legally binding (exceptions are exclusivity, confidentiality, and costs), venture capitalists regard this document as a major moral commitment.

The term sheet, as it is commonly called by venture capitalists, should contain all of the fundamental principles upon which the investment will be made. The objective of the document is to anticipate and mitigate potential risks in the life of the investment. These risks could be related to managerial challenges, operational problems, financial difficulties, and so on. The objective of venture capitalists is to devise a set of protections to address major foreseeable risks. This forces the document to be detailed (it is usually five–ten pages in length). At the same time, the document cannot contain every provision needed by venture capitalists for the future; it is impossible to anticipate all possible scenarios of underperformance or risk. The reasons for this are varied: not all the required provisions will be known or developed at the time (e.g., venture capitalists may discover some concerns during the due diligence process and want to address them in the deal structure), many specific points (e.g., procedures for executing certain rights) are discussed and agreed upon during the preparation of the closing legal documentation, and certain issues are left "open" (e.g., to be agreed upon later). In addition, the term sheet needs to be flexible enough to be able to deal with unanticipated circumstances and unforeseen risks. Consequently, the term sheet must focus on certain core principles of the partnership that venture capitalists want to instill into the legal framework. When unanticipated challenges occur throughout the life of the agreement, the two sides review the initial term sheet to refresh their understanding of the principles upon which the deal was crystallized. Notwithstanding the key principles, the term sheet usually includes the following basic elements: name and details of the firm, the amount of investment by the venture capital firm, the types and numbers of shares assumed by venture capitalists and the types held by entrepreneurs, venture capitalists' specific rights (including board representation), the use and the timing of capital, and a list of conditions precedent to funding (i.e., what conditions must be fulfilled before the deal is consummated—these may include satisfactory legal and accounting due diligence or hiring a CFO).

In signing the term sheet, the parties agree to proceed in good faith with negotiations of legal contracts based upon the business terms included in the term sheet, to put forward their best efforts to ensure the completion of the transaction by a specific date, and to do so on an exclusive basis. Venture capitalists and entrepreneurs, of course, recognize that the final execution of the transaction under the terms included in the term sheet are subject to the satisfactory results of a detailed due diligence review conducted by the venture capital firm and its advisors into all aspects of the firm.

As previously mentioned, venture capital deal structuring involves pricing, security types, and an investment vehicle. The following sections will discuss these three major components.

Deal Pricing

One of the main issues that venture capitalists need to deal with is the amount of ownership the venture capital firm will acquire. Deal pricing is a by-product of numerous critical factors. First, the range in valuation of the business must be considered. As discussed in the previous chapter, business value is never represented as a single number; instead, it is determined by a spectrum of reference points that represent the most probable valuation of the business. Deal pricing also means negotiations between the two sides of the transaction. The ultimate value of the business is determined by the market and the willingness of market participants to buy or sell an asset at a particular price. The internal rate of return must also be considered. Between the points of entry into and exit from the business, venture capitalists need to achieve a desired rate of return (e.g., IRR). Deal pricing must be set in such a way that the desired rate of return can be achieved.

In the previous chapter, we learned about the initial valuation of a business (or entry valuation). However, there is another point in time that the valuation exercise becomes important—that at which venture capitalists exit from their investment. This point in time determines the total amount of proceeds venture capitalists receive from the deal (or exit valuation). The calculation of exit valuation allows one to determine the value of the internal rate of return.

The options for determining the exit value of the investee firm are limited. Most venture capitalists rely on EV/EBITDA multiples to determine the value of a business at the end of the anticipated holding period; they do not determine the value of the business by applying the discounted cash flow model. The chief reason for this is that venture capitalists will almost certainly have a problem coming up with a credible set of financial projections beyond the fifth year. If determining the value of free cash flows in the first five years is challenging, the task of developing financial projections beyond this point is an extremely difficult task.

Venture capitalists can determine exit value through the use of EV/EBITDA multiples. EV/EBITDA multiples are the same for the entry valuation, or lower. Obviously, if the calculation of the internal rate of return works on lower EV/EBITDA multiples, the calculations of IRR will be even more compelling when higher EV/EBITDA multiples are applied at the time of exit. The use of this more conservative approach is based on the assumption that the attractiveness of the markets in which the investee firm competes in may change. Strategic investors can change their market objectives and priorities, and public markets may be less receptive to receiving a firm from a specific industry or sector. If, at the point of exit, the approach for venture capitalists is to be as conservative as possible, the only true point of flexibility in the negotiations is the entry valuation. Let's see how the IRR calculations would be made in the case of Blue Velvet.

We determined in the previous chapter that the business valuation for Blue Velvet may range between $6.8 million and $9.0 million. This represents the spectrum within which venture capitalists feel comfortable closing the deal. Let's assume that venture capitalists and BV's owners agree upon a business value of $8 million. The ownership position that the venture capitalists will assume in the firm must next be decided upon. To determine this, we need to know whether the capital provided by venture capitalists goes into the firm in the form of a capital increase or as an outright purchase of shares from BV's owners. If we assume that $3 million from venture capitalists comes into BV in the form of a capital increase (this amount of investment was determined by venture capitalists by revising the financial projections prepared by the management), then the venture capital firm's ownership stake will equal 27.3 percent ($3 million/[$8 million + $3 million]). It is important to note that the valuation of the business equal to $8 million is often called the *pre-money valuation*—the valuation of the business prior to any new capital coming into the firm. The *post-money valuation* is the value of the capital after new capital has come into the business. In this case, the post-money valuation would be equal to $11 million ($8 million + $3 million). On the other hand, if we assume that BV's owners wanted to sell their shares for $3 million (which is not the case in this situation, as the firm clearly needs additional capital), the venture capitalists would assume a 37.5 percent stake in the business ($3 million/$8 million). In the case of an outright purchase of the shares from the owners, the pre-money valuation is equal to the post-money valuation, as no new capital is brought to the firm and the capital base of the firm does not change. The situation changes only when there is a capital increase and the post-money valuation is no longer equal to the pre-money valuation. It is important to note that venture capitalists generally try to enter a business through a capital increase rather than by purchasing shares from the owners.

The exit valuation for BV is determined on the basis of the procedure described here, or $E = EV - nD$. We assume that we will exit in 2015. To determine EV for 2015, we multiply $EBITDA_{2015}$ by a conservative and discounted EBITDA multiple equal to 3; this number provides the total amount of proceeds made from the sale of the business ($22.8 million). Many venture capitalists tend to ignore the value of net debt at this point so long as the value of anticipated cash substantially exceeds the value of the debt. This is based on the assumption that the firm is likely to use the cash to repay the debt and use available cash for other investment purposes, therefore leaving a reasonable amount of cash balance in the business. This approach is considered to be more conservative, as the amount of cash is effectively ignored for the purposes of business valuation at the exit point.

Since venture capitalists own a 27.3 percent stake in the business, their total proceeds would equal $6.2 million. This represents a 2.1 cash-on-cash return from the deal (see table 6.1). It is further assumed that the venture capital firm will invest $2 million in 2011, $1 million in 2012 (as per the revised business plan; these numbers appear as negatives as they represent a cash outflow for

Table 6.1 Internal rate of return calculations based on venture capitalists' assumed exit in 2015

Cash-on-cash (multiple)	Years of investment and exit in 2015						Assumed EV/ EBITDA multiple
	IRR(%)	2011 ($M)	2012 ($M)	2013 ($M)	2014 ($M)	2015 ($M)	
2.1	22	−2	−1	0	0	6.2	3
2.8	32	−2	−1	0	0	8.3	4
3.5	30	−2	−1	0	0	10.4	5
4.2	41	−2	−1	0	0	12.5	6

venture capitalists), and that no other proceeds will be received in 2012, 2013, and 2014 (venture capitalists sometimes receive dividends if the business proves to be extra cash generative or if the firm performs well). The exit is anticipated to occur in 2015. The total IRR in this case is equal to about 22 percent. Table 6.1 also shows other IRR calculations based on different exit multiples. IRR can be calculated by using the spreadsheet or a financial calculator (the following keys: $CF_0 = -\$2$ million; $CF_1 = -\$1$ million; $CF_2 = 0$; $CF_3 = 0$; $CF_4 = 0$; $CF_5 = \$6.2$ million; IRR). If we assume that the desired rate of return is 20 percent, the initial valuation of $8 million may stand.

Let's assume, however, that BV's owners would not accept a pre-money valuation of $8 million. In this case, the question becomes to what extent venture capitalists would be able to improve upon the offer and still achieve their minimum rate of return of 20 percent. We know that in the base case, the IRR was equal to 22 percent; therefore, there is no significant possibility that the pricing could be improved (IRR would drop below 20 percent). Let's assume that all the parameters of the exit valuation stay the same with the exception of the ownership interest venture capitalists hold in BV. Different ownership interests for venture capitalists, of course, imply different pre-money valuations of the business. Table 6.2 presents these calculations. The first line of the table presents the base case, in which IRR is equal to 22 percent—this is based on the venture capitalists holding a 27.3 percent interest in BV. In the second scenario, we assume that the venture capitalists' ownership interest falls to 26 percent. The implied post-money valuation would equal $11.5 million and the pre-money valuation would equal $8.5 million—slightly higher than the initial valuation

Table 6.2 The different ownership interests of venture capitalists and implied pre-money calculations

Cash-on-cash	Years of investment and exit in 2015						Assumed VC ownership (%)	Implied pre-money valuation
	IRR (%)	2011 ($M)	2012 ($M)	2013 ($M)	2014 ($M)	2015 ($M)		
2.1	22	−2	−1	0	0	6.2	27.3	8.00
2.0	20	−2	−1	0	0	5.9	26.0	8.54
1.9	19	−2	−1	0	0	5.7	25.0	9.00
1.8	18	−2	−1	0	0	5.5	24.0	9.50

of $8 million. In this case, the IRR would be equal to 20 percent. This point effectively represents the cut-off point for venture capitalists in terms of their ability to offer a better financial proposition to BV's owners. Any capital increase based on the pre-money valuation higher than $8.5 million would result in a projected IRR of less than 20 percent for venture capitalists, which is less than their desired rate of return from the investment.

Sensitivity Analysis

Once the financial model has been created, the initial valuation has been determined, and the project returns have been calculated, venture capitalists proceed to determine the responsiveness of the financial model to changes to its key parameters. This process is defined as sensitivity analysis. The idea behind this "what-if" analysis is to see how different values of an independent variable are likely to impact a particular dependent variable under a given set of assumptions. Sensitivity analysis allows venture capitalists to predict what will happen if they deviate from a predicted course of action. The analysis is useful in scenarios in which a venture capitalist attempts to determine how changes in one variable impact the target variable; in the case of BV, the target variable is the rate of return venture capitalists receive from the project (or IRR).

Let's illustrate a few of the specific approaches venture capitalists can use. Venture capitalists can determine the impact of key business parameters on the business model and financial returns. The key business and financial parameters may relate to changes (or underperformance) in sales, profit margins (i.e., EBITDA margin), working capital items, and so on. As previously mentioned, an increase in profit margins is probably the most difficult business objective for firms to achieve; hence, venture capitalists would run multiple scenarios under different levels of profit margin. It is likely that a reduction in any of these parameters is likely to have a snowball effect or negative chain reaction on the firm's cash flow, liquidity, and ability to raise further financing. Venture capitalists change each of these parameters one at a time to understand their impact on IRR.

Another scenario involves seeing the combined impact of different business variables upon the business model and IRR when they are changed simultaneously. In addition to the most probable scenario—often called the "base case" scenario—venture capitalists run a financial model of significant underperformance in critical business areas; this is known as the "worst case" scenario. There may also be a scenario under which the firm is able to do better than anticipated; this is known as the "blue-sky" scenario. Running and analyzing both positive and negative financial scenarios is important for venture capitalists as both scenarios may imply the need for additional capital from the bank and the venture capital firm (note that unanticipated business growth brings with it the same sorts of headaches for business owners and venture capitalists as those found in situations of distress). If additional equity financing is needed, venture capitalists try to determine if they will provide an additional round of financing. If they are unwilling to do so (they may have reached their allowable limit per deal or sector, among other reasons), they must anticipate a certain level of dilution to their initial shareholding. Table 6.3 presents the impact of changes to key parameters and their impact on IRR under the three main scenarios (the worst case, the base case, and the blue-sky case).

Venture capitalists are also interested in examining the impact of the timing with which they exit upon achieving their returns. Scenarios involving both shorter and longer holding periods must be analyzed. In the case of a shorter holding period, venture capitalists

Table 6.3 Changes in key business parameters and their impact on IRR

	The worst case	The base case	The blue-sky case
Annual sales growth	15%/IRR=2%	26%/IRR=22%	35%/IRR=38%
Annual EBITDA margin	15%/IRR=17%	19%/IRR=22%	25%/IRR=35%
Working capital needs	$4M/IRR=18%	$2M/IRR=22%	$1M/IRR=25%

Table 6.4 Internal rate of return calculations based on venture capitalists' presumed exit in 2014

Cash-on-cash (multiple)	IRR(%)	Years of investment and exit in 2014				Assumed EV/EBITDA multiple
		2011 ($M)	2012 ($M)	2013 ($M)	2014 ($M)	
1.8	24	−2	−1	0	5.4	3
2.4	38	−2	−1	0	7.1	4
3.0	49	−2	−1	0	8.9	5
3.6	60	−2	−1	0	10.7	6

may receive an offer from a strategic investor or take advantage of favorable IPO market conditions. A shorter holding period may be related to a low trajectory of EBITDA or cash flow growth, both of which allow for potentially lower exit valuations. A longer holding period is generally related to poor business performance; a longer period of time is needed to reach the desired financial parameters. The effects of this scenario are considered in table 6.4, where the exit is anticipated in 2014 and the calculations are based on statistics comparable to previous examples.

In a nutshell, the sensitivity analysis should be performed around the key business drivers. The most important task for venture capitalists is to determine what these key business drivers are. For example, if the business is a restaurant, the key business drivers relate to the price per customer (how much each customer spends), the turns per table (how many times each seat in the restaurant is filled during the day), and labor and food costs as a percentage of sales. For a telecommunications firm, the key determinant is the revenue per customer. For a radio business, the focal area is the listenership data.

Venture Capitalists' Orientation toward Business Valuation

Venture capitalists often argue amongst themselves over what the proper orientation is to business valuation. The attitude selected often reflects the personal characteristics of venture capitalists, as well as their style of negotiating. Some venture capitalists are of the opinion that during the final calculations, business valuation "does not matter." If a business becomes highly successful, the entry valuation of the business becomes irrelevant, as venture capitalists make exceptionally high returns (cash-on-cash returns may be in excess of ten times). On the other hand, if a business underperforms, venture capitalists argue that they are unlikely to receive any cash from the investment. A long and protracted battle to convert a limited cash recovery into a small amount cannot be justified. These types of venture capitalists tend not to spend significant amounts of time on issues related to business valuation. Their negotiations with entrepreneurs appear easy and timely, and they express similar attitudes toward other aspects of financial contracting. Instead of focusing on issues related to exit provisions, they focus their entire attention on properly sizing up the business opportunity and conducting thorough due diligence. Consequently, this group of venture capitalists has a portfolio of firms that are either winners or losers—there are virtually no borderline investments.

The second type of venture capitalists take the opposite approach, which is best surmised by the old Irish proverb "well bought is half sold." These types of venture capitalists believe that entry valuation is critical to the ultimate success of a firm and will effectively try to "nickel and dime" entrepreneurs for every term and dollar of valuation. Consequently, deals take a longer period of time to be completed and the process is more frustrating for both entrepreneurs and venture capitalists.

No academic literature exists on the actual success rates of these approaches. As previously mentioned, the adopted style often reflects a venture capitalist's personal characteristics, their level of experience, and their track record of success. Fortunately, venture capital firms are comprised of individuals with different approaches to valuation and differing styles of negotiating; as a result, most portfolios are well balanced and diverse.

Security Types

Most financial investors, including venture capitalists, are risk-averse. Risk aversion is the tendency to avoid additional, incremental risk. Faced with financial alternatives that are equal except for their degree of risk, most financial investors choose the less risky alternative. Risk aversion also implies a positive relationship between risk and return—the more the risk assumed, the higher the required rate of return venture capitalists demand. A venture capitalist will tolerate risk better than any other type of financial investor, but will expect to receive additional compensation in exchange for assuming additional risk.

The perception of risk in a specific investment project drives the expectation for the specific type of financial security venture capitalists are likely to demand. The higher the perceived risk, the more protection venture capitalists seek. While most venture capitalists would prefer to hold an equity stake in a more protected financial instrument, the negotiating process that occurs between them and the entrepreneurs ultimately determines the type of security they end up holding in the investee firm.

The security most commonly held by venture capitalists is the convertible preferred share. This security has two distinct features: the preferred share component and the conversion feature. The primary advantage of holding a preferred share over a common share relates to the order in which shareholders are paid in the event of the firm's bankruptcy, liquidation, or restructuring. Under these circumstances, preferred shareholders will take priority over common shareholders—this is known as a residual claim. The shareholders will also have priority over common shares in terms of dividend payments (venture capitalists are less interested in this feature as they rarely take dividends from their investee firms). Preferred shares are viewed as a hybrid security because they have characteristics of both debt and equity: they are similar to debt primarily because preferred shareholders do not have any claim to the firm's profits, and they are like equity in that they may have an infinite maturity and a lower-priority claim against the firm. Venture capitalists can expect a fixed return from this security: between 2 and 10 percent per annum, payable at realization and subject to negotiation with the entrepreneurs. The conversion feature of this security provides venture capitalists with the right to convert the shares into common shares after a predetermined time or by a specific date or event. This provides venture capitalists with the option to convert when an opportunity exists to gain from a price increase in common shares. The conversion may be voluntary (e.g., when certain operational milestones are achieved, certain risks are removed, or upon any other agreement) or automatic (e.g., at the time of an IPO).

At some point in time, venture capitalists need to decide whether to retain their stake in the business, which takes the form of convertible preferred shares, or to convert. Convertible preferred shares are redeemed at face value or converted into common shares. The overall decision can be straightforward or complex. In a straight-forward situation, venture capitalists convert preferred convertible shares into common shares if the conversion value (equal to the conversion ratio, or the number of common shares that venture capitalists obtain, multiplied by anticipated or actual market price per common share) is higher than the amount of capital supplied to the investee firm. If, for example, venture capitalists supply $2 million of capital, the conversion provides them with a 25 percent stake in the investee firm, and the firm is being sold for $20 million (conversion value = $5 million [25% x $20 million]), venture capitalists would gladly convert

Most situations, however, are more complex. Imagine that venture capitalists invest two million dollars into an investee firm that is contemplating an IPO. At the time of an IPO, venture capitalists are normally required to convert their holding into common shares and, consequently, give up most of their special protections (drag-along rights, approval rights, voting-flipover events, etc.). In reality, the firm's value may reach such a low level that an ownership stake of 25 percent (adjusted by dilution from the public share issue) would be valued at less than the original investment of two million dollars. In this case, venture capitalists would have been better off not taking the firm public and retaining their capital protections in the form of preferred shares. Unfortunately, once a decision has been made, it cannot be reversed.

In many transactions, venture capitalists effectively hold two types of securities, each issued at low nominal values per share in exchange for the capital provided. The securities are known as common shares and straight preferred shares. Common shares provide venture capitalists with an ownership stake in the business determined on the basis of a pre-agreed business valuation. Straight preferred shares are only "active" as an additional protection in the event the investee firm experiences a period of misfortune (i.e., liquidation). The preferred shares that venture capitalists wish to hold may also include other features. For example, the preferred shares may include a redeemable feature where the firm buys back the venture capitalists' shares with or without an additional yield or return on them. This feature is often included in exit provisions where venture capitalists attempt to recover their capital if the agreed upon exit routes collapse. The participating rights are introduced into preferred convertible shares when venture capitalists wish to retain their priority claim and benefit from the upside potential of higher than expected profits.

While the preferred convertible share is the security of choice for many venture capitalists, many academics and practitioners argue that this type of security provides poor incentives for venture capitalists and entrepreneurs alike. Imagine that venture capitalists have invested ten million dollars in a business for a 25 percent stake in the form of convertible preferred shares. After some time, the investee firm experiences operational problems and the potential buyers are willing to pay twenty million dollars for the firm. Since venture capitalists have a preference for any purchase price equal to the value of their investment, they are effectively entitled to receive 50 percent of the contemplated purchase price, or ten million dollars (venture capitalists' entitlement to proceeds is, of course, higher than their ownership stake in the business). The venture capitalists, who may no longer see any upside potential in the firm, may be willing to dispose of the firm or liquidate the business entirely. The entrepreneurs, however, are likely to resist such actions and may even attempt to block the sale (this is easily done when management is not willing to cooperate with potential buyers) or liquidate the firm. This divergence of interest between both parties may grow further if the potential proceeds from the disposal of the business are considered to be low. If the firm is valued at below ten million dollars, the entrepreneurs will have no incentive to cooperate with venture capitalists, as they will receive no financial gain from disposing of the firm. In this case, venture capitalists would be wise to renegotiate the deal and effectively cancel the effects of any preferences to better align the financial objectives of the two parties.

Other Types of Securities

While the objective of venture capitalists is to secure preferred convertible shares in their dealings with entrepreneurs, they may have to agree to accept common shares. For example, entrepreneurs may insist on limiting venture capitalists' capital protections. Venture capitalists may also face other competitors willing to hold common shares to secure the project. In addition, in some emerging markets, preferred shares are permitted by local commercial codes, but court systems have problems recognizing the different classes of shares and the different rights enshrined in them. In an environment of shareholder "equality," preferred shares may not be granted any special rights and there is no real need to hold them.

In some cases, the level of comfort venture capitalists have with an investment project may be lower than desired. Venture capitalists can temporarily hold convertible debt, which ranks higher in priority of claim than preferred convertible and common shares. This method, however, is uncommon and used sparingly by venture capitalists. In some cases, the securities are converted into other types of securities once certain risks have been removed from the business.

Rights and Provisions

Venture capitalists use various rights to protect their economic interests. They also use different legal provisions to adjust their level of shareholding (i.e., share adjustment mechanisms or "ratchets"), create liquidity opportunities (i.e., exit inventive provisions—"drag-along" rights), approve key operational decisions (i.e., shareholders approval), and protect against unfavorable rounds of financing (i.e., anti-dilution protections). Default provisions define venture capitalists' rights and remedies if the firm and its shareholders do not adhere to the shareholders' agreement. Venture capitalists also want to improve their access to important information (i.e., inspection and information rights) and to approve transactions with related parties. All these rights are captured in the shareholders' agreements and the articles of association signed by venture capitalists and entrepreneurs. The following sections discuss each of the major clauses included in the term sheet.

Venture Capitalists' Rights

Once venture capitalists make an investment, they have two major concerns. The first is whether or not their investee firm (and thus their investment) is performing in accordance with the business plan upon which the decision to invest was made. The second relates to investment realization and whether or not exit from the investment is likely to occur within a reasonable timeframe. The rights described here aim to protect venture capitalists during the term of their investment and provide them with additional powers or remedies in the event the firm struggles. It is important to stress that these provisions are rights and not obligations—venture capitalists need to carefully consider whether they actually wish to execute these provisions.

Preemptive Rights

With these rights, venture capitalists are able to acquire new shares issued by the firm in direct proportion to their percentage holding in the firm at the time of the new issue. This ensures that venture capitalists' holdings are not diluted without consent. Let's assume that there are four shareholders in the firm—shareholders A, B, C, and the venture capital firm. The firm has a total of 200 shares issued; A has 20 shares, B has 40, and C possesses 80. Venture capitalists hold the remaining 60 shares. This represents a 10 percent, 20 percent, 40 percent, and 30 percent shareholding for each of the parties, respectively. Let's further assume that the firm wants to issue an additional 400 shares. These shares would be divided on a pro rata basis or in proportion to their level of shareholding in the firm. If the venture capitalists choose to exercise their rights, they will obtain an additional 120 shares of the new issue in addition to the shares they already hold. This equates to a total of 180 shares—exactly 30 percent of the total shares issued by the firm (180 shares divided by 600).

Venture capitalists would most likely exercise their rights under two circumstances. If the business is performing well and additional capital is likely to convert into a higher return in terms of nominal dollar value, venture capitalists may want to extend their exposure to the business. Conversely, if the firm is performing poorly, venture capitalists may wish to protect their position against a dilutive round of financing that can reduce their economic interest in the firm and limit their decision-making powers (i.e., approval rights, the representation on the board of directors).

Rights-of-First Refusal

If the firm's owners wish to sell any portion of their shareholding to an interested third party, venture capitalists have the right to acquire these shares on the same terms offered by the third party. Venture capitalists can acquire these shares in proportion to their shareholding vis-à-vis the remaining shareholders that wish to purchase the shares of the selling shareholder. Let's assume that shareholder B wishes to sell her 40 shares. The remaining shareholders have the right to acquire these shares in the following proportions: A, 12.5 percent; C, 50 percent; and venture capitalists, 37.5 percent (40/[20+80+60]). As a result, shareholder A receives an additional 5 shares (for a total of 25 shares), C acquires 20 shares (100 total shares), and the venture capitalists get an additional 15 shares (75 total shares). The new shareholding would be 12.5 percent for A, 50 for C, and 37.5 for venture capitalists.

The rationale for exercising the rights-of-first refusal is similar to that used for exercising preemptive rights. In addition, venture capitalists may want to protect against a new shareholder coming into the firm (especially when the new shareholder is likely to be disruptive to the firm's operations or exit plans) or limit an existing shareholder from becoming more powerful and obtaining the majority vote. Changes to the shareholding structure can also result in a re-negotiation of the deal, especially when one of the existing shareholders acquires more power or leverage.

Co-sell or "Piggy-Back" Rights

These rights are similar to the rights-of-first refusal, in that they deal with one of the existing shareholders looking to dispose of their stake in the firm by granting it to another third party. In the event such a disposal is considered, venture capitalists have the right to sell their shares in proportion to the level of shareholding (or on a pro rata basis) to the willing buyer. The acquisition of these shares occurs on the same terms as those offered to the selling shareholder. Venture capitalists often require that they have the right to dispose of their entire holding in the business if more than 50 percent of shares are contemplated for sale. Let's assume that the third party wants to buy 20 shares and has had initial discussions with shareholder A. If venture capitalists wanted to participate in this transaction (assuming that others were not interested), shareholder A could only sell 5 shares while venture capitalists would be able to sell 15 (20 * [60/{20 + 60}]). If the external party wanted to buy 120 shares, the venture capitalists would be able to sell their entire stake before any shareholder would be able to sell their shares in proportion to the adjusted holdings.

Venture capitalists would exercise these rights under the same circumstances in which they would exercise a right-of-first refusal.

An additional motivator would be when a new third party takes a majority stake in the firm.

"Drag-Along" and Other Exit Incentive Rights

The ability of venture capitalists to obtain liquidity from their deals is one of the most essential parts of the venture capital business. Most venture capitalists want to secure at least two possible ways of disposing their shares within a holding period of up to five years. Venture capitalists rely on a number of provisions to achieve their exit if the pre-agreed course of action in terms of achieving liquidity for the shares fails. The preferred exit route is the sale of the investee firm to a strategic investor. To achieve this, most venture capitalists insist on the inclusion of drag-along rights as a part of the exit incentive scheme. Under the terms of these rights, venture capitalists can solicit offers for shares in the investee firm. If an offer crystallizes, the entrepreneurs must sell a sufficient number of shares to satisfy the requirements of the offer. In practice, this means that venture capitalists can affect the sale of the firm (even though they are minority owners of the business) and effectively take control away from the entrepreneurs.

While drag-along rights are often regarded as an exit clause of last resort, there are others clauses that can be used. Venture capitalists may insist on redemption rights. If the firm has not achieved an exit by some desired period of time, venture capitalists will require the firm to redeem their shares in accordance with a pre-agreed timetable. A similar way of obtaining liquidity is to require the firm to pay a special dividend. These dividends normally accrue and are paid out to venture capitalists at the time of exit. Venture capitalists may also elect to either receive their initial investment or their pro rata share of the exit proceeds, plus any unpaid dividends. These dividend payout clauses also provide a guaranteed minimum return for venture capitalists. Of course, redemption and dividend payout provisions only work if the firm has sufficient cash on hand to pay them.

Change-of-Control Provisions

If a predefined set of events occur, venture capitalists may either secure the right to additional representation on the board of directors or their voting rights may increase sufficiently in order to give them control of the firm. These rights, also called "voting flip-over event" rights, normally relate to votes and controls; venture capitalists' economic interests remain unchanged. The most typical voting flip-over events relate to management committing a crime or becoming incapacitated and the poor financial performance of the firm as defined by underachievement in EBITDA or revenues. Under such circumstances, venture capitalists reserve the right to replace part or all of the management team (even though this solution is rarely adopted).

Venture capitalists will exercise these particular rights if the firm's financial underperformance is likely to reduce the valuation of the business, the exit timing becomes questionable, or if the firm's lackluster performance is attributable to the current management team. Change of control provisions allow venture capitalists to implement changes to the management structure of the firm and develop a new strategy. The change of control is either temporary (and in effect until operational problems are addressed and the firm returns to its budgeted financial performance) or permanent (lasting until the exit is achieved).

Inspection and Information Rights

Venture capitalists normally require the firm to provide them with specific information related to the firm's financial position and its operations. This information usually includes unaudited monthly financial statements, annual audited financial statements expressed in GAAP or IAS, a statement of any deviations from the agreed-upon business plan, explanations of any variance from the business plan that exceeds 5 or 10 percent of the budgeted amount, and more. Under these rights, venture capitalists have full access to information related to the firm's business, taxes, and other financial or legal matters. Venture capitalists can also audit and inspect the bookkeeping, records, operations, property, and premises of the firm at any reasonable time (financial, accounting, or legal experts may assist in this review). Normally, the costs of such investigations are borne by the firm.

There are two reasons for having these rights included in the term sheet. Venture capitalists need to have timely access to vital business and financial statistics for the firm. These statistics inform critical decisions made by the board of directors and can help to correct problems related to information asymmetry. Second, the rights allow venture capitalists the freedom to access information if they suspect any fraud, misrepresentation, or criminal behavior is occurring within the firm.

Approval of Key Decisions

Venture capitalists want to ensure that they have control over key decisions or actions related to the investee firm. A veto right allows venture capitalists to reject or refuse an agreement on a particular action. These decisions require a resolution of the board of directors, including an affirmative vote from the venture capitalists' representative. Venture capitalists will usually want approval or control over the following issues: changes to the business plan, decisions to hire or remove key management, increases in capital, the sale of shares or significant assets, liquidation of the firm, entering into very large or long-term commitments or contracts, changing the compensation of management, and arrangements constituting a conflict of interest transaction. To exercise this control, venture capitalists are usually appointed to the firm's board of directors or supervisory board. Generally, the supervisory board is comprised of persons appointed by the shareholders, including venture capitalists, in proportion to their respective levels of shareholding in the business.

Through these approval rights, venture capitalists seek to ensure that management and other shareholders consult with them over any material decisions and actions in the firm. Because venture capitalists have already agreed upon the original business plan, only variations from the plan (or any new items or actions) require their approval.

Share Adjustment Mechanisms or "Ratchets"

In the venture capital industry, share adjustment mechanisms are standard features found in the term sheet. Venture capitalists traditionally use these mechanisms to protect from the negative impact of an investee firm issuing shares at a lower valuation than agreed upon by the venture capitalists; they also moderate the risk of overpaying for a business. These mechanisms are seen as anti-dilution protections against subsequent own-rounds (offering protection on investments) and protect against stock splits, stock dividends, re-capitalization, and conversions from preferred stocks into common stocks.

Ratchets generally come in one of two forms: the full ratchet or the weighted ratchet. Full ratchets provide the most protection to venture capitalists (and have the greatest impact on existing shareholders) as they readjust the venture capitalists' shareholding as if their capital is invested at the lower valuation of any subsequent rounds of financing. Weighted-average ratchets, depending on the specific formula, effectively average out the valuation between the initial and subsequent rounds of financing. Such an approach spreads the risks of any down-rounds between the founders and venture capitalists, thereby providing a more equitable adjustment to the entry valuation. In both approaches, additional shares are issued to the venture capitalists to compensate against any dilution.

Performance-based share-adjustment mechanisms operate in a slightly different manner. In comparison to full and weighted ratchets, which aim to provide anti-dilution protection against subsequent rounds of financing at lower valuations, the focal point of performance-based ratchets is the firm's actual financial performance. Effectively, the agreed-upon entry valuation is dependent on the firm's ability to achieve specific financial milestones (often defined at EBIT or EBITDA levels). If these financial targets are not met, the entry valuation of the business is revisited and adjusted retroactively in accordance with the agreed-upon formula. An illustration of the inner workings of the ratchet formula is presented in box 6.1.

Box 6.1   The practitioner's corner: the healthy snack deal and the ratchet formula

In 2005, Colonial Partners—one of the United Kingdom's leading venture capital firms—agreed to invest eight million dollars into a newly established business focusing on healthy snacks. Healthy Snacks produced a wide range of potato chip-esque products made from apples, carrots, cucumbers, tomatoes, pears, peaches, and more. The products, unlike potato chips, were produced without the use of oil, thus significantly reducing their fat content.

Let's illustrate how a performance-based ratchet mechanism was developed by Colonial Partners to deal with a valuation problem that emerged during negotiations. Venture capitalists at the fund came up with a formula that allowed additional shares to be issued to them based on the actual results achieved by the firm in the year preceding their exit from it—this was defined as Forecast Earnings in the Relevant Year. The formula was set to adjust the venture capitalists' entry valuation on a basis in which they were compensated for 50 percent of any underperformance. The formulas are as follow:

$$\text{Reduction in Valuation of Healthy Snacks} = \frac{100 - x}{2} \times 100\%,$$

$$\text{where } x = \frac{\text{Actual Earnings in the Relevant Year}}{\text{Forecast Earnings in the Relevant Year}} \times \frac{100}{1}\%.$$

The venture capitalists acquired a 25 percent stake in the firm for $8 million in a cash-out deal. They forecasted that the actual performance of the firm in terms of EBIT up to the point of exit would be as follows: 2000—$14.82 million; 2001—$15.45 million; 2002—$20.63 million. An exit was arranged in mid-2002 based on the relevant financial performance of the firm in the year 2001. Based on the following calculations, venture capitalists received an additional number of shares, granting them 27.8 percent of the enlarged share capital of the firm. Here are the calculations that venture capitalists made to arrive at their figure.

1. $\dfrac{\text{Actual Earnings in the Relevant Year}}{\text{Forecast Earnings in the Relevant Year}} = \dfrac{15.45}{19.31} \times \dfrac{100}{1} = 80.0.$

2. Change in valuation of Healthy Snacks $= \dfrac{100 - 80}{2} \times 100\% = 10\%.$

3. Adjusted valuation of Healthy Snacks = $32 million less 10% = $28.8 million.

4. Adjusted shareholdings for venture capitalists $= \dfrac{8}{28.8} = 27.8\%.$

5. The venture capitalists' shareholdings increased by 2.8 percent from their initial stake of 25 percent.

This complex performance-based share adjustment mechanism was included in the term sheet by Colonial Partners. It was agreed that there were significant differences in how venture capitalists and the owners of Healthy Snacks were valuing the business. Under these circumstances, the only possible way to resolve the issue was to introduce a share adjustment mechanism that effectively worked as a sliding scale valuation (dependent on the firm's financial performance).

Another commonly used share adjustment mechanism is the capitalization ratchet. This financial mechanism is similar in its internal workings to the performance-based ratchet, with the difference being that the entry valuation of the business is adjusted on the basis of the total capitalization of the business at the exit (and not on the firm's financial performance). The benefit of using this type of the mechanism versus the performance-based ratchet is that it negates the argument of entrepreneurs that a cyclical reduction in EBIT or EBITDA unfairly punishes business owners (this may be true in cases where strategic investors overlook financial performance and pay a premium for a business that commands a dominant market share, owns a strong brand name, and operates an effective distribution system).

Impositions on Entrepreneurs

There are additional provisions in the term sheet that are likely to impact the relationship between entrepreneurs and venture capitalists. These provisions may limit some of the actions that entrepreneurs can take within their business. Some of the provisions discussed in this section, such as confidentiality and break-up fees, are legally binding on the two sides and carry a financial obligation on the business owner (i.e., break-up fees) or on the firm itself (i.e., transaction fees). Representations and warranties act to compliment the due diligence process, while conflict of interest provisions act to ensure proper functioning of the corporate governance systems. The following paragraphs discuss the key impositions on entrepreneurs.

"Lock-in": Given that the objective of venture capital financing is to build long-term value in the business, venture capitalists aim to ensure that neither they nor the entrepreneurs are distracted by short-term gain. Consequently, venture capitalists require all the shareholders to agree that shares are nontransferable until such time that the long-term business objectives have been achieved.

Conflict of interest: Venture capitalists require that the investee firm adopt a policy necessitating any actual or potential conflict of interest transactions between the firm and a related party be brought to the attention of all shareholders in writing for prior review and approval. A conflict of interest transaction generally includes situations in which the firm is engaging or is intending to engage in a relationship with a shareholder, board member, officer, employee, management company, or a consultant (or a person, firm, or other entity having a business, blood, or any family relationship with one of these) where the relationship involves more than the equivalent of a predetermined monetary amount in any one-year period.

Representations and warranties: Venture capitalists have a duty to protect their limited partners from being misled, misinformed, or only partially informed about the firm during the investment process. Venture capitalists require standard representations and warranties relating to the firm's activities, legal standing, and financial statements from the firm, its owners, and management at the time of the signing of the investment agreement. The term sheet merely makes the point that the two sides agree that these representations and warranties are expected to be included in final legal documentation; the actual content and wording of representations and warranties is determined during the deal closing stage and after the due diligence process has been completed. Representations and warranties force the owners, management, and the firm to provide venture capitalists with information that would otherwise be difficult or costly to establish or confirm. These disclosures are comprehensive and used to establish the potential liabilities of the entrepreneurs should the representations and warranties not be true. The entrepreneurs, and not venture capitalists, are responsible for all the liabilities of the business prior to the point in which venture capitalists enter the deal. If, for example, a tax liability is crystallized during the investment period, the entrepreneurs should be responsible for addressing this. In a case where the firm is forced to address these tax liabilities, the venture capitalists would seek additional compensation from the entrepreneurs by adjusting the business valuation or changing the division of proceeds upon exit.

Exclusivity and confidentiality: Venture capitalists require entrepreneurs to not enter into or continue discussions with any other party regarding fund raising for a reasonable period of time. The agreed-upon timeframe is normally sufficient to allow venture capitalists to investigate, process, and complete the transaction. In addition, the contents of the term sheet and any discussions between entrepreneurs and venture capitalists are treated as confidential and are not to be disclosed to third parties.

Transaction fees: Venture capitalists normally expect their investee firms to reimburse their costs after closing a deal. These costs generally relate to legal, accounting, and environmental due diligence and closing costs. For example, venture capitalists may need to hire an external expert to conduct an industrial or operational review. In other circumstances, they may require reimbursement for research materials (i.e., reports, studies) and out-of-pocket expenses (i.e., travel, accommodations). Venture capitalists do not charge for their time. That said, transaction fees vary; depending on the investee firm and the complexity of the deal, the fees can be between 0.5 and 1.5 percent of the total capital provided by venture capitalists.

Break-up fees: These fees represent the firm's contribution to venture capitalists in the event the owners breach an exclusivity or confidentiality agreement. They are also payable if the firm's owners break off negotiations when venture capitalists, acting in good faith, are still willing to pursue the investment on terms not significantly different from those outlined in the term sheet. The amount payable is normally comprised of venture capitalists' due diligence costs and legal documentation expenses plus any other penalty amounts.

Investment Vehicles

There are different types of legal structures used by venture capitalists around the world. Venture capitalists must carefully consider how to best legally structure their deals by deciding whether to utilize local or foreign vehicles (or some combination of the two) to achieve the most optimal trade-off between risk and return. Legal structures are particularly complex in the international arena. Venture capitalists in Western countries, where the legal infrastructure and courts are reliable, are likely to use simple legal structures and invest directly into operating entities. In emerging markets, where significant imperfections exist in the legal infrastructure, venture capitalists have to rely on more complex structures. This process includes using either newly created firms or special purpose vehicles (SPVs) to establish the venture locally, transfer the firm's assets and liabilities, or set up in an offshore jurisdiction. In addition, the chosen legal structure is likely to have significant tax implications for both the fund manager and the limited partners.

The key agreements used in venture capital contacting are the shareholders' agreement and the firm's constitutional documents, which take the form of articles of association, notarial deeds, charters, and other legal forms (depending on the legal jurisdiction of the firm). The shareholders' agreement is a written agreement between the shareholders of the firm that regulates the relationship between the parties and determines a course of action in the event of potential problems or disputes. The firm's constitutional documents are similar in intent to the shareholders' agreement, in that they regulate the relationship between the firm, the shareholders, the management, and the board of directors. This is a public document. However, since the shareholders' agreement is a private law contract (and is not normally made available to the public), the shareholders may not wish to disclose sensitive information to the public. The shareholders' agreement can also be easily and cheaply amended, can provide better protection for shareholders than a strict reliance on corporate or commercial law, and allows for disputes to be resolved in other jurisdictions.

Simple Deal Structures

In this form of legal structuring, venture capitalists make investments in local operating companies (LOCs). The percentage holding of venture capitalists in an LOC is equal to N, while the entrepreneurs hold a 100 percent-N stake. The advantage of such a structure relates to simplicity and cost. The two legal agreements used in this structure are the shareholders' agreement and the firm's constitutional documents. This structure is presented in figure 6.1.

Venture capitalists' rights are included in the shareholders' agreements across this and other investment structures, but only some of these rights are included in the firm's constitutional documents. Venture capitalists generally treat the constitutional documents as "more public" when there is a significant chance that the document may be shared with others (i.e., the management team, employees, the public, at the time of an IPO, and, most importantly, to potential purchasers). Therefore, most of the "controversial clauses" are included in the shareholders' agreement. Another reason that venture capitalists may limit the inclusion of their rights in the constitutional documents is that they may wish to protect their approach to deal making for competitive reasons. Consequently, share adjustment mechanisms, exit clauses and change-of-control provisions are likely to be included in the shareholders' agreement—not in the constitutional documents. On the other hand, venture capitalists' basic rights—such as preemptive rights, rights-of-first refusal, piggy-back rights, and lock-up rights—are likely to appear in two documents. Table 6.5 provides an overview of the placement of venture capital rights in different legal documents.

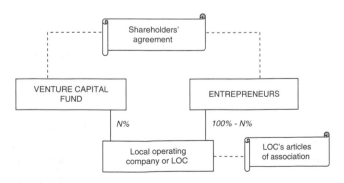

Figure 6.1 Legal structure for simple deals.

Table 6.5   The placement of venture capital rights across various legal documents

Types of protections and rights	Allocation of different rights across different legal documents	
	Shareholders' agreement	Firm's constitutional documents
Venture capitalists' basic rights:		
Preemptive rights	Yes	Yes
Rights-of-first refusal	Yes	Yes
Piggy-back rights	Yes	Yes
Lock-up rights	Yes	Yes
Share adjustment mechanisms	Yes	No
Exit incentives	Yes	No
Shareholder approvals	Yes	Yes
Anti-dilution provisions	Yes	Yes
Default provisions	Yes	No
Inspection and information rights	Yes	No
Related party transaction approvals	Yes	No

More Complex Deal Structures

In the case of a more complex deal structure, venture capitalists manage their relationships with entrepreneurs by setting up another vehicle—an SPV (either set up in the country or off-shore). There can be a variety of reasons for setting up an additional firm. First, venture capitalists may only be interested in a specific part of a business; hence, only "targeted" assets and liabilities are transferred to the SPV. The entrepreneurs may also wish to retain certain assets. Entrepreneurs commonly wish to leave some of their assets outside of the parameters of the deal and believe that holding extra real estate substantially increases the valuation of their business. Venture capitalists do not wish to pay extra for such assets unless they are critical for business expansion. This structure is also used in cases where venture capitalists see fundamental problems inherent to holding shares in the LOC (there may be a high probability of tax liabilities, e.g., or off-balance sheet liabilities that are difficult to quantify).

Under a more complex deal structure, venture capitalists would establish an SPV and hold a percentage stake (N), while entrepreneurs would retain the remaining stake (100 percent–N). The SPV subsequently acquires a 100 percent shareholding in an LOC. Figure 6.2 presents the schematic of a more complex deal structure.

There are multiple advantages to using this type of structure, both to venture capitalists and to entrepreneurs. First, venture capitalists' cash can be directed toward the LOC in the form of debt or equity.

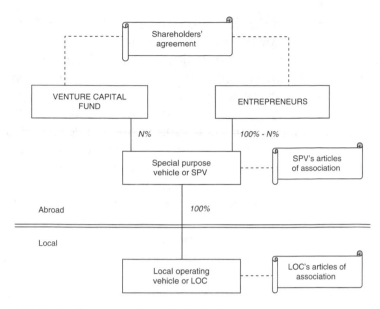

Figure 6.2 The legal structure of complex deals.

In the case of an LOC generating excess cash, the use of debt may serve as an effective way to repay the loan to shareholders in a tax-effective manner over an extended period of time (interest payments are tax deductible for LOCs and the repayment is not taxed as it is in the case of dividends, where the dividend withdrawal tax rate is generally around 20 percent). The use of debt instruments has recently become less popular due to the introduction of "thin capitalization" rules. Second, venture capitalists have more flexibility to exit if there is an option to exit through an LOC or an SPV (some strategic investors prefer to remain anonymous when making their acquisitions). Third, this structure, especially when it is set up in an off-shore jurisdiction, allows for optimal taxation in the event of a buyout. The biggest disadvantage of the structure relates to high costs for the legal and accounting advice needed to establish the structure and monitor its activities (two financial audits are required, etc.).

Multilevel Investment Vehicle Deal Structures

The legal structuring of venture capital deals in this category is complicated. Multilevel deals are predominantly constructed under special circumstances and are often associated with to government-related sectors of the economy such as telecommunications, media, the defense industry, natural resources, and so on. Any negotiated rights are captured in the shareholders' agreement, which acts as an umbrella document for the entire transaction.

As an example, let's structure a deal in the media industry. There are multiple legal entities used in this deal category. The operations of a local business are typically divided into two subgroups. The first LOC I) generally holds an operating license and deals with the day-to-day operations of the underlying business. The second (LOC II) typically acts as a sales house for the first firm (see figure 6.3). The two firms are generally "tied-up" by a cooperation agreement. Venture capitalists typically take a minority interest in the license holding firm (less than 33 percent or 49 percent). However, depending on the valuation of the underlying business, venture capitalists may also hold a minority or a majority stake in the sales house— the second firm, LOC II (where no foreign ownership restrictions are likely to apply). Both venture capitalists and entrepreneurs often establish a second vehicle—an SPV—where venture capitalists take a minority stake and the entrepreneurs hold a majority stake. This SPV also holds a small stake (30 percent, as presented in figure 6.3) in the license holding firm, LOC I. In the example, venture capitalists effectively hold a 30 percent direct interest in LOC I and a 49 percent interest in an SPV that holds a 30 percent stake in LOC I and a 60 percent ownership interest in LOC II (we assume here that the venture capitalists want to hold a majority stake in the entire

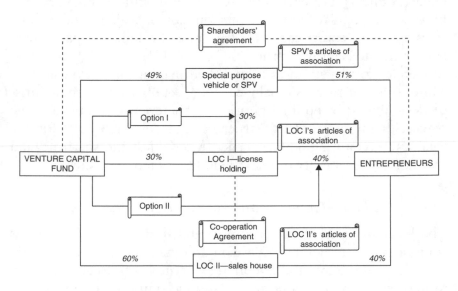

Figure 6.3   The legal structure of a multi-investment vehicle.

venture). Venture capitalists also rely on two "options" within their structuring. Through the exercise of Option I, venture capitalists are able to increase their level of interest in the SPV to achieve a majority interest in the vehicle. By using Option II, they can increase their ownership interest in LOC I directly, without the use of the SPV.

For venture capitalists, the purpose of such a complex structure is to temporarily hide their effective control of the underlying business until such time as they are able to show their holdings openly or dispose of their shares to other buyers. The key disadvantages of such a structure lie in its complexity. Venture capitalists must rely on the shareholders' agreement and other articles governing operations at various levels of the structure. In figure 6.3, venture capitalists exercise their full rights based on three sets of constitutional documents, one shareholders' agreement, and two option agreements. This structure is expensive to establish, monitor, and audit. In addition, it may be difficult to obtain full cooperation from the entrepreneurs (venture capitalists generally use a system of financial penalties to reduce the risk of noncompliance).

Questions to Consider

1. Discuss the role of the term sheet in the venture capital investment process.
2. What are the differences between pre- and post-money valuations? Provide an example of how these can be calculated in deals with a capital increase and a cash-out component.
3. What is sensitivity analysis used for?
4. What are the key exit mechanisms venture capitalists rely on? Why do these exit provisions cause so much difficulty during deal negotiations?
5. Discuss the differences and similarities (if any) between rights-of-first refusal and preemptive rights. When are these rights used and what are the benefits of these rights to venture capitalists?

Note

1. Sample term sheets can be found in the website of the National Venture Capital Association (NVCA), www.nvca.org; look at the section *Model Legal Documents*.

Menlo Ventures

Key characteristics

Year founded:	1976
Founding partners:	H. DuBose Montgomery
Number of limited partners:	N/A
Geographic coverage:	North America (1 office)
Headquarter location:	Menlo Park (USA)
Focus (if any):	Information technology
Funds under management:	$4 billion
Number of completed deals/IPO exits:	~136/~24 IPOs
Private/public:	Private
Most publicly recognized deals:	Hotmail, 3Par, Catena Networks, Chipcom, Iron Port, Acme Packet
Number of investment professionals:	13

Menlo Ventures is a leading investor in information technology. The firm manages four billion dollars of capital, and its most well-known deals include Hotmail and 3Par. The firm provides five million dollars at the seed stage and up to twenty million dollars at the later stage. In many instances, Menlo Ventures provides subsequent rounds of financing to early stage developing firms (alongside new investors).

Menlo Ventures' investment strategy focuses on firms dealing in information technology. The firm invests in different stages of its investee firms' development cycles (early-stage, expansion, to pre-IPO). Menlo pursues new ideas that disrupt existing industries or create new ones, and invests into firms that have the potential to become dominant market players in sizeable markets. For Menlo Ventures, deals come from areas related to the communications, consumer service, digital media networking, security, and mobile and Internet sectors. The firm's well-executed investment strategy is reflected in its exit statistics. Menlo Ventures has achieved 25 IPOs and over 30 trade sales to some of the world's most prestigious information technology firms, including Microsoft, Cisco, and Siemens.

The firm's strategy is executed by 13 investment professionals operating from a single location in Menlo Park, California. Menlo's staff comes from a wide range of backgrounds (industrial, financial, consulting, etc.).

Source: *www.menloventures.com.*

Chapter 7

Due Diligence Phase II and Internal Approvals

If venture capitalists are successful in negotiating the basic parameters of the transaction and the investment committee is enthusiastic toward the deal, the next step in the investment process is the involvement of external advisors. This is an expensive but necessary process during which the activities of venture capitalists are limited to providing appropriate briefs to external consultants in order to facilitate smooth communication between consultants and the potential investee firm. External advisors are involved in the investment process for between four and six weeks and their involvement normally ceases upon the submission of their final report to the venture capital firm. This report creates the basis for further interaction between venture capitalists, the investment committee, and the business founders.

External due diligence may represent a financial liability for venture capitalists. If the deal is completed, the due diligence costs are normally passed on to the investee firm (as the investee firm benefits from the findings and recommendations of external advisors). However, if external advisors make unexpected discoveries during their investigation into the affairs of the business, if the due diligence report findings are different than expected, or if discussions end for any other reason, venture capitalists are forced to cover the expenses. These costs are classified as "deal abort costs." While incurring these costs may actually prevent venture capitalists from entering into bad deals, the costs may become significant if the venture capital firm cannot successfully close the deal.

External Due Diligence

External due diligence is a formal process in which all of the firm's commercial activities are investigated by independent advisors. It is a careful inspection of the firm from most important perspectives. Specific parts of the business that could expose it to different risks are highlighted and investigated as a part of this process. External due diligence affords an opportunity to uncover any unknown factors about the business and convert them into known factors. It also involves quantifying potential liabilities or any unresolved "knowns." It is critical that venture capitalists are aware of all the facts before making a deal. This process ultimately confirms that firms that look attractive "on paper" look as good in reality.

The scope of due diligence is likely to differ, depending on the unique qualities of the business, its size and the stage of its development, its financial characteristics, the nature of the transaction (e.g., asset purchase, new firm creation, share sale), and so on. The key areas of investigation include financial, legal, and environmental reviews. The financial investigation focuses on the firm's historical data, restating financial data, identifying off-balance sheet liabilities, and investigating the internal workings of the accounting department. The investigation also focuses on the firm's predicted future performance. The legal review is an audit of all legal matters related to the firm. The main aspects of this investigation include the constitution of the firm, its title to assets, any agreements with external parties, and related party transactions. The environmental investigation focuses on waste management and other environmental concerns likely to affect the general public, as well as employee health and safety. In specific situations, venture capitalists involve other specialists in the investigative process. These special reviews may relate to technical, operational, business, commercial, or engineering due diligence. An important part of the external investigation is the performance of background checks on entrepreneurs; these reviews are conducted if venture capitalists have suspicions of criminal behavior or if irregularities are found in the firm's operational structure.

There are multiple benefits for venture capitalists who involve external advisors as an integral part of the venture capital investment process. First, external consultants provide an independent analysis and assessment of the firm that forms an important reference point for venture capitalists. These reviews either confirm venture capitalists' observations about the business, debunk them, or shed an entirely new light. Second, external due diligence helps to outline key risks in the business. Addressing or moderating these risks is likely to result in fewer problems or financial liabilities for the business in the future. External reviews also illuminate the key strengths of a firm and any new business opportunities. Third, the reviews provide venture capitalists with greater certainty around the affairs of the business in that they can underpin their confidence in historical financial numbers, financial forecasts, and the proposed business valuation. Fourth, external due diligence allows venture capitalists to better prepare for the future by allowing them to develop post-acquisition strategies. External reports may identify future opportunities for increasing revenues and decreasing costs, introducing new products and services, or improving the firm's management team. Finally, due diligence can improve the flow of information between venture capitalists and the firm, leading to an improved level and quality of communication. Conversely, there are multiple risks if such reviews are not performed. For example, the value of the business could be diminished, increasing the potential for lawsuits, financial liabilities, or disputes among shareholders.

External due diligence can be very expensive. Table 7.1 summarizes the possible range of expenses with respect to two different types of firms: smaller firms (with revenues less than $50 million) and larger firms (with revenues above $50 million). This high level of expense reflects the involvement of many professionals at different pay scales (e.g., associates, managers, partners), some of which charge between $100 and $500 per hour. Typical external due diligence costs range from $60,000 to $155,000 for a smaller firm and from $85,000 to $500,000 for a larger one (the cost of closing is not included in this calculation—these can range between $75,000 and $500,000). Additional expenses may include the cost of hiring a deal broker, local and federal government fees, taxes, and so on.

Table 7.1 An example of approximate due diligence costs (in $) for two types of firms (small and large)

	Small firm	Large firm
Limited financial review	20,000–50,000	30,000–150,000
Legal review	20,000–50,000	30,000–250,000
Environmental review	10,000–25,000	15,000–50,000
Other reviews	10,000–30,000	10,000–50,000
Total	*60,000–155,000*	*85,000–500,000*

Even though financial, legal, and environmental reviews differ in scope, the process of completing these activities is similar. External consultants commonly engage in a nine-step process, beginning with the venture capitalists' debrief and the signing of a letter of engagement and ending with the submission of a final report (see figure 7.1). This process usually takes a few weeks to complete. At the outset of the process, venture capitalists meet with external consultants. The purpose of the meeting is twofold. First, venture capitalists aim to provide background information on the firm to external consultants. Second, venture capitalists outline the key concerns. Based on this initial discussion, external consultants prepare a preliminary questionnaire (this step is usually done for larger and more complex businesses), the purpose of which is to gather sufficient information about the firm to be able to structure a more detailed questionnaire

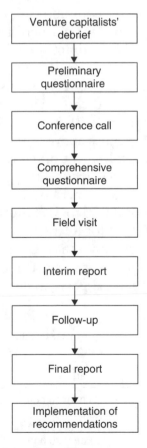

Figure 7.1   Standard steps in external due diligence.

for use later on in the process. The initial questionnaire is usually very short and is generally followed by a brief discussion between external consultants and relevant specialists in the potential investee firm. The objective of this conversation is to obtain the most current information on the affairs of the business. Once the external consultants have gathered a sufficient amount of background information, they prepare a more comprehensive questionnaire related to all aspects of the firm's operations. If existing control procedures and mechanisms in the firm are limited, the scope of external investigation is broader. Depending on the nature of the review and any key concerns raised by venture capitalists, it may take one–three weeks for the firm to respond. After the consultants review the material provided by the firm, they meet with the firm on site. This field visit generally lasts between one and five days and allows consultants to assess the competence of specialists in the firm. External consultants spend their remaining time reviewing notes, analyzing data, and preparing their report. Venture capitalists normally ask that any major issues be reported to them as quickly as possible in the form of a preliminary or interim report. Venture capitalists generally classify concerns listed in the report into three categories: deal breakers, material concerns, and minor problems. The deal breakers are concerns that fundamentally change venture capitalists' perception of the firm. These concerns significantly increase the perceived risk of the business and most commonly relate to taxation liabilities, financial fraud or criminal behavior, or certain types of commercial problems. These concerns may not be fixable and pose a permanent risk to the business. In addition, the discovery of any major issues might force venture capitalists to walk away from the deal. Material concerns represent challenges in specific areas of the business that may or may not lead to problems or liabilities in the future. These concerns can often be addressed, albeit over longer periods of time. Examples include staffing weaknesses in the financial department, declining margins, declining revenues, loss of market share, restating the financial statements, or escalating costs. Material concerns force venture capitalists to decide whether or not to renegotiate the deal. If the discoveries are significant and pose long-term risks, venture capitalists will aim to fundamentally renegotiate the deal. Minor challenges to the firm are easily addressed and implemented. These challenges relate to weaknesses in management information systems, staffing, cash management, or the management of inventory.

The submission of an interim report creates an opportunity for external consultants and the firm to discuss any uncovered problems. At this time, the firm's employees have a chance to provide their opinions on any of the concerns raised. After this, the consultants issue a final report and effectively conclude their assignment. While venture capitalists generally do not disclose the content of the final report to the firm's management and founders at this stage, they may outline key recommendations, especially if they can be implemented quickly prior to closing the deal. Ultimately, it is up to the firm to implement any changes in these areas.

Even though external reviews focus on different areas of investigation, they are interconnected and can even overlap as a part of the firm's overall risk management strategy. For example, improper environmental procedures used by the firm can translate into numerous legal challenges and result in financial liabilities. A lack of understanding of legal infrastructure (e.g., laws, regulations) can result in damaging environmental behavior. Similarly, the implementation of poor financial procedures is likely to result in tax office challenges, legal problems, and financial exposure. The misapplication of tax laws can lead to potential financial liabilities. Noncompliance with federal environmental guidelines and local community bylaws can result in financial penalties. Figure 7.2 summarizes due diligence in three areas of external investigation (financial, legal, and environmental).

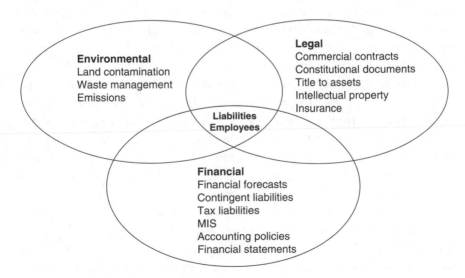

Figure 7.2   The overlap of key external due diligence areas.

The most common area of investigation within these three areas of due diligence relates to establishing the risk of monetary liabilities; the other most common area relates to employee issues.

Financial Review

It is critically important that venture capitalists receive accurate financial information from the potential investee firm. The financial due diligence report is used to validate all of the financial information received from the firm early in the process, develop sound financial forecasts, negotiate a price for the deal, and establish the framework for preparing warranties and representation clauses. The financial review also helps to identify key business and financial risks.

Venture capitalists employ accountants to perform a limited financial review (this is not a financial audit). The limited financial review reflects the "agreed-upon procedure" developed by accounting advisors and approved by venture capitalists. While the objective of the audit is to provide an opinion of whether or not the financial statements provide a "true and fair" assessment of the firm's operations, the limited financial review has a wider investigative scope and is of a more commercial orientation. Consequently, these reviews are conducted by accountants from business advisory departments—not auditors. One of the primary purposes of the review is to consider the financial forecast in the context of historical financial performance and to consider the accuracy of such forecasts. This investigation includes a review of underlying trends in revenues and costs, profitability, and liquidity. Other aspects of financial due diligence include an analysis of historical data (statutory accounts and tax returns), the current financials (year-to-date management accounts), and forecasted financial results (along with an accompanying business plan). The quality and sustainability of earnings (including any abnormalities that influence earnings), contingent liabilities, adequacy and quality of management information systems, accounting policies (whether they meet generally accepted accounting standards or international accounting standards), working capital requirements, bad and doubtful debts, employee entitlement provisions, taxation liabilities, and related party transactions are also discussed.

Firms anticipating venture capital participation are likely to complete an audit at the end of the fiscal year. If the due diligence is performed close to the firm's fiscal year-end, venture capitalists may rely on the audited figures as the basis for financial due diligence. However, because the nature of the limited financial review is forward-looking, the mere presence of the audited figures is unlikely to satisfy venture capitalists (who will bring in accountants to conduct their own investigation). If the due diligence is conducted later in the year, accountants are likely to review interim management accounts. Part of this review includes adjusting financial statements for various provisions (for obsolete inventory, bad debts, etc.). A special investigation normally focuses on taxation, tax disputes, and special tax treatments (e.g., application of tax credits).

The most common problems related to the financial review include poor quality or unreliable financial information, revenue recognition, noncompliance with tax regulations, and transfer pricing. In addition to these common financial review problems, some of the emerging markets present unique challenges (see box 7.1).

Box 7.1   International perspective on venture capital: a financial review by "interview"

In many jurisdictions around the world, legal, accounting, and taxation infrastructures do not work well. Such weak institutional systems can be abused by local entrepreneurs. Some local entrepreneurs operating in less developed countries manage multiple on-shore and off-shore vehicles that jointly constitute a single business; this creates a situation in which local authorities cannot determine the size of the business's operations and profits. In many instances, entrepreneurs operate sizeable business in this manner.

While this multi-firm, multi-jurisdictional structure may work for entrepreneurs, it is almost impossible to decipher and understand for venture capitalists. As a result, venture capitalists often call on investigative accountants to help them establish a financial picture of the entire operation.

So, how do investigative accountants do this? The task of financial advisors in this case is not to perform a limited financial review or an audit of the business; instead, they must effectively reconstruct the financials of the entire operation upon gathering and putting together data from various sources (i.e., firms) in order to create financial forecasts for the business going forward. The key challenge is to consolidate the available information into a single set of financial statements. Many pieces of this "puzzle" are obtained through interviews with managers of separate business entities; these interviews are supported with financial data.

It is perhaps surprising that venture capitalists in less developed markets are able to proceed in this fashion—perhaps they are unable to resist the temptation of pursuing an attractive business that is structured in a complex and sometimes illegal manner. The job of a venture capitalist is to continue to grow the business and transform it into a venture that is simple, transparent, and compliant with local laws and regulations. After a process of a major "legal clean-up," venture capitalists often sell these businesses to strategic investors; undoubtedly, they receive a significant "price premium" for this major activity.

Legal Review

The legal framework in most jurisdictions is complex. The risks of litigation and associated legal costs are increasing, and for most organizations, the cost of resolving a legal dispute is substantial. For venture capitalists, legal risks relate to undiscovered problems or oversights, undisclosed legal issues, or enforceable or unenforceable contractual terms. The objective of the legal review is to assess the overall "legal health" of the business. This review also serves as the basis for developing a list of warranties and representations and is used as a reference point when drafting closing legal documents. Legal reviews identify present and prospective legal problems and devise strategies to minimize exposure to claims and lawsuits. The review consists of a comprehensive screening and analysis of the firm's legal documents. These include the firm's constitutional documents (e.g., articles of association, legal deeds, or charters), title to assets, commercial agreements and third party agreements, permits and licenses, laws and regulations, employment contracts and records, employment policies and practices, minutes from board and shareholder meetings, insurance contracts, and intellectual property protections. In addition, the legal reviews identify poor record keeping, contractual language problems, and ethical challenges (such as bribes and kickbacks).

As with financial due diligence, comprehensive legal reviews vary, reflecting the size of the firm, the type of business and its complexity, the legal constitution and structure, the number of shareholders, and the regulatory framework. The most common challenges in legal audits relate to poor documentation of contracts with various stakeholders, any informal arrangements made with various stakeholders, and related party transactions.

Environmental Review

Environmental due diligence is a relatively new area of investigation. In the past, environmental reviews predominantly concentrated on issues related to land, with ground contamination as the major area of liability. Today, performing an environmental assessment of the entire firm is no longer just an option—it is a sound investment. The environmental review can be defined as the systemic identification and assessment of environmental risks and aims to define the firm's impact on the environment. The purpose of this review is to provide a detailed analysis of historical, current, and future environmental risks associated with the firm's operations and real estate. The review further aims to quantify the value of any potential liabilities.

Specific areas of investigation include waste management, the handling and disposal of hazardous materials, usage of lead-based paints, electromagnetic radiation, occupational health and safety, employee exposure to toxic materials, greenhouse gas and carbon emission, hygiene standards, pipeline routing, and product liability related to recycling obligations. Some environmental risks are difficult to anticipate and may be driven by shifts in legislation, consumer preference toward environmental issues, standards in regulatory bodies or authorities, and community expectations.

The environmental review also provides the firm's staff with an opportunity to stay abreast of new developments in environmental disclosure, institutional controls, regulatory developments, and future trends. Many countries have numerous agencies related to environmental protection; these agencies issue and update applicable regulations, amend guidelines and permitting requirements, and recommend appropriate quality assurance and control programs. Environmental consultants stress that the most common areas of concern relate to public safety.

Other Reviews

Venture capitalists rely on other types of due diligence to supplement their understanding of the business or partners involved in a deal. These reviews are not performed regularly; in fact, they often reflect specific circumstances or identified risks. The following section focuses on three types of "other" reviews: operational, commercial, and personal reviews.

In certain circumstances in which venture capitalists have limited operational experience in a specific industry or sector, or when operational inefficiencies are apparent during the initial review process, operational reviews may yield significant benefits for venture capitalists and the investee firm. Operational reviews normally concentrate on a coherent and comprehensive review of all aspects of the firm's operations. The most fundamental questions asked are whether management has been able to achieve historical goals and milestones and whether they operate the business efficiently (as compared to benchmarks). These reviews converge on primary (production, logistics, sales, and marketing) and support activities (procurement, infrastructure, human resources, technology development, management information systems). The analysis often takes the form of a value chain analysis, as it examines value chain in different product lines, linkages between value chain and performance, and synergies among product lines. Operational reviews may also focus on analyzing functional departments, departmental processes, control mechanisms, operating procedures, organizational structures, knowledge transfer, and the firm's propensity to innovate. These reviews identify operational opportunities, quantify them, and develop detailed plans to take advantage of them.

Before making an investment, venture capitalists may want to further examine certain commercial or business aspects of a firm as they relate to its future development. Young start-ups, for example, are viewed with greater skepticism because they often have to develop new market opportunities or are introducing new products and services into the marketplace. Commercial reviews aim to review the firm's future business plan and diagnose the key issues related to it. These reviews provide an analysis of the external context in which a firm operates. The review covers three general areas: a feasibility assessment, conditions of the market, and competition. The scope of these reviews may vary, but they generally assess the following components: the firm's ability to achieve its business plan, market demand, sustainability of competitive advantage, and market dynamics.

Venture capitalism is predominantly based on respectful, honest, and truthful communication between entrepreneurs and venture capitalists. Maintaining a positive relationship is as critical to venture capitalists as achieving the business, operational, and financial milestones. If the nature of the relationship between entrepreneurs and venture capitalists changes in any manner, the value of the investee firm can be affected. Changes in an entrepreneur's behavior can result in risks related to operations, approvals, decision-making, and achieving an exit. The nature of investigation in this area relates to catching any potential interpersonal complications before they arise. Venture capitalists rely on background or personal checks performed by external investigators to provide them with detailed personal profiles. It is important to note that these investigations are conducted selectively, and are not a standard due diligence requirement. The investigations reveal the personal traits and characteristics of future partners and focus on confirming the accuracy of any provided information and uncovering unknown factors. The investigation may be limited to a single country or can be conducted on an international scale. Personal background investigations aim to compile personal, commercial, financial, and criminal records into a comprehensive report. The most basic investigations focus on identity checks, employment history, education credentials, criminal records, personal debts, and bankruptcy history (personal and business). More comprehensive searches include character reference checks (based on information gathered from friends, business associates, neighbors, etc.), medical record reviews (focusing mainly on mental or psychological disorders), checks on gaps in employment or business ownership, and any histories of discrimination. These investigations are quite sensitive and can pose a significant risk to the relationship between entrepreneurs and venture capitalists prior to closing. Consequently, venture capitalists must always consider whether to openly admit to such investigations or conduct them in secrecy. If they do not disclose the investigation, they risk ruining the relationship with their partners should they discover it (the chance of such an occurrence is high if reference checks are performed). If they disclose the need to conduct the investigation (and blame the investment committee for this requirement), the entrepreneurs may become upset or distrustful—people generally do not like others poking into their personal life, even if they have nothing to hide. Consequently, many venture capitalists choose to conduct background investigations without disclosing so to their partners.

Managing External Advisors

The management of external advisors occurs in three stages. In the external due diligence phase, venture capitalists focus on hiring consultants in three basic areas—accounting, legal, and environmental. An engagement letter that sets out all of the project's details is then signed. Projects are evaluated regularly and venture capitalists receive regular verbal and written feedback. During the closing stages of the investment process, venture capitalists are likely to work with lawyers, who provide assistance with deal negotiations and the preparation of legal documents. This phase of cooperation with legal advisors is less predictable and reflects the complexities of the venture capital process. Drafting and revising legal documents is time consuming and the circumstances that surround this work can be unpredictable. Venture capitalists also hire external consultants to assist with resolving operational matters.

During the due diligence process, venture capitalists employ external consultants to perform specific tasks. The venture capitalists and the consultants will sign an engagement letter that outlines the following areas: project scope, duties and responsibilities, methodological approach, administrative relationship, reporting and output requirements or project deliverables (e.g., updates, summaries, reports), timing for project start and completion, costs (including professional and out-of-pocket expenses), and miscellaneous points. More comprehensive engagement letters also include termination clauses, arbitration resolutions, and project incentives. Consultant remuneration is normally agreed upon on a fixed price basis.

When closing deals, venture capitalists rely on lawyers to negotiate the finer points and craft legal documents. Specialists from other areas are occasionally brought in to the discussions. However, if deal discussions and closing extend beyond a six-month period, venture capitalists may revisit the need to complete another financial review. The feasibility study or market review may also require revisions or updates. The nature of the interaction between venture capitalists and lawyers may be somewhat unpredictable; this is reflective of the complexities inherent to the negotiating process, the nature of the legal profession, the mindset of potential partners, and deal fatigue. Venture capitalists are mindful that some lawyers have a tendency to engage in dialogue with the legal counsel representing the founders without necessarily progressing the deal. Remuneration is normally paid on an hourly basis.

After closing, venture capitalists aim to minimize the involvement of external consultants and resort to external assistance only in special circumstances. The benefits of temporary advisors are that the firm receives special expertise for a defined period of time, obtains support in the areas it cannot find or afford more permanent expertise in, and has flexibility within the relationship (the firm can terminate it and does not pay benefits). External consultants can assist in three areas—the offering of expertise, providing extra resources, or offering advice (e.g., opinion or evaluation). The major drawback to involving external consultants is that the firm can become dependent on them. External consultants are also expensive and may occasionally exhibit a tendency to unduly extend the project. The involvement of external consultants often indicates a weakness in the management team or operational staff. In such situations, venture capitalists tend to look for more permanent solutions.

One of the key questions is to decide whether to involve a generalist or a specialist. A generalist is a person able to provide general guidance on many issues and who has developed an ability to integrate more than one specialty into their consulting practice. The generalist focuses on tasks of integration, synthesis, and collaboration. The generalist consultant is experienced at pinpointing problems and developing a general framework for their solution. However, the generalist may not have strong implementation skills. The problems solved by generalists are larger in scope and complexity. The specialist consultant, on the other hand, has a significant depth of experience in one area and has a strong track record of project implementation.

The most popular method of managing external advisors is to require them to prepare regular status reports. During the due diligence phase, this task is considerably simple, as these assignments normally take up to six weeks to complete and are clearly set out. Venture capitalists require at least two interactions after a project commences—one after receiving the preliminary report and the other after receiving the final report. The report should include incurred costs to date in the form of time sheets (consultants normally issue monthly invoices). Tracking progress and controlling expenses during deal negotiations can prove difficult.

Most external advisors are risk averse in their presentation of the due diligence findings. This may reflect the need of external advisors to avoid any future accusations by venture capitalists that they have not disclosed all material facts about the investee firm or provided sufficient warnings. In the final due diligence reports, consultants often exhibit a tendency to magnify business problems, exaggerate their potential impact on the firm, and increase the assessment of value for potential liabilities. They may also devise negative scenarios unlikely to occur in the future. Less experienced venture capitalists may have a tendency to accept such due diligence findings as "deal breakers."

Internal Approvals

The Investment Committee

While investment officers in venture capital firms pride themselves as being the ultimate decision makers during discussions with entrepreneurs, the final authority on deals rests with the investment committee—a formal collection of individuals in the venture capital firm that has the power to legally bind the fund toward a deal. The general purpose of the investment committee is to consider deals brought to the venture capital firm and to oversee the firm's entire portfolio. In most firms, the investment committee focuses on three basic functions: establishment of the investment process, development of asset allocation, and oversight of active deals. These three functions capture the fiduciary responsibilities venture capital firms and investment committees have toward their limited partners. Within the function related to the investment process, the investment committee sets standards for internal document preparation, analysis and investigation of investee firms, due diligence criteria, usage of external advisors, and scheduling deal reviews and follow-up discussions. The committee also identifies investment timelines and sets return expectations (weighing risks versus potential returns). The asset allocation function relates to the most efficient allocation of capital toward sectors of the economy, geographic regions, the firm's development stage, and so on. This function also relates to the optimization of human resources in the venture capital firm. Investment committees are also active in the oversight of active deals. A periodic review of the investment performance of all portfolio firms is undertaken. The involvement of the investment committee may be especially pronounced at times when there are problem situations, during new rounds of financing, and at the time of exit.

Presenting a deal to the investment committee serves a number of purposes for venture capitalists. First, the committee can bring a significant amount of venture capital experience to the consideration of a single investment opportunity. Members of the committee come from different backgrounds and have different strengths and skills. In selecting individuals to investment committees, venture capital firms try to strike a balance between technical skills (e.g., operational, financial, consulting) and soft skills (e.g., deal making, intuitive capabilities). Committee members are often experienced venture capitalists themselves, and many of them are experienced in negotiating successful deals. Second, the session with the investment committee is often considered a period of "information sharing" rather than a period of decision-making. Deal leaders are encouraged to communicate without any barriers, to limit "active selling" to the committee, and to attempt to limit any personal biases toward proposed deals. For venture capital firms that have a presence in many international markets, colleagues located elsewhere may have experience completing deals in the same or similar sectors to the deal being considered. Venture capitalists stress that it is critical to tap into these resources—deals in similar industries but different geographic markets are likely to share many similar characteristics, challenges, and opportunities.

Investment committees tend to be relatively small. They generally include three or four individuals, with a maximum of up to seven; one is appointed as the chair of the committee. In experienced venture capital firms, the members of the investment committee are drawn from a pool of the firm's most experienced deal makers. In new venture capital firms, limited partners may insist on independent members being brought into the committee. Most investment committees meet regularly, once every two weeks. Prior to the meeting, the committee members receive a comprehensive information package (either a preliminary report during early stages of the deal or a comprehensive document at the more advanced stages of investigation). During official meetings of the committee, deal leaders (venture capitalists working directly on the deal) and deal promoters (senior members of the firm involved in the deal, but not in daily contact with the potential investee firm) make a 15–30 minute presentation. The presentation is followed by questions and discussions; these may be informal or scripted.

The members of the investment committee tend to focus on two basic aspects of the deal: earnings growth "disruptors" and deal fairness. In terms of hurdles to earnings growth, the basic questions of the investment committee are: "How is the firm going to be taken from its current operational performance to a 'new destination' on an accelerated development schedule?" and "Can the firm implement the value creation process?" In discussions with deal leaders, investment committee members are likely to discuss disruptors, which can sever the accelerated cycle of the firm's earnings growth. The key disruptors to growth come from many areas: market challenges, inefficient and outdated business models, poor execution, inferior management, and so on. Some of these challenges may be perceived as deal breakers. In terms of deal fairness, the members of the committee will consider whether basic protections are in place and whether the venture capital firm is overpaying for the business.

Interaction with the Investment Committee

There are multiple instances in which venture capitalists interact with members of the firm's investment committee. Figure 7.3 presents a summary of the steps in the venture capital process, along with the types of documents submitted to the investment committee and the types of decisions its members must make (these normally

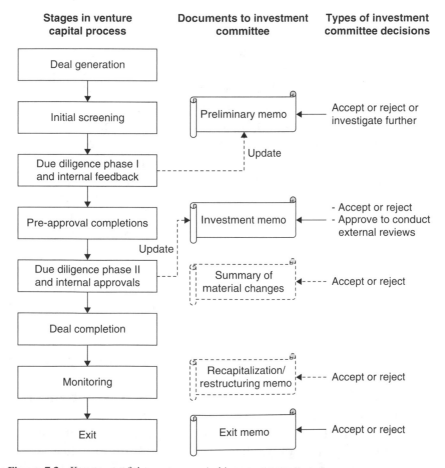

Figure 7.3   Key stages of the venture capital investment process.

relate to accepting or rejecting the deal). In the normal course of an investment, venture capitalists must prepare at least three internal documents for the investment committee—a preliminary memorandum, an investment memorandum, and an exit memorandum. The first two documents are prepared prior to deal closing and the last one is prepared prior to exit. The initial and preliminary memorandums consist of basic information about the firm and focus on areas related to the 5M principles (discussed in chapter four) and a review of the firm's financials. To prepare these documents, input is taken from the firm's information package, informal discussions with the investee firm, and due diligence. At this stage, the investment committee begins to focus on broader issues (e.g., the sector, the firm's stage of development). The investment memorandum summarizes the firm's commercial attractiveness and deal terms (agreed upon in the form of a letter of intent, heads of terms, or terms sheet). This memorandum presents a more comprehensive and complete description of the firm, with all the major risks and opportunities outlined. The document also discusses exit prospects and potential returns and summarizes key deal terms and investor protections, including exit provisions. The exit memorandum captures the venture capital firm's success in growing the business, building value, and monetizing it. It presents the contemplated returns from the deal if a specific exit avenue is pursued.

There are two other potential documents that may be presented to the investment committee. The first document represents a summary of material changes after external due diligence is completed. These reviews become the basis on which the business is reevaluated and the deal is renegotiated. The second document may be presented to the investment committee during the monitoring stage of the process, during which the investee firm may undergo restructuring, recapitalization, a merger, or any other material changes. In the case of an additional capital injection, venture capitalists effectively reconsider the deal and are obligated to present the investment memorandum with the same level of scrutiny as if they were making a new investment.

There are two types of decisions the investment committee is likely to arrive at with respect to a deal: to accept or to reject. However, during the screening and due diligence stages, the investment committee may not be able to reach a definite conclusion and may recommend further investigation into specific aspects of the firm. In later deal stages, the committee may also request that the deal be renegotiated with entrepreneurs and, at the time of exit, with potential buyers. Once these additional requests are addressed, the investment team issues a summary memorandum to the committee and the merits of the new situation are again discussed.

Discussions with entrepreneurs about the revision of captured deal terms are challenging. Venture capitalists need to present to the founders that due to new facts discovered during the due diligence process, they have identified new business risks that need to be addressed and mitigated. The identification of new risks, in turn, is likely to cause venture capitalists to renegotiate the terms of the deal or change the conditions (and timing) under which certain legal provisions are triggered. The most challenging area of discussion relates to business valuation—a revision in this area may come from an adjustment to or a restating of the firm's financial statements. If the two sides are not able to agree on a new, adjusted valuation, venture capitalists may insist on inserting other mechanisms into the legal documentation (e.g., a share adjustment mechanism or a ratchet) of the deal.

In terms of exit considerations, the investment committee may reject the venture capitalists' exit scheme (e.g., an offer from a trade buyer) and recommend that they pursue an exit at another time or through another avenue (this is especially true if valuation is below expectations). The committee may also recommend renegotiating the exit terms and conditions.

Questions to Consider

1. What is the role of external advisors in the venture capital investment process?
2. Differentiate between a financial review and a financial audit.
3. What are some of the key overlaps between the major areas of external due diligence?
4. Why has the environmental review become so important in recent years?
5. Discuss the key points in managing external advisors.

Unison Capital Partners

Key characteristics

Year founded:	1998
Founding partners:	John Ehara, Tatsuya Hayashi, and Tatsuo Kawasaki
Number of limited partners:	N/A
Geographic coverage:	Japan
Headquarter location:	Tokyo (Japan)
Focus (if any):	Buyout & spin-offs (large corporations)
Funds under management:	¥250 billion
Number of completed deals/ IPO exits:	14/N/A
Private/public:	Private
Most publicly recognized deals:	Mine-Mart, Kiriu Corporation, Drug Eleven, Orient Credit, Cosmos Life, Akindo Sushiro
Number of investment professionals:	18

Unison Capital Partners is one of the leading independent private equity firms in Japan, and is regarded as a pioneer in the Japanese private equity industry. Since its inception, Unison has raised three private equity funds and currently has ¥250 billion under management.

Unison's unique investment strategy is centered on management buyouts, spinoffs of business units from large Japanese corporations, ownership succession transactions, and leveraged buyouts. The firm relies on strong syndicate partners from around the world, including the Carlyle Group. Unison's unique strategy has been rewarded with multiple trade sales to some of the leading conglomerates in Japan, including Sumitomo and Kadokawa.

The firm maintains a small pool of staff (18 investment professionals) in its central office in Tokyo. Most of Unison's investment professionals have financial, consulting, and industrial backgrounds. In addition, the firm also relies on numerous industry advisors and consultants and a wide network of financial institutions.

Source: *www.unisoncap.com.*

Chapter 8

Deal Completion

Deal completion refers to a conclusion of the negotiation of detailed legal documents in a transaction between venture capitalists and entrepreneurs. Anxiety is felt by both sides at this point in the venture capital investment process. Unanticipated issues can often arise when the general terms of the deal (captured in the term sheet) are converted into detailed legal documents. Signing multiple copies of legal documents formally commences cooperation between venture capitalists and entrepreneurs.

Deal negotiations occur at various points in the interactions between venture capitalists and entrepreneurs. In the early stages of these interactions, venture capitalists attempt to identify any "deal breakers" that may be present in their proposal on the basic terms of the future deal. A deal breaker is a legal or business concern that is unlikely to be accepted by both entrepreneurs and venture capitalists. Once venture capitalists have established that limited points of disagreement exist, they proceed to intensify their efforts to document a deal on paper (a process that continues through other stages of the investment process). The most critical moment in the deal making process comes with the completion of the term sheet, which is accomplished prior to the presentation of a comprehensive package (in the form of an information memorandum) to the venture capital firm's investment committee. The final negotiations occur during the closing stage of the transaction, where detailed legal procedures and sequences are drawn up for various rights and mechanisms.

Deal Negotiations

Deal negotiations are the means by which an agreement that is acceptable to all parties is reached. This agreement serves as the basis for the business relationship going into the future. Venture capitalists rely on their ability to recognize certain behavioral tendencies, good communication, persuasion, and their presentation abilities to minimize the adversarial aspects of the interaction and to bring the parties together. A quote by John Kinross, a founder of 3i, best captures the approach of most experienced venture capitalists during the negotiation process:

> You must make it easy for the other person to agree with you, not difficult as many people do. You must aim to win his confidence, without that you face an uphill struggle. You start by going over the areas where there is little or no difference between you. You will dwell on these things giving them the maximum amount of importance. Having laid out as wide a basis as possible, you only then move to difficult areas.

This quote underlines the importance of knowledge, preparation, and dedication to understanding the other side's point of view.

Venture capital negotiations are complex and time consuming. The dynamics of negotiations are often driven by the entrepreneurs' deal making experience. For example, venture capitalists may choose to immediately proceed to full-stage negotiations if they are dealing with experienced "serial" entrepreneurs. In these conditions, venture capitalists immediately offer a comprehensive term sheet describing detailed mechanisms for anticipated procedures. The experience of both parties allows the negotiations to move quickly and constructively. Interestingly, break-up points are also easily reached. On the other hand, young entrepreneurs with no deal making experience are cumbersome and time consuming to deal with. These initial interactions are difficult for venture capitalists, who need to simultaneously act as educators, partners, and opponents. Many venture capitalists choose to take an incremental approach to negotiating—they start with a short document (e.g., a letter of intent) as the basis for their negotiations and subsequently progress the negotiations to a point where a more comprehensive document can be introduced. The advantage of this approach is that a relationship is built through the continuing discussions, and the complexity of the discussed issues is allowed to increase incrementally.

Seasoned venture capitalists are aware of the limitations of relying on legal documentation in deal making. If trust, mutual respect, honesty, and integrity are the foundational blocks of the interaction between the parties, the relationship can sustain severe tests in the future. Legal documentation provides guidelines for the relationship—both sides use it to remind themselves of mutual obligations, responsibilities, and rights. Legal documents also act as reminders of once established principles that can be used to deal with unanticipated events. However, if positive interpersonal relations break down, the value of the legal documentation greatly diminishes. Since these documents are unlikely to foresee all the eventualities in the business, the two sides will be required to engage into new discussions. In hostile circumstances, the two sides will often assume adversarial modes. Even "water-tight" legal documentation can be strained by a lack of compliance, vengeance, or greed on the part of an opposing party. Venture capitalists often remark that even the best legal protections are no match for the damages caused by poor interpersonal relations.

Venture capitalists often compare their business negotiations with entrepreneurs to the process of building a bridge from both sides of the river. While this analogy may not reflect construction and engineering principles, it underscores the need to develop a mutually supportive structure, as the two sides are interdependent of one another until the final point of exit (the relationship often continues beyond this point in time). The nature of the rapport developed between the two sides is likely to be subjected to minor strains and major stresses. The relationship is likely to survive if the foundations of it are strong and a mutual understanding exists between the two parties.

Venture capital negotiations have a number of unique characteristics. First, they are comprehensive, encompassing many functional areas of the business and the personal behaviors of all shareholders. Second, they are future-oriented. Venture capital negotiations focus on a plan that can achieve the firm's future market success, better its competitive position, increase its profitability and market share, and, above all, grow its value. Third, the negotiations are emotional. From the entrepreneur's point of view, they include "selling out" a part of their own business to a new partner. From the venture capitalists' perspective, they involve personal engagement—a venture capitalist's personal credibility can be damaged if things go wrong. The relationship is regularly tested by changes in business fortunes, personal circumstances, and market situations. Last, venture capital negotiations are legal in their orientation. Anticipated business behaviors are captured in legal documentation that describes the basis of business conduct in the venture and between shareholders.

Benefit Selling

Both venture capitalists and entrepreneurs need to "sell" themselves to the other party during their initial courtship. Venture capitalists believe attractive entrepreneurial firms are likely to be pursued by multiple venture capital firms. A business owner normally has a preference for concluding a deal with a venture capital firm that he knows well personally or that differentiates itself by establishing a special relationship with him. Fostering a strong personal relationship is effectively the means by which venture capitalists are able to investigate the commercial characteristics of an investee firm and secure preferential deal terms. Interpersonal connections are useful even if the venture capital firm ultimately decides not to pursue the deal. If an interpersonal relationship is not achieved at the outset of the courtship, venture capitalists are unlikely to be invited to participate further down in the investment process. Entrepreneurs must also sell themselves to venture capitalists. Venture capitalists have multiple investment opportunities and choose only the ones where they can see themselves building value in cooperation with entrepreneurs. In any case, development of a strong rapport between both sides is seen as a prerequisite for future cooperation.

Experience suggests that developing a strong interpersonal relationship is heavily dependent on demonstrating to the other side that one's affairs, business, personal needs, and aspirations are well understood. A potential partner must be able to meet the needs of the other party and satisfy their aspirations. A common communication technique used to develop strong interpersonal relations (based on identifying needs and satisfying them) is called "benefit selling." A skilled practitioner of benefit selling utilizes the interactions between the two parties to build the relationship, advance negotiations, and acquire information to make a proper assessment of the firm and its founders.

Table 8.1   Examples of benefit selling by venture capitalists

Entrepreneur's statement	Key entrepreneurs' concern	Venture capitalist's statement
"We have built a solid management team—it is critical to our future."	Management retention	"Our firm sees management as critical to any success. This is why we often offer a stock option program for management."
"A part of our growth strategy is to acquire firms in our industry in other geographic markets."	Acquisition execution	"Our firm has a strong track record of assisting firms in expansion plans. Affecting acquisitions is one of our strengths."
"We need capital quickly."	Deal completion time	"We aim to close deals in three months. Our internal process is designed to minimize deal completion time."
"We like cooperating with local people."	Geographic proximity/ appreciating regional differences	"Our offices are located in your area. We understand the needs and circumstances of agricultural enterprises in the region."
"My business needs $10 million in further financing and I need $0.5 million myself."	Business and personal finances	"Our firm has sufficient capital to satisfy your needs. We always strive to achieve the best possible financial mix to limit the founders' dilution. We are also open to cash out situations."

Benefit selling favors asking questions and seeking clarifications over the provision of information and active selling. Questions should be asked for about 80 percent of the interaction. The objective of these questions is to clarify needs, assign relative values to these needs, crystallize aspirations, and understand fears. The individual who asks questions and is interested in clarification is perceived to be interested in his discussion partner. On the other hand, the individual who talks incessantly is perceived as focused only on his or her own needs. Let's observe how benefit selling works in the venture capital setting. Table 8.1 presents an entrepreneur's sample statements, their key concerns, and possible responses by venture capitalists.

Common Negotiation Strategies

Negotiation is a process by which compromise is reached on the division and allocation of resources, rights, responsibilities, and obligations between parties. The process involves three basic strategies of negotiation: distributive, integrative, and interorganizational.

Distributive negotiation focuses on agreement between the two sides along a single point of concern. This strategy can be based on a discrete distribution of fixed resources (e.g., cash), business parameters (e.g., business valuation), and rights (e.g., approvals). In contrast, integrative negotiation is multidimensional, in that it simultaneously focuses on many issues or concerns. Integrative negotiation focuses on creating synergies and values, thereby expanding the universe of possible reciprocal exchanges of value. Integrative negotiations are about securing the best possible agreement for all concerned. This kind of negotiation is based on cooperation and integration rather than on competition and the discrete division of a limited resource. Interorganizational negotiation involves resolving the internal conflicts that occur among stakeholders representing the same negotiating team. For example, there may be different groups of shareholders attempting to achieve different objectives (e.g., dividend payout versus profit retention; expansion versus stability), making it difficult for the firm as a whole to maintain a consistent negotiating position. In such a case, interorganizational negotiations may be used to solidify the bargaining position of all shareholders into a single, homogenous group. The most common negotiating strategies used in the venture capital setting are distributive and integrative. Interorganizational approaches are used in situations where the shareholders or venture capitalists (in a syndicate, e.g.) need to arrive at a common negotiating position vis-à-vis the other side.

Some venture capitalists argue that the methods of negotiation described earlier are mutually exclusive and incompatible; others believe that most negotiating sessions involve a combination of different methods. Venture capitalists argue that while the integrative negotiating approach focuses on creating value, or effectively increasing the "pie," the negotiating sides may eventually get to a point in which the goal is to distribute the pie, or claim value. If the universe of possibilities and values is increased, an exchange of value becomes easy.

Distributive Negotiations

Distributive bargaining may be defined as a competitive negotiating strategy used when parties are in conflict over a single issue. This form of negotiation represents a closed system of mutual exchange, effectively becoming a "zero-sum" situation—the more one side gets, the less the other side receives. It is a *win-lose* approach to arriving at a solution and a process by which a concession is extracted from the other side. If neither of the sides is willing to give in, the bargaining session ends in a break up.

Some venture capitalists and entrepreneurs try to simplify the bargaining process by focusing on financial issues. If the issues present in a negotiation are perceived solely on the basis of cost and benefit, the negotiation is often limited to the discrete distribution of numeric values. The best example of a numeric issue may be the valuation of the firm, of which the two sides may hold different perceptions. Negotiation over the price becomes a process of distributive bargaining (to the extent that one side wins and the other loses). Figure 8.1 presents an example of distributive negotiations.

Each negotiating team engaged in distributive negotiations sets negotiating targets (the preferred and acceptable range of solutions on certain issues) and "walk away" or resistance points (the minimum or maximum it can accept before ending discussions). The goal of each party is to use available information, previous discussions, body language, and other clues to establish the opposing party's walk away position and attempt to negotiate a final result that is closer to its own predetermined walk away point.

Venture capitalists employ different tactics using this approach. For example, some venture capitalists choose to open negotiations

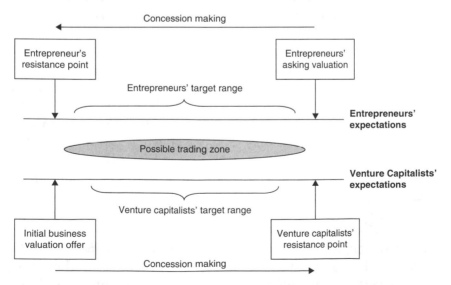

Figure 8.1 An example of distributive negotiations related to business valuation.

with high demands and extreme positions, providing a signal to the other side that the road to settlement is long and significant concessions may be required. The danger in this situation is obvious—an extreme opening approach may alienate the other side and irreversibly damage the relationship between the two sides. Furthermore, if the extreme offers are rejected by the receiving side and subsequent offers are developed by the proposing side, there is strong potential for a loss of credibility on the part of the proposing side. Other venture capitalists prefer to open negotiations closer to their ultimate objective. While the different tactics used need to account for available alternatives (e.g., Best Alternatives to a Negotiated Agreement, or BATNA), negotiating skills, and preparation, most venture capitalists attempt to land their opening positions within an acceptable range of the opposing side. If the initial offer falls within the receiving side's acceptable range, further discussions are possible and counter offers may be made; otherwise, offers can be rejected without a clear next step in place.

The advantage of distributive bargaining is that it can be used to resolve disputes where limited options are available and the situation cannot be resolved in any other way. This is especially true when it comes to the division of proceeds or business valuation; the process is relatively simple and straightforward as a single issue is involved (multidimensional negotiations present a greater challenge). There are, however, many disadvantages to using this technique. Distributive bargaining is often viewed as competitive, and forces the two negotiating parties to take extreme positions during their discussions. It may also force sides into a "take it or leave it" situation. Over the course of their negotiations, the parties will often come together by finding a point of central tendency or mutual acceptance; parties focusing on their differences usually further exacerbate conflict. Furthermore, focusing on maximizing the outcome or on attempting to win as much as possible from the other side on a single issue may strain the relationship between the parties. As such, distributive bargaining is often perceived as inefficient in a venture capital setting.

Integrative Negotiations

Integrative negotiations are multidimensional and iterative. The process is based on understanding the concerns of the other side, converting and integrating these concerns into a package, and proposing a comprehensive solution. Ultimately, this form of negotiation operates within a two-part approach, based on a condition and an offer—an "if..., then..." formula. In other words, one party says, "if you do this, then, I offer that." Integrative negotiations continue until a deal is reached or all possibilities are exhausted. The underlying premise is that the two sides negotiating the deal attribute different values to different concerns. A realization of this fact establishes trading zones, as opposed to labeling each opposing concern a mutually exclusive issue. Trade-offs—mutually exclusive acceptable exchanges of value—are an essential component of integrative negotiation. When each side values an issue differently, a concession on a point of greater value to one side than to the other can be exchanged for a concession on another issue where the values are reversed. Skilled venture capitalists seek to build a package of interrelated trade-offs. Skilled negotiators often say to the other side, "Nothing is agreed until all is agreed"—a statement that implies achieving compromise along a multidimensional spectrum of issues. Complete packages comprised of different critical components are traded during these negotiations. No deal is effectively final until the two sides agree upon a complete package of issues. The process is integrative in that it provides answers to three basic questions: "What do they want it for?," "What is it worth for them to get it?," and "What happens if they do not get it?"

Let's observe how integrative negotiations work using a simplified example. Imagine that venture capitalists are dealing with a successful serial entrepreneur operating in the pharmaceutical industry. This entrepreneur has a track record of developing new pharmacological solutions for various gastrointestinal problems. She is looking to establish a new business with venture capital financing. We further assume that the key negotiating issues are reduced to three main components: business valuation of the venture (or its pre-money valuation), the amount of personal contribution made by the entrepreneur to the venture, and the percentage level of EBITDA underperformance above which venture capitalists may assume control of the business. The initial positions of the two sides are summarized in table 8.2. This table also presents the ranking of each side's issues; this ranking indicates the possible trading zones. For venture capitalists and entrepreneurs, assessing the other side's ranking, or the value they attach to various issues,

Table 8.2   Example of distributive negotiations on three issues

	Venture capitalists' opening offer	Venture capitalists' ranking	Entrepreneur's verbalized position	Entrepreneur's ranking
Pre-money valuation	$4.0 million	2	$5.0 million	1
Personal $ contribution	$100,000	1	$0	2
% EBITDA underperformance	≥30%	3	≥50%	3

comes from asking questions, gathering information, and testing assumptions.

With respect to the three most important issues, venture capitalists proposed the business valuation at four million dollars, required a personal contribution of one hundred thousand dollars from the entrepreneur, and expected that more than 30 percent underperformance in the venture in any given year would constitute a failure to achieve key financial milestones (providing them grounds on which to assume control of the business by way of a voting flip-over event). On the other hand, the entrepreneur valued her business at five million dollars and did not want to make any financial contribution into the venture, believing her track record of success to be sufficient enough evidence to prove the likely success of the new venture. She also believed that her missing the forecasted EBITDA by more than 50 percent would be construed as material underperformance. While the values proposed by the entrepreneur are not significantly different from those suggested by venture capitalists, there are opportunities to make concessionary trade-offs and affect the deal.

Table 8.3 presents an evolution of the negotiating positions proposed by the entrepreneur and venture capitalists. In Stage I of the discussions, venture capitalists reduce their expectations for the personal financial contribution to $75,000, but also reduce the entry valuation of the business to $3.7 million. They retain the EBITDA underperformance measure at less than 30 percent, as initially proposed. Stage II presents the entrepreneur's response and indicates a strong commitment to the entry valuation ($5.0 million). The entrepreneur also concedes to make a personal contribution equal to $50,000. For venture capitalists, a personal contribution is often an important indicator of an entrepreneur's commitment to the

Table 8.3 Progressions of negotiations through six stages from initial positions described in table 8.2

	Stage I—VC	Stage II—Entrepreneur	Stage III—VC	Stage IV—Entrepreneur	Stage V—VC	Stage VI [deal agreed] Entrepreneur
Valuation (million $)	3.7	5.0	4.3	5.0	4.5	4.8
Personal $	75,000	50,000	150,000	150,000	200,000	200,00
% EBITDA	≥30	≥45	≥35	≥45	≥40	≥40

venture, as it indicates whether the entrepreneur is willing to place some of her personal money at risk alongside the capital provided by venture capitalists. A small reduction in the expectations for the trigger of the underperformance clause also occurs. Stage III presents the trade-offs venture capitalists are willing to make. Venture capitalists are prepared to increase the entry value of the business in exchange for the entrepreneur's personal contribution to the venture. The entry value is increased to $4.3 million and the personal contribution requirement is increased to $150,000. Further flexibility is also shown for EBITDA underperformance, which is reduced to 35 percent. Stage IV outlines the entrepreneur's rigidity with respect to business valuation, but willingness to match the venture capitalists' expectations for personal contribution. Stage V demonstrates the venture capitalists' continued willingness to trade an increase in business valuation against an improvement in the amount of personal contribution. The proposed amount of personal contribution at this stage of discussions ($200,000) exceeds the value of venture capitalists' initial expectations ($100,000). Stage VI captures the terms of the deal on the three most important issues. At this stage, the entrepreneur is no longer willing to continue the previous trade tied to valuation versus personal contribution. The result of this position is a reduction in valuation expectations to $4.8 million and an agreement to make a personal contribution equal to $200,000. The value of the EBITDA trigger point is settled at 40 percent, a half-way compromise between the two sides' opening positions. In summary, the parties achieve success along the lines of their most important issues: the entrepreneur achieves a business valuation close to her opening position while venture capitalists secure the entrepreneur's personal contribution above their initial expectations.

Making concessions and trade-offs is important when concluding venture capital deals. When each side at the negotiating table values a business concern differently, a concession on a point of greater value to one side can be exchanged for a concession on a different point. How value is assigned to different issues may not always be logical, clearly verbalized, or even justified. As previously discussed, preparation prior to negotiation is needed to understand the key needs of the other side and what values are ascribed to them. Closing a deal usually follows the same sequence: confirm needs, explore values and trading opportunities, and prepare a package of key terms.

The following section explores the most important trades venture capitalists can make in their pursuit of deal making. Figure 8.2 summarizes a possible sequence of venture capital negotiations and available trade-off zones. The double solid line in the figure indicates common instigators for discussion while the dotted line indicates the possible concession. Venture capital negotiations usually begin with a discussion around valuation, which is often the first point of contention raised in the negotiation. Perhaps mistakenly, valuation often represents the most critical deal breaker for entrepreneurs. Venture capitalists must decide whether the valuation range proposed by the entrepreneur is generally acceptable within comparable transactions and proceed to obtain concessions around

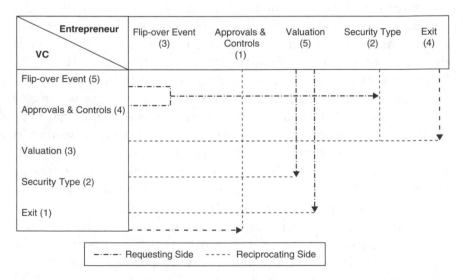

Figure 8.2   Trading zones in venture capital negotiations.

their most pivotal issues, namely exit provisions (including drag-along rights) and the type of security (preferred convertible shares, with full liquidation rights). If the valuation range is outside of the venture capitalists' comfort zone (thereby creating IRR below expected levels), further discussions do not occur. The second critical issue for entrepreneurs (and also for venture capitalists) relates to exit provisions. This issue is usually raised early on in negotiations, when venture capitalists aim to maximize the "tightness" of exit provisions. Most entrepreneurs find it difficult to accept the sale of their business to a strategic investor—they instead prefer to buy back the firm's shares from venture capitalists later in the process, if possible. Exit provisions are often viewed by entrepreneurs as an assault on their independence. Similar reactions are also seen over venture capitalists' approval and control provisions; entrepreneurs may attempt to soften exit provisions by offering more strict controls in this area.

There are numerous advantages to using the integrative approach when negotiating. First, this negotiating technique inevitably creates multiple opportunities to increase the universe of possible trades and areas of mutual advantage; it often leads to a *win-win* situation for all parties involved. This scenario is made possible by the fact that each side values issues differently. With this approach, all parties may win, or at worst, neither party may appear to lose. Second, the integrative approach creates multiple opportunities to build a strong relationship between the parties. Multidimensional trade-offs often tend to maximize each sides' satisfaction. The two sides often "test-drive" multiple issues and resolve them successfully, thus forming a track record of working together successfully on business problems. Third, this approach to negotiating protects both sides against making unwanted concessions on any single issue. The parties are unable to concede thin-sliced deteriorations to their positions; in other words, they cannot be "salamied" by the other side. The disadvantage of integrative negotiations is that they are complex. The negotiator must first resolve easy-to-deal-with issues that are unlikely to be deal breakers and effectively reduce an outstanding list of issues to a manageable level (ideally to about five–seven major issues) before entering into integrative bargaining; it is extremely difficult to deal with many issues at the same time. Dealing with multiple issues simultaneously requires strong analytical skills, enhanced reasoning, problem solving, and preparation.

Entrepreneurs' Approach to Venture Capital Negotiations

Since venture capitalists are normally more skillful negotiators than entrepreneurs, this section is dedicated to providing some hints to entrepreneurs on how best to interact with venture capitalists. Venture capital negotiations are complex and often overwhelming to entrepreneurs. It is important for entrepreneurs to obtain external assistance when dealing with venture capitalists (this is especially important for first-time entrepreneurs seeking this type of financing). The advisors may be lawyers, accountants, consultants, former venture capitalists, and so on. These advisors should have closed at least two deals with venture capitalists in the past. Ideally, the entrepreneur will also have a chance to employ a lawyer and a business specialist somewhere along the way (lawyers are normally less versed with financial issues than business specialists).

While venture capital term sheets are normally filled with numerous clauses, restrictions, procedures, and mechanisms, only a handful of these terms are likely to really affect entrepreneurs. Some terms proposed by venture capitalists are relatively standard for the industry and no amount of discussions are likely to change them (even though flexibility always exists in deal making). The two most important areas of concern for the entrepreneur are retaining operating freedom and maintaining the ability to make decisions in a timely manner. The issue of valuation, often viewed by entrepreneurs as the most important selection criteria and negotiating point, should be seen as a secondary issue. If the underlying business develops well and is successful, venture capitalists and entrepreneurs will almost certainly be satisfied with the final result.

Agreeing to work with a venture capital partner experienced in the entrepreneur's industry may be more critical than any legal terms negotiated in the final deal. Serial entrepreneurs that have been financed by multiple rounds of capital by venture capitalists often confirm the importance of having quality partners in a deal. This usually translates into superior financial performance, a better chance of obtaining further financing (debt and equity), and stronger exit prospects. Securing the right venture capital partner may mean waiting for them (they are usually busier than other venture capital firms) and refusing to work with less optimal financial partners.

Nothing motivates venture capitalists more than the possibility of a good investment prospect landing in the hands of competing venture capital firms. Experienced entrepreneurs work to expand their pool of possible credible financial partners and avoid signing letters of intent too early in the process (this often precludes other venture capital firms from pursuing the deal). If the entrepreneur has multiple venture capital firms interested in the business, the chances of securing a strong partner on favorable business terms increases significantly.

Legal Closing

Legal closing is the process of signing and exchanging all agreements between entrepreneurs and venture capitalists. At the time of legal closing, all appropriate changes are made to the firm's constitutional documents and venture capitalists are appointed to the board of directors. The changes made to amend the appropriate legal documents reflect the newly established capital structure and enshrine venture capitalists' rights. Most closings occur smoothly, with the documents often initialed the day before by official signing; however, some closings are characterized by last minute negotiations and amendments. On occasion, deals fall apart at this juncture. The process of rethinking exit provisions can trigger negative thoughts in entrepreneurs.

There are different ways of dealing with the payment for the acquired shares and the issuance of the share certificates. It is possible to reach a complete conclusion of the deal at closing. Venture capitalists bring a certified cheque issued by the bank to the firm (in the case of a capital increase) or to existing shareholders (in the case of a share purchase) and the firm issues certificates of ownership. The new owners are subsequently entered into the company's register. However, the flow of capital and the issuance of share certificates can be delayed. Venture capitalists may sign a subscription agreement and agree to pay for the shares a few days later. The share certificates are issued when venture capitalists actually pay for the shares in accordance with the subscription agreement (note that in some jurisdictions, no share certificates are issued and ownership is reflected by registering the new owners in the company's register and, subsequently, in the court register). Other scenarios are also possible at the time of closing. For example, the parties may enter into an escrow agreement and delay the payment of capital until some conditions are met.

During legal closing, the parties involved are represented by lawyers. The lawyers ensure that the parties are satisfied over the closing conditions or the conditions precedent to closing; they are also responsible for filing changes to the firm's constitutional documents. Lawyers also draft appropriate board and shareholders' resolutions that are signed at closing to reflect the new ownership structure and the division of power among different shareholder groups.

Legal Documents

There are at least four standard legal documents used in venture capital closing that need to be drawn or amended: the firm's constitutional documents, the shareholders' agreement, the management agreement, and the registration rights agreement. The relationship between the shareholders and the firm is regulated in the firm's constitutional documents (articles of association, memoranda of association, legal deeds, trust agreements, charters, etc.). These constitutional documents are formal regulations governing the relations between shareholders, directors, and management and are commonly filed with courts. The constitutional documents outline the procedures for operating the firm's internal affairs. In many jurisdictions, they are required for the legal establishment of the firm (in some jurisdictions and in certain legal forms of a business, shareholders are given time to file the constitutional documents after registering the firm). Constitutional documents include information pertaining to share issuance, voting rights, dividends rights, restrictions, approvals, and so on, and are developed on the basis of the business law commensurate with the appropriate legal jurisdiction (Companies Act, Commercial Code, etc.). They often supplement local laws in areas where it leaves them operational flexibility, enabling the shareholders to establish specific legal processes reflecting their unique circumstances. These laws can be amended by shareholders' resolutions provided that they meet the voting restrictions included in the general business law or in the documents themselves (shareholders may increase voting thresholds above those anticipated by law). Constitutional documents are not private documents and may be viewed by banks and other financial institutions, management and employees, business partners and stakeholders (i.e., unions, suppliers), the legal system, consultants, and advisors.

In a situation where the number of shareholders is small and there are multiple issues to manage, shareholders may choose to supplement the firm's constitutional documents with a shareholders' agreement. This agreement provides significant assistance to the shareholders in managing and controlling the affairs of the business. The shareholders' agreement is one of the most important documents in venture capital contracting as it directs and guides partners' conduct. The document typically includes clauses related to management decisions and approvals, transfer of shares, dividend policy, standard shareholders' rights (preemptive rights, rights-of-first refusal, etc.), voting control mechanisms (i.e., flip-over events), voting provisions, exit procedures (i.e., drag-along rights), dividend policy, information rights, dispute resolution, share adjustment mechanisms, representations and warranties, appointment of directors, and so on. This document is private and strictly confidential—it is not available for public inspection. It also outlines any conditions precedent to closing that need to be fulfilled prior to the deal being consummated; these may include the completion of due diligence, management contracts, insurance policies, and so on.

The signing of the management agreement must occur prior to the actual transfer of any capital by the venture capital firm. The management agreement is signed by the key members of the management team and often includes agreements made with the founders (who are often a part of the management board). It defines key managerial compensations (including performance expectations, bonuses, and stock option programs), obligations, grounds and covenants for termination (for cause and not-for-cause), non-compete clauses, and intellectual property protection clauses. The employment package also includes "key-men" insurance, which insures the lives of key executives with all proceeds payable to the firm.

The registration rights agreement provides venture capitalists with the right to require the firm to prepare, file, and maintain a registration statement on the appropriate stock exchange at its own expense in order to achieve the sale of shares to the public in the initial public offering (should venture capitalists wish to do this). Filing a registration statement is one of the key steps in the IPO process. There may also be other documents drafted at the time of legal closing, such as a business plan (many provisions of the shareholders' agreement are grounded in the business plan), a subscription agreement (where venture capitalists agree to purchase shares and provide payment for them), an escrow agreement (where the payment for acquired shares is deposited into a third party's account and released upon the satisfaction of outlined conditions), a side agreement (a contract made outside of publicly known documents or contract law), and a comfort letter (a document outlining moral commitments, e.g., an entrepreneur's intention with respect to an exit).

Internal Requirements for Venture Capitalists

The legal closing triggers venture capitalists to conclude their internal process, ultimately leading to the transfer of capital. The process begins with an internal resolution made by the venture capital firm's investment committee. The committee passes the resolution as a formality, as the deal and its legal terms have been discussed many times earlier in the process and the deal has already been officially approved (albeit without formal paper work). The resolution outlines any concerns that the committee has regarding the deal; these concerns are phrased as guidelines or references for venture capitalists.

The last part of the resolution usually relates to the preparation of the custodian bank instruction letter. This letter is forwarded to the venture capital fund's designated bank (where cash draw-downs from limited partners are deposited), a financial institution, or a trust in order to instruct it to send the appropriate amount of capital to the investee firm. If there is no sufficient capital in the fund's account, venture capitalists must issue a notice of draw-down to their limited partners (venture capitalists normally maintain sufficient amounts of cash to fund at least two deals with an average anticipated deal size). The custodian letter specifies the amount of cash, the number and type of securities acquired by the venture capital fund, and the date of anticipated completion of the cash transfer; it also outlines the details of the receiving bank. The receipt of the custodian letter by the bank triggers the transfer of cash.

The last step in the process is the receipt of share certificates by the custodian bank. Share certificates are held in deposit by the bank on behalf of the limited partners. These shares are converted into cash at the time of the investee firm's exit or can be distributed *in specie* at the time of the fund's closure if it is not successful in liquidating its assets.

Questions to Consider

1. Discuss limitations of relying on legal documentation in legal closing.
2. Differentiate between distributive and integrative negotiating approaches. Which method is more appropriate for venture capital negotiations?
3. What are the most common trading opportunities in venture capital negotiations?
4. Under what circumstances should entrepreneurs seek assistance from external advisors during venture capital negotiations?
5. Describe the major steps in legal closing for venture capitalists.

Temasek Holdings

Key characteristics

Year founded:	1974
Founding partners:	Richard Magnus, Halimah Yacob, Pang Cheng Liam, Rajamanickam Vemala, Hohd Salleh Marican, Benedict Cheong, and Goh Yong Siang
Number of limited partners:	N/A
Geographic coverage:	Asia (3 offices) and South America (2)
Headquarter location:	Singapore
Focus (if any):	Asia region
Funds under management:	$172 billion
Number of completed deals/ IPO exits:	N/A/N/A
Private/public:	Private
Most publicly recognized deals:	Bank of China, Standard Chartered, Singapore Telecommunications, Singapore Airlines, Singapore Power
Number of investment professionals:	~380

Temasek Holdings is one of the largest investment firms in Asia. Over 75 percent of the firm's investment focuses on the regions of Singapore (31 percent of total investment), North Asia (27 percent), and South Asia (7 percent); the remaining amount is invested in OECD countries. The firm actively manages $172 billion of assets.

Temasek's investment activity revolves around four major themes: transforming economies (pursuing industries that correlate with economic transformation), growing the middle class (investing into firms that are fueled by a growing affluence in the middle class), deepening comparative advantages (increasing the market potential of firms with strong comparative advantage), and supporting emerging champions (supporting absolute market leaders). This approach to investment has led Temasek to commit about 33 percent of its funds to financial services, 26 percent to telecommunications and media firms, and 13 percent to transportation and logistics businesses. Temasek has achieved an average return of 16 percent compounded annually since its inception.

A total of 380 investment professionals from 22 countries affect Temasek's investment strategy. Its staff operates from 5 different countries (China, India, Vietnam, Brazil, and Mexico). The company takes pride in making strong social contributions; it established Temasek Cares, a one-hundred-million-dollar public foundation, to assist underprivileged, poor, disabled, and needy families in the Singapore region.

Source: *www.temasekholdings.com.*

Chapter 9

Monitoring

Once the investee firm has been funded, venture capitalists focus on the following key considerations: maintaining the operational efficiency of the business, developing the business according to the pre-agreed upon business plan, achieving operational and financial milestones, and performing operational reviews and audits. The achievement of operating efficiencies anticipated in the business plan is reflected in the strength of operating margins (at EBITDA and EBIT levels) and cash flows. Monitoring these financial parameters ensures that the business is unlikely to experience any financial surprises that may require the business to restructure, make changes to the management team, or inject additional capital. The agreed upon business plan effectively forms an "operational bible" for key stakeholders in the business, including entrepreneurs, venture capitalists, and management. The business plan outlines key operational milestones that need to be met at every facet of business development if the business is to achieve its long-term goals.

Management, owners, and venture capitalists actively scan the industry in which their firm operates. The main purpose of this activity is to ensure that the firm's competitive position is strong, that there is a good match between the firm's core competencies and market opportunities, and that the target customers are well served. In addition, scanning the external environment allows for the evaluation of opportunities that were not anticipated in the original business plan. These opportunities may include new product or service development, acquisition or merger opportunities, new strategic partnerships or alliances, and geographic expansions. All shareholders must carefully evaluate these developments, as capturing new opportunities is likely to require additional resources (both financial and human). The evaluation of these external opportunities must not undermine the value of the core business; the business needs to be financially strong, have addressable operating risks, and be well-managed or else new opportunities will aggravate existing operating risks. A strong execution of these activities is reflected at the time of exit, which represents the ultimate test of success in developing and growing the business.

Four aspects of venture capital investment make it necessary for venture capitalists to be active investors: asymmetry of information, an extended period of illiquidity, high entrepreneurial and business risks, and the inability to predict future business challenges. Any asymmetry of information that venture capitalists are faced with throughout the investment process can cause significant agency risks, and an extended period of illiquidity can result in a questionable exit scenario or returns. The high entrepreneurial and business risks associated with the firms in which venture capitalists invest are equally problematic. Venture capitalists, like entrepreneurs and management, are unable to predict the future of a business. In order to reflect current market conditions and changes in business opportunities, business plans, operational goals and shareholders' agreements need to be regularly revisited and revised after the initial deal is closed.

This chapter focuses on two specific aspects of venture capital monitoring. The first section focuses on being an effective director to a single deal. In this scenario, venture capitalists aim to maximize a single deal's value. Venture capitalists, however, are also mindful of the fact that their firms are comprised of a collection of deals. Given that a venture capital fund has limited financial and human resources, it needs to optimize its use of these resources across all of its portfolio firms.

Corporate Governance and Venture Capital

Recent financial abuses around the world have reignited discussion on the principles related to corporate governance. Public debates, legal proceedings, and social outrage have spurred government involvement in this matter. Legislators in different countries have focused on introducing corporate conduct standards aimed at adopting a set of commonly accepted corporate governance principles that treat all shareholders equally. These standards include the establishment of corporate standards for accountability and control over management, the improvement of the transparency of financial reporting, and resolving inherent conflicts of interest. For venture capitalists, there is perhaps another reason to focus on corporate governance—strong corporate governance can help firms optimize their financial performance.

Corporate governance initiatives are related to the agency problem. An agent is a person who has the implied or actual authority to act on behalf of another. The owners whom the agents represent are the principals. In a normal situation, the firm's managers are the agents and the shareholders are the principals. Agents have a legal and ethical responsibility to make decisions that further the interests of the principals. When the interests of the agents and principals conflict, the agency problem results. Firms spend ample time and money to monitor and reduce agency problems; these outlays are called agency costs. One of the most common examples of an agency cost is an accounting audit of the firm's financial statements.

The agency problem arises in the venture capital setting for at least three reasons. The first relates to information asymmetry, which occurs when both management and the founders have more data or better access to information than venture capitalists. The founders, by virtue of starting up the business, have superior knowledge of the firm and direct lines of communication to staff at different levels of the organizational structure. Management is involved in the business on a daily basis and has the best and most accurate access to information. Venture capitalists, on the other hand, receive monthly or quarterly reports that may or may not include all relevant information. While venture capitalists receive audited financial statements at the end of the fiscal year, these financial accounts are aggregated, the auditor's opinions are brief and standardized, and some of the operational statistics may be missing. Second, the goals and interests of venture capitalists and management may be mismatched. It is important to note that both the founders and venture capitalists have significant ownership stakes in the business and their goals may be well aligned; of course, there are also multiple instances in which their objectives will diverge. In such situations, a conflict may arise vis-à-vis management. For example, management may be reluctant to seek and support exit initiatives if it means that the new buyer can replace the existing management team. Such a situation may significantly shorten management's tenure and reduce its lucrative compensation package. Third, conflicts may arise between venture capitalists, founders, and other shareholders as their circumstances and expectations change. New situations may not be reflected in contractual arrangements. The severity of these conflicts can vary, especially when the financial performance of the firm is poor and the potential payoff for founders and venture capitalists changes from what was originally anticipated. Additionally, the founders may wish to continue with the business and become reluctant to seek an exit as anticipated in the contract. On the other hand, venture capitalists may seek to promptly dispose of the business if its future prospects appear weak and they are unlikely to receive any significant proceeds from the deal.

Venture capitalists use a wide range of techniques—including incentives, punishments, and managerial processes—to align the interests of management and founders and achieve a "win-win" situation for all stakeholders. These mechanisms aim to align the common interests of all stakeholders, to reduce asymmetric information advantages of one party over another, and to curtail opportunistic behavior. The mechanisms may be formal (e.g., board of directors' meetings, legal documents such as the shareholders' agreement or the firm's constitutional documents, requests for additional information, etc.) or informal (off-site meetings, business correspondence, informal meetings with other staff, field visits to exhibitions, trade shows, trade conferences, etc.).

The definition of corporate governance has evolved over the years and varies from country to country. It can generally be defined as the system or mechanism by which firms are directed or controlled to achieve their objectives, management performance targets, and financial milestones. Corporate governance can be classified into four functions: financial control and accountability, conflict of interest resolution, performance enhancement, and value maximization. On occasion, venture capitalists come across unique ethical issues that cannot be easily classified in one of the categories described earlier and are difficult to deal with (see an interesting ethical case in box 9.1).

Financial control and accountability is an essential function in any firm. This function is often fulfilled by the appointment of

Box 9.1 Ethical considerations in venture capital: Russkoye Radio—pay or not to pay

Russkoye Radio FM is a Moscow-based local broadcaster. Alexei Obornikov, Russkoye Radio's founder (80 percent shareholding), and Natasha Strelaya, the company's managing director (20 percent), currently own the business. The station attracts around 20 percent of the local advertising market and has a listenership of around 7 percent. It broadcasts from one 1-kW transmitter and has a technical reach of 2.8 million listeners or 25 percent of Moscow's population. Obornikov acquired Russkoye Radio for RB* 25 million (about $1 million). He subsequently obtained $5 million in venture capital financing from two local venture capital firms. The proceeds were dedicated toward building the super-regional network consisting of leading local radio stations in key cities in Russia.

The company achieved growth in excess of 40 percent per annum in the last two years. In 2005, it had sales of RB 6.3 million and reached RB 10.7 million in 2006, which was 15 percent above budget. The business was profitable: the EBITDA margin was 15 percent in 2004, 13 percent in 2005, and 28 percent in 2006. Russkoye Radio was established in 2000 and has a seven-year broadcasting license, which was due for renewal in the middle of 2007. Given that the station has adhered to the conditions of its broadcasting license, Russkoye Radio's shareholders did not expect any problems with the renewal process. Russkoye Radio focuses on Russian's fastest growing sectors of the economy (financial services, automotive, telecommunication, and retail sectors). Sales to these sectors account for approximately 40 percent of total revenue. Russkoye Radio's clients include leading international and Russian companies in these sectors such as IKEA—Swedish furniture store, Auchan—French grocery chain, and Rustel—Russian mobile telephony operator.

In contrast to the open playing field in print media, the radio and TV broadcasting market is subject to stringent regulations. The key element of broadcasting regulations in Russia was the 1995 Russia Audio Visual Law. It determines the status of public broadcasters, the licensing, the programming obligations of broadcasters, the registration of retransmission of program services by cable operators, and finally the collection of broadcasting fees. The main regulatory authority in the industry is the Russia National Broadcasting Council (RNBC). Members of this national radio and television board are appointed by parliament with the chairman nominated by the president of Russia.

The transmission of a program service in Russia requires authorization in the form of a license issued by RNBC. This requirement applies to entities that transmit a program service from Russian territory, use a frequency or technical means situated in Russia, and entities established in Russia even when they transmit to Russia from another country. The Audio Visual Law also limits the direct participation of foreign capital in a license to 33 percent. Russian citizens residing in Russia must have majority representation in the governing bodies of the licensee company. In addition, the law stipulates that advertising may not exceed 15 percent of total airtime, with a cap of 12 minutes out of every hour. Finally, the law requires a minimum level of domestically originated programming.

In early 2007, Obornikov was asked to meet with a representative of the Russia National Broadcasting Council. He was told that Russkoye Radio was unlikely to receive an extension of its broadcasting license beyond the year 2007. From his informal sources, Obornikov learned that he would have to transfer $100,000 into an unidentified cash account in Switzerland to secure the license. Obornikov wondered what alternatives he should consider and what to do. He immediately thought of a number of possible solutions (e.g., making the unofficial payment, not paying it, approaching other members of the Council, taking legal action, ignoring the situation entirely), which he wanted to discuss with his venture capital partners.

Ethical Consideration
Ethics, or rather a lack of ethics, is a recurring theme in business and venture capital, especially in emerging markets. Ethical behavior involves "doing the right thing," but defining "the right thing" can be difficult. The problem here relates to how each individual has his or her own set of values. Every society adopts a set of rules or laws that prescribe what it believes to be the "right thing to do." In a sense, laws are a set of rules that reflect the values of the society as a whole, as it has evolved. It is also important to recognize that individuals have the right to disagree on what constitutes the right thing to do. In other words, there may be multiple solutions for ethical issues and challenges, and these solutions will depend on the involved individuals' values. As with most debates that center on ethical and moral questions, there is no definitive answer.

The broader question in this situation is whether ethics are relevant in venture capital. This raises at least two important issues. First, although business errors can be forgiven, ethical errors tend to end careers and terminate future opportunities for venture capitalists. This is because unethical behavior eliminates trust—and without trust, a business cannot operate effectively. Second, the most damaging event a business can experience is the loss of public confidence in its ethical standards. Trust and credibility are essential to achieve success in business in the venture capital industry.

*RB stands for Russian currency—Ruble.

---

an external auditing firm that provides reassurance to management, the board of directors, and shareholders as to the firm's financial performance; this is accomplished in the form of financial audits. Compliance audits, on the other hand, focus on determining whether the firm's managers are following certain procedures, bylaws, and other provisions included in the firm's constitutional documents (articles of association, deeds, charters, etc.). Other reviews, such as operational audits, examine the firm's internal procedures to determine its internal efficiencies. Venture capitalists rely on financial control and accountability for a variety of reasons. For example, they monitor the financial performance against the forecasted budgets and respond to any underperformance. In addition, they understand that their success in achieving a profitable exit is connected to the quality of the financial data provided to potential buyers at the time of a trade sale or the firm's listing on the stock exchange. Venture capitalists also use the financial control function to verify whether entrepreneurs and management are adhering to the terms of legal agreements (e.g., a share adjustment mechanism is based on financial performance and may result in an adjustment of the level of ownership between shareholders). Last, financial controls are used to award management bonuses and stock option programs.

Conflict of interest arises when a stakeholder's actions or intentions have the potential to benefit the personal interest of one or a group of individuals at the expense of other shareholders. The most common instances of conflict of interest involve management or the business owners using the firm's assets and financial resources for their own private use. Other examples include instances in which bonuses or stock options are awarded unjustly, unqualified family members are appointed to senior management positions, and loans or lines of credit are provided to individuals (these off-balance sheet transactions are especially difficult to identify). Some conflicts of interest can arise in the corporate boardroom. Poor corporate oversight, lack of director's independence, and dual CEO-chairman roles are often quoted as the chief reasons for the largest corporate governance failures. Resolving conflicts of interest within investee firms is a prerequisite for a successful investment. Venture capitalists regularly encounter conflicts of interest in the transactions they enter into and understand that unless they resolve these critical issues, their ability to realize full value from the deal may be jeopardized and the distribution of economic value may not be in accordance with the agreed upon deal.

Corporate governance is more than a mechanism for resolving the problems of financial control and conflict of interest; it also places focus on the enhancement of a firm's performance through the directors' impact on strategic decision-making. An effective board of directors is involved in a variety of activities, including helping management to resolve specific business problems while overseeing the firm's strategic direction. Such involvement can take a variety of forms, including occasional active counseling to the CEO and top management, continuous involvement and participation in contemplated projects, helpful assistance to management, and crisis management. Active participation from the board is often associated with a superior level of financial performance. Many academics argue that directors need to be more involved in strategic decision-making processes to ensure the firm's compliance with corporate governance controls and strong market performance. In the context of venture capital, the active involvement of venture capitalists is a must. Active interaction between venture capitalists, management, and founders is a prerequisite for the proper development and implementation of strategy. Venture capitalists regularly participate in decision-making processes involving key personnel, budget approvals, and the development of the strategic plan.

The concepts of performance enhancement and firm's prosperity are inherently connected with value maximization and realization. A well-implemented strategy can translate into a significant increase in sales and profits for the firm, thereby leading to higher business valuation. For venture capitalists, implementing well-developed business strategies creates value. Venture capitalists also engage in "corporate grooming" activities prior to divestment. These activities include simplifying the legal and corporate structure of the firm, negotiating strategic relationships that can increase the value of the firm in the future, and resolving outstanding technical and environmental challenges. Venture capitalists will also occasionally employ external consultants to affect divestment.

Effective Directors

Venture capitalists typically adopt a hands-on participation style with their investee firms through their appointment to the board of directors. Venture capitalists' active participation at the board level carries significant benefits for investee firms. In fact, venture capitalists often cite active participation at the board level as a defining characteristic of venture capital.

The board can be an effective avenue by which to implement monitoring mechanisms to control management and is often critical in introducing corporate governance initiatives and instilling continued focus on financial performance. The value added services venture capitalists provide often reflect their commitment to the firm, which, in turn, increases the quality of communication and its intensity. Boards also offer an excellent venue for interaction between venture capitalists, other shareholders, and management. The level of interaction between the firm and venture capitalists may vary. Firms tend to rely on venture capitalists for business know-how, access to capital, business networks, and experience. In such roles, firms—especially younger ones—become dependent on venture capitalists for a wide range of advice, resulting in resource dependency.

Assistance to a firm can come throughout the normal course of a business or during a crisis or emergency situation. During the normal course of a business, venture capitalists fulfill a number of roles. First, they serve as sources of information. Access to venture capitalist networks (which are comprised of investors, financiers, bankers, and regulators) provides a business with timely access to information, which can become the foundation for strategic decision-making. This, in turn, translates into effective assistance to management when they are developing and revising their business plans. Access to venture capital networks can also lead to strategic alliances or partnerships, as venture capitalists have specialized knowledge of specific industries or sectors. Second, venture capitalists promote the efficient and effective use of the firm's available resources. This orientation toward optimizing resources can translate into new product development, the timely introduction of products and services to the marketplace, and an increase in export activities. Third, venture capitalists are effective at identifying management gaps, filling them promptly, and building well-rounded and talented management teams. Venture capitalists are able to do this by tapping into their wide network of contacts, which often include previous investee firms and competent managers with whom they have worked. A change in management most often occurs in the areas of finance and accounting. Venture capitalists also help to design compensation packages for senior and middle managers and view their being involved on the board as a way in which to provide complementary services to management. Fourth, venture capitalists are sensitive to issues related to exit. The presence of a venture capitalist alone can confirm the quality of the management team and the firm in trade sales and IPO situations.

In special circumstances or during emergency situations, the role of venture capitalists can shift. Venture capitalists may step in as interim CEOs or managers in order to solve certain business or operational problems. Since the role of venture capitalists is not to get involved in the day-to-day running of the business, these assignments continue until replacement managers can be found and rarely exceed six months.

It is important to note that there is a point in the relationship between the founders and venture capitalists at which the monitoring costs outweigh their potential benefits. Ultimately, there are limits to which venture capitalists are likely to support their investee firms. In such situations, venture capitalists may decide to force a fire sale (a sale at below invested capital), conduct an orderly winding-down of the business, or force its bankruptcy.

Effective Venture Capital Directing

There are at least four main categories of responsibilities for venture capitalists: oversight, review, compliance, and leadership. Oversight relates to the task of monitoring the performance of the management team and the CEO. CEOs and managers are held accountable for performance. Management is required to prepare, revise, and resubmit their strategic and operational plans to the board of directors and is held responsible for the achievement of these plans. Oversight also involves venture capitalists using the firm's management as a sounding board for their ideas and plans. The review process relates to the proper allocation of resources and the achievement of financial performance as agreed upon in the business plan. These tasks are achieved in the context of the existing external environment. Changes to the external environment often force the business to change the way it conducts its affairs. Knowing the industry allows directors to be prepared for more timely responses to windows of opportunity and emerging market niches. Compliance relates to adherence to various internal documents and external laws pertinent to the firm. The internal legal documents are likely to include the shareholders' agreement, articles of association or deeds, and any internal bylaws. The external documents influencing the conduct of the firm include relevant commercial and civil laws, environmental protection acts, government regulations, taxation laws, and so on. For venture capitalists, directorship also means providing leadership, establishing policies and procedures for different business scenarios, and being accountable to the firm and its limited partners. The process requires that appropriate controls and monitoring capabilities are in place. In short, having a place on the board requires venture capitalists to strike an appropriate balance between financial performance now and in the future.

Committees are becoming increasingly popular within venture capital financing, in part because they represent an excellent way to allocate responsibilities among board members and make more efficient use of their time and expertise. The firm will usually have an audit committee and a compensation committee; another popular example is the executive committee. The audit committee focuses on the oversight of financial reporting and financial disclosure. In short, the committee ensures that the firm's accounting is kept in accordance with generally accepted accounting principles (GAAP) or international accounting standards (IAS). The main tasks of the audit committee include overseeing the following functions: financial reporting and disclosure, compliance with laws and regulations, accounting policies and procedures, internal financial control systems and internal auditing systems, and the appointment and oversight of external auditors. The compensation committee focuses on establishing a compensation strategy for the CEO and the senior management team. This committee effectively approves the amounts and types of compensation (including cash and equity based remuneration), reviews the overall effectiveness of the compensation systems, ascertains the appropriateness of compensation packages based on the firm's actual financial performance, and approves any employment agreements, severance, and retirement packages. The work of the committee is done in consultation with the full board. The executive committee functions on behalf of the entire board in special situations or under certain circumstances, such as in times of emergency or crisis or in the interim period between regularly scheduled board meetings. The committee provides recommendations for ratification by the complete board. Other committees (e.g., finance committee, board development committee, fundraising committee, resource development committee) also provide opportunities for venture capitalists to interact with members of the management team.

All members of the board of directors, including venture capitalists, have a fiduciary responsibility to act in the best interest of the firm; this requires board members to not only exercise care of duty and show loyalty toward the firm, but to act in good faith. To act in good faith means to use the privilege of membership on the board of directors for purposes benefiting the firm and not for personal gain, and to avoid any personal or corporate conflicts of interest. For venture capitalists, the hierarchy of responsibility also extends to the protection of their own class of shareholders and limited partners. When in conflict, at least theoretically, venture capitalists' fiduciary responsibility to the firm should prevail. However, venture capitalists' desire to achieve maximum profits at exit can sometimes come into conflict with a desire by other stakeholders to grow the business. If things are going well, other shareholders, especially the founders, may wish to avoid the exit scenario in spite of the fact that they may have already agreed upon a specific exit scheme.

Active interaction with the firm's CEO, who is the center of gravity in the firm, is a prerequisite for being an effective director. It is important for venture capitalists that their relationship with the CEO is strong at the time of board meetings and during informal sessions. Venture capitalists often volunteer to participate in committee activities and seek additional assignments. Generally, they possess expertise in at least one specific area that the CEO considers valuable to both himself and to the firm. Sometimes, venture capitalists over-interpret their role and act as if they run the business rather than encouraging and advising the CEO; this often occurs in situations where the venture capitalists come from a corporate background, where they were senior managers or even CEOs themselves.

Numerous skills are required to be an effective director. Such personal qualities as integrity, independence, objectivity, sensitivity, and commitment are key considerations. In addition, venture capitalists must possess ethical awareness, honesty, accountability, confidentiality, and responsibility. However, a group of individuals with strong business acumen and strong personal characteristics may not constitute an effective board. The board's performance depends on the quality of communication and interaction between its members and those members' desire to work as a team. Individuals with financial and managerial skills as well as strong personal attributes are usually the most effective members.

When venture capitalists make their initial investment, the board may need to be restructured. This change can occur early in post-closing when venture capitalists assume their board seats for the first time and can result in a number of challenges. Boards of entrepreneurial firms often include the founder's family members or friends, as well as the firm's initial financiers (likely private individuals) or local angel investors. Venture capitalists often recommend that the founders change the composition of the board of directors (in some cases, this will be one of the conditions of closing the deal). The number of seats may be reduced, as the logistics of scheduling a meeting and maintaining open communication channels between shareholders can prove difficult if the board exceeds seven members. If the venture capital deal is syndicated, a lead investor will often assume a seat on the board, while other venture capitalists may secure "observer" (nonvoting) seats.

When the board functions properly and effectively, the opinions offered by its members can be instrumental to the development and success of the firm. On the other hand, dysfunctional boards can create significant problems for the CEO, the management team, and the shareholders. Boards generally try to pass resolutions and reach agreement by consensus, but if a decision needs to be made by a vote and different points of view prevail, the board can become dysfunctional. There are numerous moments in the life of an investment when the board is tested and relationships between shareholders are strained. In certain cases, the CEO may have to be replaced. This is quite common in a situation where the investee firm develops quickly and the required skill set for the CEO changes very rapidly. If the CEO recognizes his shortcomings, the situation can be easily resolved; if the CEO continues to believe in his skills despite the noticeable underperformance of the firm, the situation can grow increasingly difficult to manage. The case gets even more complex when the CEO is the founder and the largest shareholder. Shareholders' objectives may also evolve over time. This evolution often relates to divestment, especially in cases of substantial financial underperformance by the firm. In such cases, the fact that venture capitalists often hold preferred shares (which provide them with liquidation preference) may result in partial or full cash recovery for them and no capital recovery for the remaining shareholders. Such an eventuality normally acts as a strong motivator for the other shareholders and quickly works to destroy any goodwill between venture capitalists and the remaining parties. Issuing additional equity at a lower valuation than the last round can also negatively affect board relationships. Such a down-round can dramatically dilute the stake of any shareholder, including management.

Private and Public Boards

There are significant differences for venture capitalists between being a director of a private firm and that of a public firm. When the investee firm is private, venture capitalists enjoy significant minority shareholder protections and controls, including the right to change the management team (i.e., flip-over events), the ability to withstand reduction in business valuations (i.e., ratchets), and the ability to affect exit (i.e., drag-along rights). They also have strong approval rights in key decision-making areas of the business. Many of these protections are written into the shareholders' agreements and the firm's constitutional documentation.

Once the venture capitalists' investee firm becomes public, however, venture capitalists lose most of (if not all of) their protections, beginning with preferred shares (which are converted into common shares), management controls, exit mechanisms, and approval rights. In addition, when the shares are initially quoted, venture capitalists' ability to dispose of them may be compromised by underwriters. All public shareholders are also subject to the regulation regime of the local stock exchange and additional regulations (i.e., the Sarbanes-Oxley Act). Directors representing venture capital firms are also limited in their ability to dispose of shares in a public firm.

Monitoring and Managing Information

Venture capitalists generally monitor the performance of their investee firms by analyzing a confidential package of information prepared by the firm (these reports may be monthly or quarterly). Venture capitalists also ask for annual performance evaluations and summaries. The interval of reporting varies. Generally, venture capitalists require monthly reporting from younger firms or firms that have experienced operational or financial challenges and quarterly reports from mature firms. The reports generally include financial and operational updates. The key objective of venture capitalists is to receive a complete set of financial statements. Additional information on the firm's operational performance can include a new customer list, new product lists or new lines added, the markets entered, changes to the distribution channels, new competition entering the market, the activities of competitors, and any significant pricing changes. In short, the report must cover all relevant information that may impact the risk of the venture, its financial performance, and exit potential. In addition, the firm may report different activities as requested by the shareholders' agreement or articles of association. Annual reports include similar information to that found in monthly or quarterly reports. In addition, venture capitalists require audited financial statements and an annual business plan for the next fiscal year that is a part of a rolling three- or five-year plan. Information from the board packages, as well as any other information obtained during board meetings, is commonly used by venture capitalists to prepare their internal summaries for the fund's supervisory board and limited partners.

Many venture capital firms also insist that their investee firms undergo an external appraisal at least once every two or three years. An external consultant, either known to venture capitalists as an expert in the field or from a reputable consulting firm, usually performs this task. The purpose of such a review is to perform a 360-degree audit of the firm and compare it to other industry benchmarks and leading market players. Many venture capitalists hold the view that even if the external review generates one or more good ideas in terms of executing the business plan or increasing operational efficiencies, innovation initiatives, and new product or service lines, the exercise proves worthwhile. Such reviews may offer additional investment opportunities and profits for the firm. Other venture capitalists are skeptical of such reviews on the assumption that they are unlikely to discover new facts. These skeptics, however, commonly resort to such reviews when their investee firm experiences operational or financial challenges.

It is unlikely that venture capitalists will know everything about their investee firms; often, venture capitalists wish to boil the information down to a few key facts. Venture capitalists monitor firms by reviewing the vital signs of the business and examining its key milestones. Any achievements are compared with the original business plan—the foundation upon which venture capitalists made their investment. All the members of the board, including the CEO, generally agree on the vital signs of the business. However, these key matrices vary from business to business. In a marketing firm, the key vital signs can include profitability per consumer. In the restaurant business, they may include average ticket price and "turns per seat." In the radio business, key markers relate to listenership data; in the software business, they involve new systems installed, the deal closing life cycle, and backlog. The reporting systems and the vital signs venture capitalists monitor change over time. This change is reflective of the firm's evolution through different stages of its life cycle, changes in the external environment, market and operational risks, and the firm's capital needs. The reporting is usually qualitative and descriptive.

Troubled Investments

Venture capital is about making investments in a wide spectrum of firms in different industries with varying degrees of risk. It is a game of averages. Most venture capitalists appear to follow a "two-six-two" formula: two superior deals, six single-digit return or no return investments, and two write-offs. Others quote a more successful track record of performance that follows a "three-three-four" pattern—more successful deals, but also more problem situations. In any case, at any point in the life of the fund, venture capitalists are likely to experience financial distress in one or more of their investee firms.

The causes of financial distress in firms vary, but generally fall into one of the following categories: poor management, unwise expansion, intense competition, excessive debt, massive litigation, or signing unfavorable contracts. Most distress cases involve cash emergencies. The "silent" warning signs include delays in receiving financial information, frequent personnel changes, changes to accounting policies, restatement of financials, customer complaints about product or service quality, or recurring visits to the bank to seek additional lines of credit. More subtle cases become visible when venture capitalists examine board packages showing deteriorating trends in the firm's financial performance. These trends include declining margins, increasing losses, declining market share, increasingly high "cash-burn," and deteriorating financial ratios.

Depending on the severity of the problem, venture capitalists have a variety of possible options from which to choose. For one, they can engage in a turnaround (or workout effort). Such an initiative is likely to involve significant time pressures on venture capitalists and require additional financing. In such a scenario, issues related to management may need to be dealt with, including potentially firing the CEO. In an extreme situation, one of the directors may need to step in as interim CEO or general manager. Second, if the firm's financial performance is deteriorating, but the challenges do not threaten an immediate loss of the firm's liquidity, venture capitalists may decide to sell the firm (most likely through a "fire sale"). A fire sale involves selling the business for less than venture capitalists invested in it and requires venture capitalists to take a partial write-off on the deal. Such a disposal may require venture capitalists to invoke some of their rights (i.e., drag-along rights, liquidation preferences, voting flip-over events). Depending on the liquidation preference negotiated in the deal, different classes of shareholders will receive different payback percentages or no paybacks at all if the sale amount is low. Third, when the firm's financial situation is beyond recovery, venture capitalists may decide to "pull the plug" on the business. While this is an emotionally difficult decision for venture capitalists, it can sometimes be the only available solution to dire financial problems. The process involves filing for bankruptcy and the orderly winding-down of business activities. In some situations, venture capitalists may dissolve the firm while the firm still has cash in the bank. In these cases, the role of the board changes. Members of the board can face lawsuits from parties unhappy with the turn of events and significant legal consultations may be required to address issues related to credits, financial institutions, employees, and customers.

Troubled investments make it difficult for venture capitalists to maintain their composure. Most venture capitalists pride themselves on their ability to diagnose firms and investment opportunities. If an investee firm gets into trouble, the reputation of the venture capitalists involved will suffer. Many venture capitalists also tend to second-guess their analysis and decisions, and may have a problem "pulling the trigger." In addition, venture capitalists have a natural tendency to "protect" their investments and reject any sensible criticisms of their deals. That said, venture capitalists instinctively understand that unexpected events represent significant career risk.

Turnaround or Workout

Turnaround or workout is a formal process or approach used to assess the firm's situation and to develop clear recommendations for the firm to move forward. For venture capitalists, a workout may include a troubled or underperforming firm. The main objective for venture capitalists is to minimize the loss from the deal and maximize the return. The following sections focus on the basic steps and key considerations involved in a turnaround or workout situation. The steps in turnaround are relatively simple, though the specifics differ from case to case. The key steps include due diligence, background preparation, developing a plan, and implementing a plan.

Workout Due Diligence

No matter what venture capitalists decide, the first step in any crisis situation is to understand the severity of the operational and financial challenges facing the firm. The focus shifts from growth to survival. Venture capitalists first conduct a thorough due diligence of the firm in a very short period of time. This process involves the use of external advisors (operational, accounting, and legal) to pinpoint issues and recognize key problems and is likely to involve a review of the firm's financial statements (especially the cash flow, the cash balances, and the burn rate). The process helps venture capitalists to determine how much time they actually have before the firm loses liquidity. The goal is to focus on cash generation and preservation, but in most cases it costs money to cut costs and recover sales. The income statement is then reviewed to understand the true costs and expenses associated with fixing the problem. During this stage, venture capitalists also focus on legal documentation, with an aim to thoroughly revisit the shareholders' agreement and the firm's constitutional documents in light of new circumstances.

Venture capitalists know the importance of conducting their own due diligence rather than relying on someone else's findings and conclusions. As a consequence, they are actively involved in discussions with management, employees, and external advisors.

Background Preparation

Turnaround or workout situations require the cooperation of all stakeholders, including the board, all shareholders, management, employees, customers, bankers, suppliers, and other creditors. It is critical that venture capitalists understand which stakeholders are willing to be involved in the process and which will be pulling in their own direction. Once this is determined, venture capitalists normally keep all of their supporters informed of both good and bad developments. Venture capitalists understand the importance of maintaining their commitments. If a promise has been made to repay a certain portion of the loan on a specific date, venture capitalists need to hold to their commitment in order to keep bankers interested in the process.

One of the most critical steps of the process involves determining the role of the current management team. Most managers are unfamiliar with crisis management and lack experience in turnaround situations; in some cases, they may even be responsible for the crisis at hand. If venture capitalists decide to terminate the CEO and/ or other members of the senior management team, they generally select an interim CEO in advance and line-up any additional support that the remaining management team might require. Terminating the CEO generally causes some delays in the implementation of the plan, as venture capitalists, along with their lawyers, need to decide upon the reason for termination (cause or not-for-cause), prepare appropriate termination documents, brief the interim CEO, prepare a press release, and release internal communication statements. Depending on the complexity of the situation, this process can require a significant amount of time. If the option to terminate the CEO is chosen, any actions are usually performed swiftly. If multiple terminations are to occur, venture capitalists perform them all at once. Experienced venture capitalists are aware of the potential disruptions caused by terminating the CEO.

Developing a Plan

While the specifics of a plan differ from case to case, there are simple rules venture capitalists try to follow when developing one. The turnaround plan is generally simple and centers on a small number of priorities. This plan aims to bring immediate stability to the firm. The major priority is cash management. Venture capitalists will focus on establishing control over cash, prioritize payments, and co-sign every expense to be paid. Others priorities include meetings and negotiations with customers, suppliers, and, most importantly, bankers. Meetings with these stakeholders are critical to the development of future steps.

The workout plan may include selling a part or a division of the firm, reorienting the business, or entirely changing its focus. This plan may involve the provision of further financing to the firm. In order to simplify the plan's implementation, venture capitalists seek to ensure that all stakeholders reach a consensus over the proposed actions.

Plan Implementation

Once the plan has been developed and all parties are in agreement with its contents, the plan is executed. Implementation efforts generally focus on cash management, right-sizing the business, and maintaining open lines of communication with all stakeholders.

Heavy focus is placed on meeting priorities and achieving operational and financial milestones.

Unexpected Rounds of Financing

The investee firm may require an emergency round of financing. Venture capitalists' approach toward dealing with such a situation depends upon whether or not their partners choose to participate in this round of financing. Figure 9.1 provides a brief overview of possible responses or routes available to venture capitalists in four specific situations.

If all of the shareholders, including venture capitalists, agree that an emergency round of financing is necessary and agree to provide it (Quadrant 1), their actions will be swift and decisive (this is usually to the benefit of the firm). The shareholders will generally invest on a pro rata basis. If the shareholders agree that they will not provide additional financing to the ailing firm, the firm may face imminent failure (Quadrant 4). The objectives of the involved parties may diverge with respect to cash recovery. In these situations, venture capitalists will rely on their liquidation preferences and try to minimize their loss from the deal. The other shareholders and management, usually holding common stock, may not receive any proceeds.

There are other scenarios also likely to cause strain in the relationship between venture capitalists and other shareholders. If the other shareholders cannot participate in the emergency round of financing (Quadrant 2), venture capitalists are likely to issue the shares at lower prices, effectively diluting the stake of the remaining

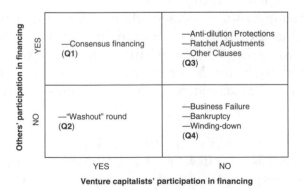

Figure 9.1   Venture capitalists' potential actions vis-à-vis the behavior of other shareholders.

shareholders to zero. Venture capitalists assume that if other share-holders are not willing to provide additional capital, they are effectively saying that the business is worthless (as the business is likely to fail without an injection of additional capital). Another problem that venture capitalists must address is how to provide an incentive to management, which is negatively affected by the washout round, to react positively to a dilutive round of financing. If their goal is to retain key managers, venture capitalists need to offer them additional shares. The allocation of these shares is usually based on financial performance and the achievement of milestones. Before proceeding with such a drastic scenario, venture capitalists attempt to confirm that bridge financing is not available from other sources. Down-rounds are potential legal minefields for venture capitalists, who are likely to encounter conflicts of interest as directors on the board and as shareholders (they owe fiduciary responsibilities to both of these capacities). Ironically, the legal risks can be magnified if the firm actually succeeds in its turnaround efforts, as the diluted shareholders can sue over a breach of fiduciary duty when approving a wash-out round of financing.

If venture capitalists are not able to participate in additional financing (Quadrant 3), they are likely to rely upon their built-in protections. The key clauses here are anti-dilution protections and the ratchet mechanism. The anti-dilution protections protect venture capitalists if the firm's valuation is reduced significantly during the next round of financing (venture capitalists normally introduce a price floor on the value of the business). Ratchets, either full or weighted, can adjust the entry valuation of the firm on the basis of its financial performance or value. If the firm is underperforming, venture capitalists are likely be entitled to additional shares. Venture capitalists can also rely on liquidation protections (based on preferred convertible shares) and drag-along rights, as well as their ability to control the board through voting flip-over rights.

Any capital provided by venture capitalists is likely to have a number of conditions attached to it. The key concern for venture capitalists is to decide under what conditions and circumstances they are willing to provide additional capital to the firm. First, venture capitalists expect to receive a revised, more realistic, and achievable set of financial projections. The financial projections allow venture capitalists to judge the value of the business if it survives the turnaround or workout. Second, an emergency round of financing usually causes venture capitalists to have serious reservations about the management team. The key questions here are: Is the firm still basically sound? Is industry-wide turbulence affecting all firms? Is the firm out of cash or out of business? Is this a case of "good money after bad"? Third, venture capitalists are likely to revisit their existing legal protections and reconsider whether they are still sufficient. They are also likely to insist upon additional protections related to business valuation, control, and additional preferences, or require changes to or strengthening of the management team. To proceed with any additional financing, venture capitalists need formal approvals. This process requires venture capitalists to prepare internal documents and seek approvals from their investment committees. Such internal requirements place additional pressures on venture capitalists to act swiftly.

Valuing Portfolio Firms

As a part of their investment monitoring, venture capitalists report the status of their portfolio firms to their limited partners (this is usually done on a quarterly basis). This disclosure involves reporting the value of each firm in the portfolio. This information is important to both venture capitalists and limited partners. Assigning values to portfolio firms provides limited partners with an overview of how well venture capitalists are performing throughout the value creation process. Through the quarterly exercise of valuation, venture capitalists formally review their deals and set priorities for maximizing the value of their portfolios.

The European Private Equity and Venture Capital Association (EVCA) has been one of the most active organizations in developing and revising the guidelines used by venture capitalists to value portfolio firms. Its standards have been widely adopted around the world, with some minor modifications reflecting the nature of venture capital in different geographic markets. The major difficulty in valuing venture capital deals comes from the fact that these investments are mostly illiquid and the true value of the firm is ultimately determined upon a full and complete exit (i.e., the sales of all shares held by venture capitalists).

The EVCA dictates that the value of firms should be reported on the basis of a fair value, which is defined as "the amount for which an asset can be exchanged between knowledgeable, willing parties in an arm's length transaction." However, without tangible confirmation of the price that may be received for the firm, the process of determining the interim fair value of the firm is subjective. Nevertheless, assigning value rests on a detailed consideration of specific conditions of the business, as well as the specific legal terms upon which the deal was consummated.

The valuation methodology applied by venture capitalists to business valuation reflects the firm's nature of business and the industry, its stage of development, its success in achieving operational and financial milestones, its unique features and circumstances, and the availability of comparable data on the industry. In circumstances in which a deal has been recently closed, using the deal costs as the valuation basis represents a conservative approach to valuation. However, using the cost-based approach to determine the long-term carrying value of the firm can backfire because the firm's value may actually erode over time. If the deal was completed some time ago, the valuation or the price at which another shareholder invested into the firm can be considered as the more prudent means of arriving at a fair value for the business. This methodological approach is even more pronounced if the amount of the new investment was relatively significant, if some or all of the existing shareholders participated in the round at the agreed valuation, and the new shareholders negotiate similar rights and protections as those available to the existing shareholders.

In the absence of any new investments made into the firm, venture capitalists rely on subjective measures. For example, venture capitalists resort to earnings multiples (especially for established businesses). A number of earnings multiples are applied, including price/earnings (P/E), enterprise value/earnings before interest and taxes (EV/EBIT), or enterprise value/earnings before interest, taxes, depreciation, and amortization (EV/EBITDA). These multiples can be used on the basis of the firm's historical (the most conservative approach), present, or perspective financial numbers. Venture capitalists obtain these multiples on the basis of a basket of market-based multiples that come from public firms or recently completed transactions in the private sector. The EVCA guidelines suggest that these earnings multiples and the resulting valuations may be subject to the "marketability discount," which reflects factors such as exit readiness of the existing shareholders and their level of cooperation in the matter, stock market conditions, and the underlying business and financial conditions of the firm. The EVCA suggests that these subjective discounts may be between 10 and 30 percent, depending on circumstances.

For younger firms (given the absence of profits in early years), the discounted cash flow (DCF) method may be a more appropriate method of valuation. However, DCF is only recommended as cross-check methodology for more mature firms and is not to be used as a primary method of valuation. Occasionally, venture capitalists may employ industry valuation benchmarks even though the EVCA does not recommend them as a main valuation method. These benchmarks may include "price per subscriber" (for television businesses), "price per listener" (for radio businesses), "price per bed" (for hospitals or retirement homes businesses), and "price per 1 percent of market share" or "price per volume of output" (for businesses in fast moving consumer goods industries). In the case of firms quoted on the stock exchange, the EVCA suggests quoting the investment on the basis of bid prices. Table 9.1 summarizes valuation methodologies recommended by EVCA in relation to the firm's stage of development.

There may be circumstances upon which venture capitalists decide to reduce the value of the firm. This reduction in value can occur for a number of reasons. First, the investment may be impaired. A firm's value can erode if it is unable to reach specific operational and financial milestones and if its development is lagging behind what is outlined the development plan. Other conditions include significant adverse changes to the firm's business prospects, meaningful

Table 9.1   A summary of the valuation guidelines provided by the European Private Equity and Venture Capital Association

Firm's stage of development	Firm's economic conditions	Suggested valuation methodology	Time limitations
Early-stage deals (seed, start-up)	• Limited revenues • No profits • Poor cash flow	• Cost-based • Price of recent capital increase or share sale • If above not available, discounted cash flow or DCF	• Up to one year • Up to one year after capital increase or share sale
Early-stage (including turnaround, restructuring)	• Some revenues • Limited profits • Limited cash flow	• Cost-based • Price of recent capital increase or share sale • If above not available, industry benchmarks • If above not available, DCF	• Up to one year • Up to one year after capital increase or share sale
Other stages	• Strong revenues • Maintainable profits and cash flows	• Earnings multiples • Price of recent capital increase or share sale	• Up to one year

negative changes to external environments (market, legal environment, economic outlook, regulatory framework, etc.), breaches or defaults on any banking provisions, significant changes to the management team, and the deterioration of general market conditions. Second, confirmation of value erosion can come from market evidence suggesting that subsequent rounds of financing are likely to occur on significantly worse pricing and contractual terms. Venture capitalists may receive preliminary indications from external parties that their investee firm is not as well perceived in the marketplace as they might think it is; these external parties then make preliminary offers to either participate in a capital increase of the firm or in its outright sale. Third, other shareholders may not be in support of exit and actively resist the sale.

Portfolio Optimization and Prioritization

Venture capitalists need to maximize the value of their entire portfolio rather than the value generated by a single firm. To address this concern, venture capitalists internally prioritize deals. This process involves developing certain criteria and using it to allocate firms to different clusters. For venture capitalists, the objective of such an analysis is to place their time and energy into the "winning" firms and to deal effectively with the "losers."

Let's imagine that a venture capital firm has $250 million under management. It has already liquidated 15 of its investments and has received total proceeds equal to $341 million (this is already in excess of the initial capital provided by limited partners). The venture capital firm still has 10 active deals at different stages of development and varying business prospects. The total cost of these investments is equal to $146 million. The fund managers estimate that in the best case scenario (target valuation), the venture capital firm would be able to return $160 million in proceeds from these 10 deals; in a more pessimistic scenario (likely valuation), this number would equal $108 million. Table 9.2 presents a compilation of the fund's investee firms, along with costs and target and likely valuations.

Let's assume that the fund is looking to establish operational priorities to maximize the value of its portfolio. A review of table 9.2 confirms that the composition of the fund's portfolio varies—five deals are likely to lose money (two of which may be total write-offs) and five deals are likely to return at least the cost amount (four of

Table 9.2   A summary of portfolio firms in a sample venture capital fund

Firm type	Cost (million $)	Target valuation (million $)	Likely valuation (million $)
Restaurant[a]	26	50	26
Software developer I[b]	11	11	11
Business incubator [d]	10	2	1
Telecom [d]	3	1	0
Building materials[c]	8	8	4
Software developer II[d]	18	1	0
Radio station[c]	11	11	7
TV station[b]	22	30	22
Land reclamation[b]	16	25	16
FMCG[b]	21	30	21
Total value expected	*146*	*169*	*108*
Already distributed		341	341
Total value of fund		*510*	*449*
Cash-on-cash return		*2.04*	*1.76*
IRR on initial value of capital (%)		*7.38*	*5.79*

Note: [a]Fund makers; [b]Meaningful refunders; [c]Underperformers; [d]Dogs.

these have at least some upside potential). With respect to the performance of the fund and the current assets, one can make the following observations. First, the venture capital firm needs to convert all the portfolio firms with value potential into strong performers in order to assure a two times cash-on-cash return to their limited partners. These firms include the Restaurant and Land Reclamation businesses, which appear to have the strongest return potential. A sound performance by these two investments will move the overall performance of the fund into the desired range. Second, the fund needs to sell its remaining "high potential" investments—these firms are performing well, and the fund has priority liquidation clauses that guarantee a return of capital while maintaining some upside potential. Third, while it is always desirable to maximize the cash recovery from any deal, the actual expected returns from the five underperforming deals are unlikely to make any significant difference to the venture capital firm. Venture capitalists are unlikely to worry about the fortunes of such deals when they are performing in such a manner.

The venture capital firm should also establish criteria to ensure the effective allocation of human resources to the best prospects. These criteria may include the firm's potential to meet or exceed budgeted financial milestones in terms of sales and profits ability, the exit potential and interest from strategic buyers, the level of cooperation between all the stakeholders on the exit issue, the existence of strong downside protections for venture capitalists, and so on. The fund may subsequently divide investee firms into four or five categories and establish priorities on which to work with them. These categories may include: "Fund Makers"—investee firms that have a strong opportunity to return in excess of 2 cash-on-cash and may be instrumental in generating the desired level of capital to limited partners; "Meaningful Refunders"—firms that have strong return potential, but less than those in the first category; "Underperformers"—investee firms off track in terms of performance, but with the potential to return at least 50 percent of invested capital; and "Dogs"—firms that lose money and are generally believed to be write-offs. The footnotes in table 9.2 show the assignment of deals to these different categories.

In any portfolio, venture capitalists dedicate the best people to the best prospects. They also supplement investment officers leading the best deals with additional resources to realize the full potential of these firms. One investment officer may be assigned to deal with the "dogs" so that the involvement of senior people in those deals can be minimized. In other circumstances, venture capitalists may rely on other syndicate partners in the deal to lead the process if their level of shareholding is small or if they find that they cannot influence the decision-making process or outcome in any meaningful way.

Questions to Consider

1. What is the purpose of the monitoring function in the venture capital investment process? What are the key questions that venture capitalists must ask during this phase?
2. What aspects of venture capital investing make it necessary for venture capitalists to be active investors?
3. What are the key corporate governance challenges in venture capital investing?
4. Discuss the components of effective directing.
5. Differentiate between being a director in a public and a private firm. What are the key challenges in each situation for venture capitalists?

Russia Partners

Key characteristics

Year founded:	1991
Founding partners:	Drew Guff, George Siguler, and Donald Spencer
Number of limited partners:	N/A (EBRD)
Geographic coverage:	Russia (2 locations), Ukraine (1)
Headquarter location:	Moscow (Russia)
Focus (if any):	None
Funds under management:	~$1 billion
Number of completed deals/ IPO exits:	50/N/A
Private/public:	Private
Most publicly recognized deals:	MTV Russia, Syktyvkar Pulp & Paper, Radio-7, EPAM System, Kontakt Insurance
Number of investment professionals:	~25

Russia Partners was one of the early entrants into the Russian market and is also one of the leading private equity firms in the region. To date, Russia Partners has raised four private equity funds and currently manages over one billion dollars of capital. The firm has completed approximately 50 transactions, including MTV Russia and Syktyvkar Pulp & Paper.

Russia Partners pursues a wide range of deals, including privatization deals, new entrepreneurial ventures, and co-investment opportunities with strategic partners. Its investment strategy is based on investing into local firms with strong market positions, committed and complete management teams, and sustainable barriers to entry. The firm provides capital for expansion and modernization. Russia Partners has a wide sectoral orientation, which includes advertising and publishing, construction materials, consumer and household products, financial services and leasing, IT, logistics and distribution, and more.

The firm employs 25 people. Russia Partners regards itself as one of the most experienced and stable groups of investment professionals. The cadre is comprised of Western-educated local staff and Western partners with international private equity experience. The firm maintains two offices in Russia (Moscow and Samara), one in the Ukraine (Kiev), and one in New York.

Source: *www.russiapartners.ru.*

Chapter 10

Exiting

The initial years of cooperation with an investee firm focus on increasing efficiencies, reaching operational milestones, and meeting financial forecasts. At some point in the deal (normally between years two–four), venture capitalists begin to shift their discussions with management and other shareholders away from issues related to the business and toward those related to the exit and its timing. Other shareholders generally place less importance on this issue than venture capitalists, in spite of the fact that many entrepreneurs actually see themselves going public. If an investee firm has been performing well according to its business plan, achieved considerable market share and brand awareness, developed a strong customer base, and maintained a strong future outlook, venture capitalists will focus their attention on the most profitable mode of exit for the business. In these circumstances, the investee firm is likely to have already lured interested buyers or been approached by investment bankers promising a successful initial public offering (IPO). If the firm's development has not proceeded according to plan, the spectrum of profitable exit choices diminishes significantly. In the most critical situations, the firm may be liquidated and venture capitalists may face the prospect of writing-off their investment to zero. In less extreme cases, venture capitalists may dispose of their shares to the highest bidder (founders or management) or attempt to reignite interest in the business through recapitalization or a merger with another firm in the sector. Venture capitalists must also decide whether to navigate the exit process by themselves or to hire external advisors. If the decision is made to seek public listing, the process becomes easy for venture capitalists, as underwriters will effectively manage the entire process.

Exit represents an orchestrated way of cashing out a venture capital investment in a portfolio firm and is the monetization of cash committed to the deal by the virtue of a trade sale, an IPO, or other means. The exit is the fundamental core of the venture capital investment model; it aims to maximize the value of the investment and, at the same time, secure optimal opportunity for the firm to grow after venture capitalists have left the firm. Exits normally occur three–five years post closing, although there are many circumstances under which an exit can occur sooner. A unique perspective on exit is described in box 10.1.

The ultimate proceeds that venture capitalists make from the sale are subject to taxation on capital gains. The determination of

---

Box 10.1 The practitioner's corner: "Not all good companies are good investments"

There is a famous joke about venture capitalists. "Why do venture capitalists never keep their backs to the door?" the joke asks. The answer: "Because they must always keep an eye on the exit." As the joke suggests, the exit is one of the most critical parts of the venture capital process; it is the goal that all venture capitalists wish to achieve.

A managing director at one of the leading venture capital firms in Europe had two unique principles that guided his thoughts with respect to evaluating exit scenarios for potential investments. It must be mentioned that this investment officer has never lost money for his fund and has never had a single write-off in his investment career—an outstanding accomplishment given that the professional track record of most venture capitalists includes at least one or two "meltdowns." The two principles can be summarized in the following manner:

1. Not all good companies are good investments;
2. IPO is not an exit.

Let's consider what is meant by the two statements and why they are significant. The first principle stresses the fact that investigating a potential investment candidate and its commercial attractiveness and ascertaining the exit probability are distinctly separate thought processes. In one case, the potential investee firm may have strong and growing profits, a leading market position, a unique product offering, a top-notch management team, and excellent expansion plans, but if the owners are not keen to allow venture capitalists to reach a liquidity event, such an investment is not likely to work for venture capitalists. There is no benefit for venture capitalists to invest into a commercially attractive business only to be stuck with it in the long term. Venture capitalists would be better off investing into a less attractive firm where the exit goals are well aligned between their own and those of the founders.

The second principle—later softened to "IPO is not necessarily an exit" by the managing director—underscores the fact that venture capitalists rarely achieve a full exit at the time of an IPO. In some cases, they are allowed to sell some of their shares at the time of an IPO; in most cases, however, they are required to retain their shares for a lengthier period of time. This highlights the point that venture capitalists are not well trained in managing firms that are publicly listed.

the tax liability upon the disposal of the asset depends on a variety of factors, including the local tax regime, the legal and jurisdictional set up of the fund manager (off-shore or on-shore), and special arrangements that exist between the fund manager and the limited partners. Venture capital firms are normally set up as "flow through" entities from a taxation point of view, as proceeds from the disposal of any business move to the partnership (the fund) and are distributed to limited partners without having to incur any tax at the fund level.

Exit Preparation

Because every investee firm is different, a development plan to achieve a successful exit takes into consideration a number of factors at two levels: the macroeconomic level and the firm's individual level. Some of these factors, especially those related to macroeconomic trends, are outside of a venture capitalist's sphere of influence and control. At the macro level, venture capitalists consider the economic cycle and anticipated growth rates, the nature of the industry, the cycle of financial markets, the costs of borrowing, and so on. The anticipated timing of the exit is perhaps the most critical factor that influences the value of the investee firm. At the beginning of the economic cycle, strategic investors actively seek out opportunities for business expansion; they are also more willing to pay premium prices for acquisitions. In public markets, P/E multiples, investor confidence (both at the institutional and retail level), and the appetite for new opportunities are high. These conditions reverse at the end of the cycle. Strategic investors mostly look inward to their own businesses and focus on controlling their costs rather than on expansion. As public markets are often volatile, investors tend to be more cautious of new issues; they may also delay their investment decisions and seek value opportunities.

To ascertain the firm's readiness at the micro level, venture capitalists are likely to consider business development, business expansion, and achievement of milestones and operational goals, as well as trends in profitability and sales. It is also important that a complete and competent management team without any apparent weaknesses is in place.

Background Investigation

An investigation into a firm's exit potential is critical to venture capitalists. There is nothing worse for a venture capitalist than to be stuck in a well-run business with no strong exit potential and a lack of shareholder support for achieving one. At the time initial due diligence is performed, venture capitalists effectively make an educated guess as to how much the investee firm will be worth at the time of exit. As discussed in chapter six, this is usually done on the basis of EBITDA multiples, based on public firms and transactions in the private sector. The initial judgment made on the valuation is tested at the time of the actual exit—at this time, all the information venture capitalists need to more-precisely ascertain the value of the business will be available.

Since the two primary modes of exit are IPOs and trade sales, venture capitalists tend to concentrate on investigating these exit scenarios prior to their closing the deal. In the case of an IPO, venture capitalists will try to identify a number of critical factors, the first of which is the geographic options for an IPO. This process requires an analysis of both local/regional and international exchanges and is considered critical. While IPOs generally tend to be underpriced, local firms are generally better received in local or regional markets because the firm can rely on strong brand awareness and in-depth coverage from local analysts (this may improve the overall liquidity of the stock). Cross-listing on different exchanges is also a possibility for most firms, as this can assure additional price stabilization, exposure to more institutional investors, more access to cash, and increased stock liquidity in the aftermarket. Second, once a decision has been made about the preferred mode of exchange, venture capitalists investigate whether the potential investee firm is likely to meet the various thresholds for admission to the chosen exchange. Meeting the financial considerations necessary for listing the firm is critical. Most countries have at least two exchanges—junior and senior. The financial requirements for these markets vary, but they generally relate to the firm's level of sales, profitability, liquidity, and the value of its assets. For example, to reach a primary market in most countries, the firm needs to achieve sales of at least $50 million and have net profits of at least $2 million; the offering should not be less than $20 million. If a potential investee firm is unlikely to meet the criteria for listing, an IPO will likely not materialize. Third, venture capitalists must investigate the recent history of IPOs in their preferred market. This process is likely to yield information about IPO pricing, subsequent trading ranges, under- or overrepresentation in the chosen sector, the preferences of the local investor community, and more. The investigation also often includes discussions with local underwriters and financial institutions.

Information on exit potential through trade sales is more difficult to access, as limited public data exits on private sector deals. In this exit mode, venture capitalists tend to rely on their internal data, sector reports, or informal discussions with consultants (who are often involved in merger and acquisition activities on behalf of strategic buyers). The potential acquirers may be existing market players or new entrants into the market. Existing market players are likely to investigate the market performance of firms as captured in market share statistics, customer brand awareness data, brand loyalty, and so on. Strategic investors are often frustrated by the fact that they are not able to grow their businesses fast enough and that local firms with less financial resources continue to be market leaders (strategic investors generally outspend local entrepreneurial businesses). For new entrants, the considerations are similar, but at least two areas are perceived differently—the effectiveness of the distribution structure and the management team. New entrants will seek immediate access to a strong logistics infrastructure. They also realize that finding and training management in local markets is difficult and takes a considerable amount of time. Venture capitalists aim to understand the strategic fit between acquirers and their investee firms. Many venture capitalists believe that firms with at least ten million dollars in revenue and one million dollars in net profit enjoy the broadest market for a trade sale.

Due to the limited availability of information related to trade sale opportunities, venture capitalists may contact the local or regional offices of strategic investors to further reinforce their geographic expansion plans. While strategic investors are unlikely to reveal their precise market plans, venture capitalists can obtain general information related to their potential exit prospects through informal conversation. Such a direct approach is more common once the deal has been completed. In many cases, these innocent "get to know you" conversations result in future merger or acquisition opportunities. Venture capitalists know the value of staying on the radar screens of strategic investors.

The timing of an exit is difficult to predict. While venture capitalists try to be deliberate when planning an exit and act in accordance with a preferred schedule of events, they are open to more opportunistic exit scenarios if the possibility presents itself. Figure 10.1 presents a time continuum, charting firms at different stages of their development, along with their most likely mode of exit. In general terms, strategic buyers either acquire successful start-ups almost instantly or wait to see the rollout of their business plan. Start-ups enjoy the shortest exit timeline, particularly if they own proprietary technologies, innovative products, or present new market opportunities to strategic investors. Start-ups are especially attractive to strategic investors if their valuation range falls within $20 million–$30 million. For most attractive start-ups, an exit can easily occur within 18 months of their obtaining venture capital funding. While numerous successful start-ups have gone public in markets around the world—especially those dealing in Internet technologies, pharmaceuticals, and biotechnologies—an IPO is not achievable for the vast majority. Consequently, the IPO is not listed on the graph related to start-ups as a likely mode of exit during a firm's early stages of development.

Expanding firms that are supported by venture capital are likely to enjoy the second shortest exit timing. These "expansion plays"

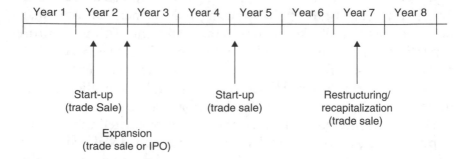

Figure 10.1 The continuum of exit options and firms at different stages of development.

can become viable trade sale and IPO candidates. An exit can occur as soon as 24 months after the venture capitalists' cash contribution is translated into tangible expansion results. Start-ups that have not been acquired by strategic investors after achieving venture capital funding may take longer to exit than expansion deals. These firms become viable IPO candidates if they are "rejected" by strategic investors in the early stages of their development. Firms undergoing restructuring and re-capitalization take the longest time to exit. In such situations, venture capitalists must effectively rebuild the firm.

Grooming Investee Firms for Exit

Exit activities differ with the anticipated mode of exit. While general business principles apply in most exit cases (maximizing profits, growing sales, improving market share), the priorities are different in each scenario. In the case of a trade sale, strategic buyers are particularly interested in market share, brand awareness and loyalty, strong local management, and distribution structures. While achieving operating efficiencies is important, strategic investors take a broader view of the venture. Strategic investors can improve the profitability of a business almost instantly by incorporating it into their network of raw material sources, providing improvements to it by benchmarking it against other businesses owned by them, or introducing sophisticated management planning resources (e.g., ERP, ERM). Venture capitalists seeking a trade sale as their preferred exit route must therefore focus on introducing new and innovative products, developing strong relationships with stakeholders in their distribution structure (regional or local distributors, service providers, retailers, etc.), and developing a challenging geographical market (maybe in a new country or geographic region). The firm's interim level of profitability is of less concern; greater focus is placed on the nontangible aspects of the business described earlier.

In the case of an IPO, preparation is multifaceted and includes different areas of the business. One of the priorities is to build public confidence in the firm's management and corporate governance regime. This process involves filling any gaps in management and providing appropriate motivational schemes for managers (e.g., stock options programs). Appointing distinguished and well-respected individuals to the board of directors achieves the second purpose.

Venture capitalists also focus on "cleaning up" any undocumented or poorly constructed legal agreements, including those related to personal loans, distribution arrangements, and intellectual property rights (e.g., patents and trademarks).

Common Modes of Exit

Multiple modes of exit are available to venture capitalists, including trade sales, IPOs, sales to financial investors, buybacks, liquidation, and so on. Figure 10.2 presents a map of the most common modes of venture capital exit. Two criteria related to business value and liquidity were selected for charting the exit universe. Maximizing proceeds from investee firms allows venture capitalists to meet the limited partners' return expectations. Liquidity assures that the business valuations of investee firms are converted into cash in the most expedient manner possible. Exits can be full or partial. Occasionally, venture capitalists will decide upon an intermediate step—an equity release where a small portion of their stake is sold to a third party. The options included in Quadrant I of figure 10.2 are the most preferred exit modes for venture capitalists. These options assure maximum value and liquidity. While there is a general perception that IPO yields the highest amount of value to venture

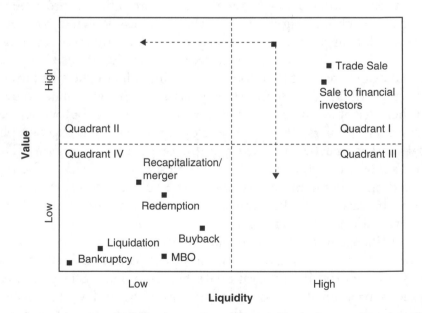

Figure 10.2   The map of the major exit possibilities in venture capitalists' investments.

capitalists, full liquidity in IPO situations may not be assured—this reflects market conditions, securities regulations, underwriter preferences, and so on. The sale of an investee firm to a strategic investor or financial institution almost certainly completes the relationship between venture capitalists and investee firms. Another option involves selling shares to a financial institution. Quadrant II of the graph is not filled, but may include IPO exit cases with the possibility of declining liquidity due to a poor aftermarket for newly listed firms—the valuation of investee firms can remain relatively high, but the achievement of full liquidity will be delayed. There are no options listed for Quadrant III, as well—the public listing of firms may fit into this category if the stock price declines significantly while the firm's stock enjoys strong liquidity in the secondary market. Quadrant IV includes a combination of compromised investment exits, as well as partial and total write-offs. In the case of buybacks, redemptions, and MBOs, venture capitalists are likely to receive a portion of their invested capital back in the form of a one-time payment or on a payment schedule. Re-capitalization, restructuring, or merger options may ultimately create value, but the initial liquidity timing can be severely compromised and a chance for a future liquidity event may not develop for some time. Winding-down or liquidating the business concludes the relationship with the investee firm in a negative manner.

Preferred Modes of Exit

The following sections discuss the two major preferred exit routes: trade sale and IPO. A third, less common option is to sell to financial investors. Table 10.1 summarizes the main advantages and disadvantages of these three options. Many venture capitalists tend to initially investigate the trade sale option, as they are attracted to the immediate payout it offers and a full exit from the deal. Trade sales also offer venture capitalists a special "merit badge" that can be promoted to their limited partners and other entrepreneurial firms—being able to persuade strategic investors to purchase their investee firms confirms their skill at picking winners.

Trade Sale
Trade sales are attractive to venture capitalists due to their strong pricing potential and instant liquidity. This method of exit includes

Table 10.1 Advantages and disadvantages of the three most desired exit routes

Mode of exit	Advantages	Disadvantages
Trade sale	• Simplicity and cost—low cost compared to IPO • Complete exit • One party to deal with • May achieve premium pricing	• Confidentiality—a purchaser will request access to sensitive market and financial information • Management and/or founder may oppose • Warranties—all shareholders need to provide warranties and indemnities • Escrow arrangement—a purchaser is likely to hold back a portion of the agreed price
IPO	• Price—IPOs may provide highest price • Attractive to management and remaining shareholders • All shareholders can time their own exit • Provides a liquidity event for exiting shareholders • Limited or no warranties provided by venture capitalists	• Release of nearly all minority investor protections • Additional restrictions on share sale brought by the underwriters and stock exchange regulators • High cost of listing and maintaining the listing • Disappointing earnings could significantly reduce the firm's value • Pressure to achieve regular profits • Potential for additional liability under securities regulations
Sale to financial investors	• Complete exit	• Difficult to identify potential purchasers • Lower valuation compared to trade sale and IPO • Route only available to selected firms • Long time to complete

the sale of shares in the business or the sale of selected assets (strategic investors may be interested in select parts of the business that match their existing business structure or strategy).

Strategic investors purchase either established businesses or early stage firms. The reasons for these acquisitions are different. Strategic investors are looking for strategic compatibility—the business has to be a good fit. The most common reasons for acquisition include achieving operational efficiencies and economies of scale, increasing market power, and achieving growth quickly and cheaply. Mature businesses are bought for their strong market presence, customer base, and brand recognition. Start-ups or early-stage firms are acquired for different reasons. Strategic investors rely on newly formed firms for new products and services, innovative ideas, or new ways of connecting with customers. Small firms acquired by strategic investors essentially act as research and development centers for larger market players. Many attributes of these young entrepreneurial firms can convert into strong growth and potential profits down the line.

During the trade sale process, a purchaser is likely to require warranties and representations about the state of the acquired business. These requirements may also be interconnected with indemnifications and escrow arrangements. Venture capitalists often argue that they should not have to provide any warranties to strategic investors because they are not involved in the day-to-day management of the business (pointing to management as the only source of warranties). Ultimately, however, venture capitalists agree to provide warranties and indemnities to trade buyers, and to escrow arrangements for up to twelve or eighteen months.

Venture capitalists have numerous tools at their disposal to affect exit. The most common features include drag-along rights, share adjustment mechanisms, management control mechanisms, and put options. In the case of resistance from management or remaining shareholders, they can rely on sanction mechanisms or on methodologies to increase the "level of pain" to the uncooperative parties. These tools include forced redemption of venture capitalist shares, forced dividends only payable to venture capitalists, firing the management team, or diluting management shares. While sound on paper, these legal clauses can be difficult to enforce and execute. Many venture capitalists come to realize that if shareholders and management change their minds regarding the exit, they may be forced to renegotiate the terms of the deal or pursue a legal route that can diminish their exit prospects and the value of the business.

Let's examine an example of how venture capitalists can structure an exit clause to effectively increase the "threshold of pain" to other shareholders over time. The development of such a mechanism always follows a detailed analysis of the firm's exit prospects. Negotiating an exit provision is one of the most challenging clauses in venture capital contracting. Venture capitalists must focus on assuring liquidity while the founders resist being forced out of the business. Let's assume that venture capitalists have negotiated a softer exit provision clause (as is the case in many situations). In this

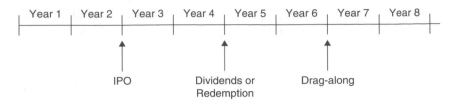

Figure 10.3   An example of sequencing exit arrangements.

example, venture capitalists are not able to ensure that their drag-along rights will come into effect shortly after closing, so they construct a mechanism that provides incentives to the founders over the life of the deal. This "step-wise" mechanism is presented in figure 10.3. Venture capitalists may initially agree with the founders to focus on obtaining a public listing in the two-year period post closing. The window of opportunity to achieve exit generally lasts for two years (such timing theoretically allows for achieving an IPO until the end of the fourth year). At the end of year four, venture capitalists can start to force a sequenced series of liquidity events, achieved through the redemption of shares or paying special dividends (these benefits only accrue to venture capitalists). If paying out cash to venture capitalists is not possible due to the firm's poor financial condition, venture capitalists may resort to a "last-stop" option—drag-along rights (year six). Such a mechanism can reduce the founders' anxiety over premature disposal of shares and allow venture capitalists to achieve liquidity in an orchestrated and deliberate manner.

Instead of selling to one strategic investor, venture capitalists may choose to pursue multiple investors in a tender process—a strategy that has grown in popularity within the venture capital community in recent years. While such a process offers strong potential for premium pricing, it also offers risks—the process may alienate some or all investors. The process also increases the risk that a larger number of investors will have access to sensitive information about the firm. A consulting firm normally navigates this process on behalf of venture capitalists and other shareholders.

Initial Public Offering

An exit through initial public offering includes the sale of the firm's shares to the public, followed by a listing of the shares on the stock exchange. To venture capitalists, the attractiveness of this option usually relates to pricing. Achieving liquidity can continue to be a concern. Venture capitalists realize that even though business valuation can be attractive at the time of an IPO, the stock price may shift downward quickly, totally erasing the premium price advantage of the IPO when compared to other exit options. In short, the total proceeds from an IPO can be significantly lower than the price offered by a trade buyer.

For venture capitalists, the IPO option may offer different liquidity conditions determined by underwriters or investment dealers. In some circumstances, venture capitalists are able to fully exit during an IPO due to significant demand for shares; this might occur in the case of an outstanding firm with sound financial fundamentals, a strong market position, and unique development prospects. In most cases, however, the IPO represents only a partial exit; venture capitalists are allowed to sell up to one-third of their holdings at the time of the IPO while the remaining shares can be sold only after a period of twelve–eighteen months (a similar lock-up is also imposed on management).

The steps in the IPO process are well understood and include cleaning up the financial and legal matters of the candidate firm, choosing the underwriter, participating in due diligence, preparing and filing the registration statement, preparing a prospectus, conducting a road show, building "the book," and setting the issue price. While the process is relatively straightforward to follow on most exchanges, venture capitalists must make critical decisions along the way. At one such time—the moment in which the final price of the issue is determined—venture capitalists (and other shareholders) may reconsider whether or not to proceed with the IPO. In some instances, the underwriters may have been too optimistic in estimating the value of the business at the outset and may suggest an issue price per share at below the minimum of the initially quoted price range. In such a circumstance, venture capitalists must carefully decide whether or not to continue with the IPO. The trade-off is the achievement of expected premium price versus loss of minority right protections (including the ability to affect an exit through other means). Venture capitalists may also lose liquidation preferences (venture capitalists' preferred shares are converted into common shares). If the issue price is not seductive enough, the trade-off may not be worth the loss of the protections.

At other times, venture capitalists must decide whether or not to be on the board of directors of the newly listed firm. The trade-off here for venture capitalists is whether to sit on the board of directors and maintain an ability to influence decision-making, or maintain the ability to dispose of their shares in a timely manner. In most exchanges, trading regulations prohibit insiders from trading stock freely. Insiders—such the firm's employees, management, or directors—are not allowed to engage in trading on their own accounts or to execute or direct trades on behalf of the firms they work at if they are privileged to material and insider information (defined as information that can affect or be reasonably construed to affect the firm's stock price). Most exchanges provide long lists of what constitutes insider or material information. In the case of an expanding business that often wins customer contracts, borrows funds, engages into acquisitions, and amends expansion plans or capital expenditure programs, the board of directors may not have many opportunities to dispose of their shares (given the insider trading regime). The only time venture capitalists are able to trade is when the general public is presumed to have the same knowledge as insiders. According to most securities legislation, everyone should have equal access to information that may affect their desire to trade securities. This symmetry of information normally occurs around the time in which quarterly and annual statements are issued. Insiders are specifically forbidden to trade prior to the release of these statements or before other public announcements are made.

The major advantage of an IPO is its ability to obtain liquidity for all the shareholders, including venture capitalists, without alienating any stakeholders and management. The major disadvantage of this option for venture capitalists relates to liquidity risks.

Sale to Financial Investors

A sale to a financial investor, whether an investment fund or another private equity firm, may be considered when the business generates repeatable cash flows and pays regular dividends, but has limited growth potential (making it less attractive to strategic investors). Financial investors may be interested in taking an equity stake in the private firm or encouraging it to obtain an IPO (where they can benefit from the steady stream of dividends the firm pays out). Another variation of selling to financial investors involves effectively "recycling" the deal to another venture capital firm or to existing financial investors in the form of a secondary buyout. This buyout may have a different timeline for holding assets and may include other development plans for the business (e.g., combining the firm with an existing portfolio firm).

Compromised Exit Strategies

A compromised exit can occur as a result of two main events: financial underperformance by the business and a lack of cooperation from shareholders. If the firm underperforms financially, venture capitalists aim to minimize loss from the deal. If the business is performing well, but the shareholders (the management and founders) are uncooperative with respect to exit, venture capitalists are unlikely to extract maximum value from the deal (conflicts or legal disputes on this issue delay exit timing and can destroy value). The exit scenarios described here are backup ones.

A buyback represents the purchase of the venture capitalists' ownership stake by the founders. In essence, the founders provide an exit for venture capitalists and effectively reassume full ownership of the business. This exit option may involve a put option arrangement (where the investor has the right to sell shares) and a call option arrangement (where the founders of the firm have the right to buy shares). This option presents multiple challenges for the founders and venture capitalists to navigate around. The first challenge relates to the valuation of the firm. In the case of a well-performing business, and given venture capitalists' high return expectations, pricing can become a major concern. In the case of business underperformance, venture capitalists wish to extract maximum value and want to avoid selling at just any price. If the shareholders have not anticipated a buyback as an exit eventuality at the outset of the process, whether by fixing the price (an annual hurdle rate of return may be applied) or by developing a formula (based on P/E or EBITDA multiples), they resort to a third party valuation (usually performed by a reputable consulting firm). If the price for the business is agreed-upon, a more serious problem relates to obtaining financing (normally from the bank) to execute the purchase. Even though the leveraged buyout (LBO) market has been developing quite well in recent years, it is cyclical. If the banks agree to provide financing, they are likely to demand strong collateral, including shares, firm assets, and personal guarantees from the founders.

Exit through redemption is similar to a buyback, with one notable difference—venture capitalists require the firm (rather than existing shareholders) to purchase shares and to cancel them, thereby reducing the total number of outstanding shares. Similar valuation and financing issues arise as in the case of buybacks. While redemption may not be practical if the firm does not have sufficient cash to redeem shares, this mechanism usually provides an effective incentive to management and shareholders to focus on exit considerations. If venture capitalists trigger redemption and the firm is not able to fulfill its obligations, they can assume control of the board of directors and force business liquidation.

A merger with another business represents no immediate liquidity for venture capitalists, but it may offer the potential for value creation at some time in the future. In this situation, venture capitalists willingly sacrifice liquidity in an attempt to generate some value from the deal. Venture capitalists will assume ownership in the larger business, which is likely private (if venture capitalists convert their shares into a public firm, they often have fewer concerns about liquidity). A merger with another business often relates to the scale of the investee firm—the firm has likely not developed according to plan in terms of business growth. Consequently, the business may be too small to be of interest to strategic investors or to list publicly. Despite the fact that a merger can sometimes be the only option for venture capitalists, it has multiple drawbacks. The role of venture capitalists in the business can be diminished if they assume a lower ownership stake in the new venture; they may not be invited to sit on the board of directors if their smaller investee firm joins a significantly larger business (in such a case, observer's rights are normally granted). In such a scenario, venture capitalists are also likely to give up legal protections as a result of the merger. The prospects for a liquidity event may worsen and, ultimately, the only way an exit may occur for venture capitalists is if they sell their stake to the combined business (usually at a heavily discounted price). Many venture capitalists discover the hard way that the intentions behind mergers can change and that deal agreements fall apart. The investee firm may also be required to disclose sensitive information to a potential merger partner that is a direct or indirect competitor in the marketplace.

MBO represents an acquisition of the firm by its management. In this exit scenario, management purchases the business from existing shareholders, including venture capitalists. While an MBO can occur in any situation, most commonly it is executed under less favorable business circumstances. Management relies on the assumption that a turnaround or restructuring of the business is possible and value can be generated. This situation often arises when significant differences exist between shareholders with respect to the strategic and operational direction the business should take or when management may be convinced that the decisions of shareholders have impacted the business. In some cases, the sale of the business to management may represent the only real exit opportunity for venture capitalists; hence, the valuation that they can obtain from this exit scenario is low.

Undesirable Exit Scenarios

In an attempt to limit their committing human resources into the deal, venture capitalists may discontinue efforts to actively work with investee firms. In such cases, the investee firms will almost certainly have underperformed and venture capitalists will have explored other exit potentials resulting in no other avenue. The most common methods used to close the relationship are liquidation and bankruptcy. The procedures of these options differ among legal jurisdictions.

If shareholders exhaust all possibilities of keeping the business alive and see limited value in it, the liquidation option is the best way in which to achieve the closure of the relationship with the investee firm. Liquidation, also referred to as a winding-up of the business or its dissolution, is a process of redistributing the assets of the firm to shareholders. Liquidation may be compulsory or voluntary. The firm, the board of directors, or creditors can drive compulsory liquidation; venture capitalists may have rights to force liquidation even if other shareholders disagree. Applications by creditors are uncommon. Voluntary liquidation occurs when the firm resolves to voluntarily wind-up its affairs. Liquidation begins when the firm passes an appropriate resolution. Broadly speaking, liquidation is conducted in four steps. First, a liquidator is appointed to represent the interests of all creditors and shareholders. This occurs when the shareholders pass an appropriate resolution or when the court makes the order to appoint a liquidator.

Second, the appointed liquidator collects the assets of the firm (including uncalled or unpaid capital), establishes the list of liabilities, sells the assets, and settles the creditors in order of priority: secured creditors (those that have a charge over the firm's assets) → liquidation costs → wages and salaries → unsecured creditors (e.g., vendors; in proportion to the size of claim) → any interest on debt → debt owned to shareholders (e.g., unpaid dividends) → shareholders. If the firm is solvent, the shareholders or the board of directors can oversee the process (though this rarely happens). If the firm is insolvent, creditors can be placed in charge of the process by applying to the court. Third, the liquidator distributes any surplus funds to all shareholders in accordance with the order of priority—venture capitalists rely on their liquidation preferences in this situation, but may not secure proceeds. Finally, the liquidated firm is formally dissolved and removed from the firm's register.

Bankruptcy represents the firm's inability to pay its creditors, or its becoming insolvent. As is the case with liquidation, two types of bankruptcies exist: voluntary (initiated by the firm) and involuntary (initiated by creditors). The major aims of bankruptcy, however, are to address the firm's financial distress, to allow for its rehabilitation, and to effectively extend its existence through reorganization. While business reorganization cannot create a market for or improve the operational efficiency of the business, it can free up cash from servicing debt to permit operations, prevent creditors from liquidating assets, and renegotiate contracts that put the firm at a disadvantage. An inherent part of the bankruptcy proceedings is the development of a workable plan that allows the firm's creditors to pay back their debt. This plan must be accepted by creditors, shareholders, and the court. Bankruptcy proceedings allow the firm to continue its operations and to use its revenue and profits to settle creditors' claims; keeping the business alive is in some cases the best way in which to maximize a creditor's claim recovery. In some instances, bankruptcy proceedings are similar to liquidation—the process includes dividing the firm's assets among creditors. The bankruptcy process is overseen by bankruptcy courts or trustees appointed by the court. Bankruptcies involve a significant commitment of shareholders' and management's time to interact with the court and its declared procedures, lawyers, and creditors. While firms can emerge from the bankruptcy process, their value to shareholders is usually significantly diminished.

Challenges to Exits

Exits are difficult to orchestrate, navigate, and execute. The major reasons for this include changing circumstances around major stakeholders and changing fortunes for the business. These circumstances are captured in figure 10.4, which describes the firm's stage of development as well as associated market, financial, and exit risks. The first stages of the firm's development seem to share many common financial and business risks and are grouped together. Common similarities are also visible within the last two stages.

The goals of founders and management may change over time, as can the liquidity requirements of venture capitalists. The independence,

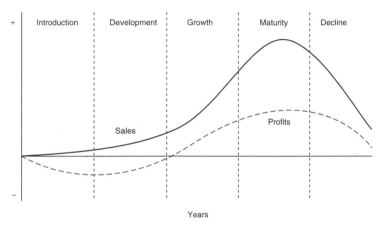

Stages	Introduction	Development	Growth	Maturity	Decline
Business Risks	• Prototype does not work • Increased competition • Inadequate management • Product too expensive		• Competition • Inability to attract management to affect growth • Expansion too aggressive	• Loss of market share • New technology erases initial advantages • Management and key employees depart	
Financial Risks	• Insufficient business funding • Excessive cash burn		• Financial losses • Difficulty in raising additional capital • Expansions drive profits and cash flows down	• Strong decline in sales and profits • Inability to reinvigorate business with other products or services • Rapidly declining profits and cash flows	
Market Risks	• Market too small • Technology proves inferior		• Poor market share • Limited product acceptance	• Declining market share in a declining market	
Exit Risks	• Trade buyers not active in market • Volatile IPO prospects		• Trade buyers build own operations • Poor public stock aftermarket	• No market for "secondaries" for financial investors	

Figure 10.4 Firm's stages of development and associated business, financial, and exit risks.

status, and lifestyles of founders and management are directly related to a strongly performing business; management also enjoys high salaries and regular bonuses. On the other hand, venture capitalists approaching the end of the partnership may wish to change their corporate strategy and shift their investment focus to show a strong exit in anticipation of upcoming fund-raising activities. These changes in expectations can cause disagreements among stakeholders.

A lack of alignment of goals at the time of exit can be further complicated by discussions pertaining to the business valuation of the investee firm. Even if the business is performing well, the founders may continue to believe that their business is worth much more than it actually is and become unwilling to settle for the offered price. Conversely, if the business is performing poorly, they see their "sweat equity" being diminished in value.

The potential for the founders to receive lower than their desired valuation for their firm, along with venture capitalists' liquidation preferences (which may consume all proceeds from the sale), can create significant tension on the board of directors. In order to secure a timely exit, venture capitalists attempt to decipher how to provide incentives to shareholders and how to retain management's support. The second problem is especially critical for venture capitalists because management may abandon the business as a result of redistribution of proceeds (strategic investors are likely to lose interest if this occurs). Venture capitalists generally address this problem through "management carve-outs," where a portion of venture capitalists' proceeds or shares is relocated to management upon their meeting some specific operational goals.

Changing circumstances in an investee firm's business conditions and its financial performance during exit discussions negatively influence exit prospects. If the decline in the financial performance is severe, but temporary, exit may be delayed for some time (pending improvement to business circumstances and financial performance). Strategic investors, for example, are likely to monitor the business for some time before making a final decision. Trade buyers may restore their interest in the firm after it has improved its business operations even though the turnaround has not yet become visible in financial data. If an IPO is being contemplated, the underwriters will recommend that at least two positive quarters of improved financial performance should pass before the listing efforts are resumed. If the deterioration of the business is permanent, venture capitalists may reduce their valuation expectations.

Any underperformance by investee firms brings venture capitalists to an important decision—namely, whether to accept a lower valuation of the business and proceed to an exit or to wait for a recovery to try and exit again. Many venture capitalists admit that this key judgment call comes when determining the severity and permanent nature of the firm's underperformance. As previously observed, many venture capitalists tend to hold strong emotional attachments to deals and tend to overlook financial underperformance in hopes of a quick turnaround some time in the future. These turnarounds rarely happen, and regret over not selling the business at a higher valuation almost always occurs. The key consideration is whether the business is likely to grow in value well above the rate of return initially expected by venture capitalists. If, for example, venture capitalists expect a 30 percent growth in value from the deal, and the business has underperformed for two years, the investment has to achieve a rate of growth significantly higher than 30 percent to capture the original value-building trajectory. If one assumes that EBITDA multiples are likely to stay at their current levels, any recovery in the valuation of the business can only come from significant improvements to EBITDA. The reality may be that such a sharp recovery in EBITDA is not feasible, and in such a case, the decision to dispose rather than hold may be the correct one.

Questions to Consider

1. Discuss the advantages and disadvantages of the three major exit options from the entrepreneur's point of view.
2. List the key activities firms backed by venture capital are likely to engage in prior to exit.
3. Discuss key challenges to exit and how venture capitalists may prepare for them.
4. Propose an exit procedure for an entrepreneur who does not want to agree to drag-along rights.
5. Compare liquidation versus bankruptcy from the venture capitalist point of view.

The Blackstone Group

Key characteristics

Year founded:	1987
Founding partners:	Stephen A. Schwarzman and Peter Peterson
Number of limited partners:	N/A
Geographic coverage:	North America (2 locations), Asia (3), Europe (1)
Headquarter location:	New York (USA)
Focus (if any):	Opportunistic
Funds under management:	$44.7 billion
Number of completed deals/IPO exits:	138/N/A
Private/public:	Public
Most publicly recognized deals:	Hilton, Harrah's Entertainment, Freescale, Mega Bloks, Sunguard, Michael's, Deutsche Telekom, TRW, Sirius
Number of investment professionals:	~100

The Blackstone Group is a complex global investment firm. Its business includes corporate private equity, real estate, marketable alternative asset management (including hedge funds and funds-of-funds), and financial advisory services. Blackstone went public in 2007 and trades on NYSE (symbol: BX). It manages about $45 billion in private equity capital. Some of Blackstone's signature deals are among the largest ever done; they include Harrah's Entertainment ($31.3 billion), Hilton ($26.9 billion), and Freescale ($16.0 billion).

Over the years, Blackstone has migrated away from its initial investment strategy focused on leveraged buyouts to pursue a more opportunistic investment strategy. Its wider investment spectrum now includes pursuing growth opportunities, early-stage firms, significant minority-stake deals, public-to-private deals, and distressed debt situations. In some of these deals, Blackstone becomes contrarian by investing into traditional industries such as oil refining, coal, automotive parts, and commodity chemicals. Blackstone also invests in more modern sectors, such as healthcare and pharmaceuticals, financial services, the food and beverage industry, and hospitality. Investing alongside major corporations is one of the signature characteristics of Blackstone. Since 1987, Blackstone has developed 48 corporate partnerships with some of the world's leading industrial firms, including AT&T, Sony, General Electric, Vivendi, GM, Mitsubishi, and NBC Universal.

Among Blackstone's personnel are 100 investment professionals and 22 senior partners, many of whom have backgrounds in private equity and consulting.

Source: www.blackstone.com.

Chapter 11

New Frontiers in Venture Capital and Private Equity Investing

With over $2.2 trillion raised and nearly $1.5 trillion invested over the period between 1998 and 2007, the venture capital and private equity industry continues to be an important asset class. The industry is a strong contributor toward supporting firms deploying new technologies, increasing sales growth for expanding firms, developing export markets, increasing employment, and reducing rates of failure. For limited partners, the venture capital and private equity industry provides access to private firms that would otherwise not be possible.

With that said, there would appear to be some turbulence on the horizon for the venture capital and private equity industry. The most basic challenge is that the industry is suffering from too many investors, with too much capital under management. This frequently leads to deploying excessive amounts of capital to investee firms, investing into firms that should not be funded, "artificially" inflating entry valuations, and realizing depressed returns. Other challenges are multidimensional and structural; they relate to proposals for increased government regulations and oversight, the limited partners' desire for improved liquidity, more orientation toward emerging markets, overhauling the operating model for venture capital and private equity firms, a reconsideration of the industry's compensation scheme, a difficult exit environment, and possible reduction of allocation toward the industry.

The venture capital and private equity industry is currently looking to redefine itself as it works out current capital excesses. For many firms, the search for a new operating model may involve entry into international markets, focusing on new sectors of the economy (e.g., green energy), setting up different organizational structures to allow easier access to liquidity, and addressing the other concerns raised earlier.

Key Trends in the Industry

Regulation of the Venture Capital and Private Equity Industry

In the wake of the recent subprime mortgage crisis, many governments, research centers, security market regulators, local and international monetary agencies, and central banks around the world are calling to introduce measures and legislation aimed at preventing any potential threats to the financial stability that may come from the venture capital and private equity industry. These institutions aim to focus on reducing systemic risk in a broadly defined financial system. Systemic risk is a risk faced by the financial system or the entire economy; it is the risk of the collapse of the entire financial system or of a single economic shock that may ignite a chain of negative economic consequences. Such negative events can lead to institutional failures, financial market disruptions, or the collapse of entire economies.

The venture capital and private equity industry initially appeared on the radar screens of regulators when it was collapsed with hedge funds into one problem area. The regulators' central thesis was that the two types of investing were broadly similar and needed to be managed in a similar manner. The extension of the regulators' reach toward venture capital and private equity also comes from a belief that there is a growing trend of disintermediation, involving various financial institutions effectively obtaining access to capital without going through the traditional banking system (historically, banks have been the regulators' sole focus when assessing systemic risk). The intense focus on the industry also reflects an increasing trend toward using leverage in private equity transactions (the period between 2005 and 2008 has seen some of the largest leveraged buyout transaction records). Consequently, regulators on both sides of the Atlantic (the United States and the European Union) have embarked on new initiatives to regulate their respective venture capital and private equity markets. Many regulators believe that the venture capital and private equity industry has magnified and exacerbated the financial crisis. The European Union has already developed a detailed regulatory proposal, while the United States has outlined a broad legal framework to give local authorities almost unlimited inspection rights on venture capital and private equity firms. The two approaches are discussed in detail in the following sections.

The responses of respective local venture capital and private equity associations to these regulatory initiatives have differed. The National Venture Capital Association (NVCA) of the United States has been focused on persuading the regulators to drop their initiative altogether (such initiatives undertaken by NVCA were successful in the past). The European Private Equity and Venture Capital Association (EVCA), which represents associations from a number of EU member countries, seems to have accepted that regulations are forthcoming. Unlike NVCA, EVCA sees the proposal as an invitation to negotiate and settle on reasonable terms.

The Private Fund Investment Advisors Registration Act—The United States

In the summer of 2009, the Department of Treasury in the United States introduced a draft regulatory proposal entitled the *Private Fund Investment Advisors Registration Act of 2009* (the Act), which effectively requires the vast majority of venture capital and private equity funds to register with the Securities and Exchange Commission (SEC) under the terms of the *Investment Advisers Act of 1940* (the Advisers Act). The Act broadly increases the Treasury's ability to monitor the industry's activity and determine whether it poses systemic risk to the financial system in the United States. The Act requires venture capital and private equity firms managing assets in excess of $30 million to register with the SEC under the Advisers Act (this low threshold effectively applies to almost every single industry participant). Specifically, it requires venture capital and private equity firms to maintain regular filings with the SEC (disclosing information related to capital under management, use of leverage, trading practices, off—balance sheet activities, etc.), to adopt compliance procedures, and to make any documents available to the SEC as determined "necessary or appropriate" for the protection of investors or assessment of systemic risk. The examination may be periodic, regular, or special. The Act also provides the Treasury and the SEC with broad rule-making and disclosure requirements, which change as the Treasury, SEC, and other associated regulatory institutions (i.e., the governors of the Federal Reserve System, the Financial Services Oversight Council) deem appropriate. The Act also requires venture capital and private equity firms to disclose information to investors, creditors, and any additional parties during transactions.

The NVCA has voiced a number of arguments against the Treasury's initiatives. Some of these arguments have merit, while others appear somewhat contradictory to the general understanding of what constitutes sound venture capital and private equity activity. First, the Association argues that the Treasury has not fully understood the real causes of the financial crisis and it is, therefore, unduly punishing the venture capital and private equity industry with the current proposal of an "umbrella" regulatory framework. Second, NVCA argues that it does not create any systemic risk to the financial system as "it does not use leverage." This argument is perhaps related to venture capital investment into smaller entrepreneurial firms and leaves out the private equity component of the industry (which uses a significant amount of leverage and which the Act also regulates). The industry's use of complex derivatives is indeed quite limited. The Association also claims that the requirements are likely to place undue burden on smaller venture capital and private equity firms that may not have the staff to deal with the regulatory requirements. The industry claims that the role of the regulators should be to support entrepreneurial ventures and not to fulfill bureaucratic requirements. Finally, the industry argues that it does not manage enough capital to warrant such draconian disclosure measures and such a high level of scrutiny. This argument was perhaps made in comparison to the hedge fund industry and unduly diminishes the role of venture capital and private equity in the U.S. economy.

The Directive on Alternative Investment Fund Managers—The European Union

In April of 2009, the European Union tabled a proposal known as the *Directive of the European Parliament and of the Council on Alternative Investment Managers* (the Directive), which provides a comprehensive, 50-page proposal aimed at addressing the potential risks posed by the venture capital and private equity industry to the broader financial system. The document focuses on six types of potential risks related to the stability of the financial system: macro-prudential (systemic) risks, micro-prudential risks (i.e., market, liquidity, and operational risk), investor protection (i.e., information disclosure), market effi-ciency and integrity (i.e., trading techniques), impact on market for corporate control (i.e., transparency concerns), and impact on compa-nies controlled by investment firms (i.e., misalignment of objectives, lack of transparency and public scrutiny, use of debt financing). While the Directive specifically observes that the venture capital and private equity industry has not contributed to systemic (macro-prudential) risk, and acknowledges the difference between hedge funds and ven-ture capital and private equity funds, it argues that some of the firms in the industry are vulnerable to other risks.

The Directive is aimed at venture capital and private equity firms with capital in excess of €100 million (about $150 million), with a more modest threshold of €500 million (about $750 million) set for funds, which do not use leverage and offer redemption within five years of inception. The Directive makes calls for additional corpo-rate governance, transparency, and reporting requirements for the industry. Specifically, it includes requirements for registration with local authorities of member states in the European Union, disclosure and notification, restrictions on leverage, the reduction of manage-ment fees, amendments to compensation structures, the maintain-ing of capital reserves, the application of new valuation procedures (appointment of an independent valuator), custody and depository arrangements, and approval over investor marketing material. The transparency requirement forces the industry participant to file an annual report, along with audited financial statements.

More critically, the Directive forces investee firms into disclo-sure. When venture capital and private equity investors take more than a 30 percent stake in an investee firm, and if the investee firm meets certain requirements (employees more than 250; turn-over >€50 million or/and assets >€43 million), it becomes required to disclose information to the local authorities. This disclosure requirement is perceived as similar in complexity and rigor to the requirement for publicly listed firms. The legislation also requires investee firms to disclose their commercial information (and finan-cial data) if they have rendered control of the firm to venture capital and private equity firms (the Directive exempts small and medium-sized enterprises from such disclosure).

The guidelines in the European Union not only deal with sys-temic risk, but also extend into the social and political spheres. Many European politicians argue that a recent wave of leveraged transactions has led to employment reduction, the selling-off of assets, "milking off" firms, and curtailing growth opportunities. It is further argued that such activity may not be perceived as beneficial to firms, their employees, and European economies. Many are calling for the venture capital and private equity industry to become more publicly accountable.

In June 2009, the EVCA issued its comprehensive response to the proposed Directive and provided the underlying reasons for their position. The rebuttal argued that many of the functions anticipated in the Directive (such as custodian arrangements and valuation methods) are already in broad alignment with the Directive and therefore limited legislation is required. The EVCA also argues that the level of threshold to firms with capital in excess of €1 billion should be increased, that capital requirements should be withdrawn, that marketing material approval needs should be revised, and that the transition period for compliance with the new European Union regulations should be extended.

In conclusion, it looks like new regulations for venture capital and private equity firms are inevitable for the two largest venture capital and private equity markets, the United States and the European Union. The industry will be required to determine what changes are reasonable to accept in terms of disclosure, and which do not constitute undue burdens on the human resources and finances of industry players. In addition, consideration must be given to the possible disclosure of sensitive information so as not to influence the competitive strategies of market participants.

Limited Partners' Desire to Increase Access to Liquidity

Venture capital managers receive capital from a variety of sources, including financial institutions, public and private pension funds, university endowments, private foundations, funds of funds, corporations, high net-worth individuals, and more. The capital is normally "frozen" for a period of ten years (the usual life span of a venture capital or private equity fund), without the possibility of early redemption. Any attempt to withdraw the commitment is usually met with severe financial penalty. The capital providers do not provide all the cash at once; rather, they require draw-down notices or capital calls from the venture capital or private equity firm and are required to act promptly on the request (the funds generally call down additional tranches in 10 percent increments, depending on the deal pipeline).

As the recent financial and subprime crises revealed, all capital providers are sensitive to economic cycles. While they generally plan for cyclical increases in their need for capital, more severe economic fluctuations are likely to force limited partners to look for alternative solutions. During the recent financial crisis, many venture capital and private equity firms saw a delay in receiving capital from their limited partners; some were even outright told that the next tranche would not be forthcoming for a short period of time. Many funds were also told to delay their investment activities. Others, perhaps less fortunate venture capital and private equity firms, were asked to entirely renegotiate their capital commitments.

There are at least three possible solutions to reorchestrate the long-term period of illiquidity that limited partners are exposed to. First, venture capital and private equity firms can be established within shorter periods of time. Such action is possible for venture capital and private equity firms with exceptionally strong deal pipelines and that are capable of deploying large amounts of capital in relatively short periods of time. This time period, however, should not be less than five years, as the venture capital or private equity fund manager must have sufficient time to quickly deploy capital and seek realization within the next two–three years. While this may be possible for some funds, it will not be an option for the majority of them.

Second, venture capital and private equity firms can offer an option arrangement to limited partners. The option could be offered in increments where limited partners would be able to voluntarily participate in any round of incremental cash draw-downs. The industry may require additional compensation for providing such an option to limited partners. Ultimately, this option could become a viable alternative for strong performers in the industry and a difficult mechanism to offer for the weak ones. Since limited partners look for performance and liquidity, they are likely to reward venture capital and private firms that are providing strong and repeatable returns with additional capital.

Third, the simplest mechanism for limited partners is to hold capital in a "highly liquid" security. Such an action can result in two possible scenarios. The venture capital and private equity firms may establish operations as public entities, whose shares are listed on the stock exchange. There are already several examples of publicly listed private equities on stock exchanges around the world, with the most notable being KKR. The public orientation of venture capital and private equity would have equal benefits to institutional and individual investors alike. For institutional investors, the solution would create timely access to liquidity. Individual investors would receive access to a new class of investments that was not open to them in the past due to high capital entry requirements (normally at least $500,000). Alternatively, liquidity may be obtained by relying on a secondary market where investors' commitments are bought and sold to venture capital and private equity funds (this already represents a sizeable market, estimated at some $60 billion). The sellers view this secondary market as an opportunity to gain liquidity, reduce their ongoing funding commitment, change their asset allocation strategy, and reduce exposure to an underperforming fund manager. Buyers see this market as a way to selectively enter specific funds, achieve more diversification, and test the funds' performance. As an additional bonus, entry into these venture capital firms can occur at a discounted price.

Growing Strength of Emerging Markets

The vast majority of venture capital and private equity investments have been directed toward Western markets. The industry's investment in Western countries accounts for about 85 percent of the total investment pool (emerging markets consume the remaining amounts of capital). Western markets have traditionally been a source of deals and have provided the most profitable exit opportunities.

The case for emerging markets as the primary recipient of venture capital and private equity capital in the future can be supported by at least five arguments. First, the economies of emerging markets such Asia, Latin America, South America, and Central and Eastern Europe have been experiencing growth rates that are three or four times higher than those of Western countries. This fact is difficult for venture capitalists and private equity investors to ignore. While emerging markets are often only properly assessed by Western investors when a crisis occurs in their home market, they are likely to be receiving a steadily growing allocation of capital. Second, emerging markets have traditionally achieved stronger returns (albeit while generating a higher level of volatility). Third, emerging markets are becoming stronger in terms of innovation. While there has always been a strong pool of scientists and academics, a technically skilled labor force, and creative and innovative managers (who have experience from Western corporations) in these markets, such groups were unable to commercialize their inventions in order to achieve global recognition and market presence. With a growing focus on and orientation toward research and development, these economies are likely to emerge as the next fastest growing innovation centers in the world. Fourth, emerging markets have recently enjoyed a profound improvement in the quality of their local talent. There is a growing trend among academics, business managers, and entrepreneurs toward re-immigration to their home countries. Return-immigrants can secure local jobs at salaries comparable to or even exceeding those they can achieve in Western countries, and they can enjoy a higher standard of living when compared to Western markets. Fifth, Western venture capital and private equity markets are overcrowded; there is too much money chasing too few deals. Consequently, entry valuations increase and returns continue to be under pressure.

Limited partners can attack emerging markets in at least two ways. First, they can attempt to invest into these markets directly by supporting the local venture capital and private equity community and local players. While local operators can be relatively inexperienced, they often have great access to deals, understand the local business environment, possess knowledge of local language and customs, and have access to a local network of contacts. The market niche to support local entrepreneurial firms and corporate initiatives in these markets has predominantly been filled by smaller investment firms that have grown into sizeable operations (more than two billion dollars), achieved consistent deal flow, and developed a strong market reputation. Many of them have also established their subsequent funds and have a loyal following among limited partners. Second, limited partners can "motivate" their Western-based general partners to set up operations in emerging markets, whether as an independent operation or on an affiliated basis (with a local partner). The world's biggest venture capital and private equity houses have been relatively slow to set-up operations in these markets. While a few of the largest venture capital and private equity firms established operations in these markets more than a decade ago, the vast majority still do not have any presence at all, or they have established their presence only recently.

Overhauling the Venture and Private Equity Capital Model

The current operating model of venture capital and private equity investing is under siege for a variety of reasons. First, venture capital and private equity firms are becoming multidimensional investment houses with widely spread industry focus and different geographic orientations. Many large investment groups have significant stakes in nontraditional transactions such as real estate holdings, alternative asset classes (such as derivatives), debt instruments, and public equities. Second, venture capital and private equity firms are getting larger. This has resulted in significant management fees for the industry; in many instances, these fees have been uncoupled from financial performance and returned to limited partners. In a matter of a few years, small venture capital and private equity firms can be converted into global investment conglomerates, focusing on multiple asset classes, sophisticated financial products, different geographic regions, and quantitative analysis. Capital flows seamlessly from one asset class to another. For many firms, venture capital and private equity investing represents a small part of their overall business. If this trend continues, many venture capital and private equity firms will effectively depart from the industry, leaving a potential gap in the financial marketplace. This leaves limited room for financing small and medium-sized enterprises, the traditional recipients of financing from the industry. Third, the current model for the industry (especially private equity) is significantly grounded in access to leverage. Funds have skillfully taken advantage of cheap bank financing to magnify returns. Due to the financial crisis and forthcoming regulations on the financial sector, access to cheap financing may be temporarily suspended or permanently lost. Last and most importantly, the long-term annual returns of venture capital and private equity firms have been declining. Average returns are broadly comparable with those achieved by investing in public equity markets. Many industry experts comment that the returns achieved in the past can no longer be realistically achieved. Even though the venture capital and private equity industry has seen sporadic high returns (in excess of 20 percent per annum) in short-run periods (i.e., 1961, 1967–1969, 1972, 1980, 1983, 1999–2000), returns in the low-to-mid teens are more realistic in the interim periods (this is broadly comparable to long-term returns from public equity markets). Venture capital managers seem not to be able to obtain premiums for illiquidity.

The current model of venture capital and private equity investing is not transparent and can be confusing to limited partners. This confusion has been exacerbated by the emergence of crossover funds (i.e., owning shares in public and private firms) and integrated funds (i.e., investments across different classes of assets, including debt, real estate, derivatives, etc.). Anticipating the future evolution of the venture capital and private equity industry in this respect is challenging. In addition, economies and industries move in cycles. The industry may undergo structural changes that will either lead to the development of a new paradigm or a return to past-practices (where the industry revolved around the "business of building businesses," rather than on the indiscriminative pursuit of returns in whatever form they may come).

Dismotivational Management Fees

Another point related to the lack of effectiveness of the current industry's business model relates to compensation. Venture capital and private equity firms are compensated on a 2–20 percent basis: an average of 2 percent management fee and 20 percent carried interest above the limited partners' contributed capital. Many industry experts feel that venture capital fees are dismotivational. They claim that venture capital firms can effectively siphon off capital from limited partners by "showing up to work." They further argue that the 2 percent management fee was appropriate when the funds were smaller. The compensation structure is not motivating performance when venture capital and private equity firms have billions under management.

Many limited partners are already looking into this concern, and there are multiple solutions to it. The fees for some funds are already structured on the basis of actual performance (e.g., realization over a specific time period), reaching strategic and operational milestones, and capital deployment rates. These newly designed compensation schemes reflect variations in actual human resource commitment and actual operational costs over the holding period.

Challenging Exits

Exit prospects for venture capital-backed firms are normally cyclical. At the beginning of the economic cycle, strategic investors actively seek out opportunities for business expansion; they are also more willing to pay premium prices for acquisitions. In public markets, at the peak of the economic cycle, P/E multiples, investor confidence (both at the institutional and retail level), and the appetite for new opportunities are high. These conditions reverse at the end of the cycle. Strategic investors mostly look inward to their own businesses and focus on controlling costs rather than on expansion. As public markets are often volatile, investors tend to be more cautious of new issues; they may also delay investment decisions and seek value opportunities.

In addition to cyclical variations to exit prospects, there are some structural concerns. With trade sales, for example, many experts believe that the speed of emergence of new technologies and applications makes it virtually impossible (and even unprofitable) for the market to absorb and effectively utilize them. This may be especially true for new start-up firms in the fields of information technology, Internet applications, telecommunications, biotechnology, and so on. Consequently, strategic investors may not be willing to pay substantial amounts for acquisitions. The most widely quoted "sweet spot" for acquisitions falls in the range of valuation between $30 million and $100 million.

For public markets, two structural issues seem to be raised. First, the cost of achieving an IPO listing continues to be prohibitively high. Second, even if investee firms manage to obtain a public listing, there are concerns related to maintaining liquidity for listed entities. The aftermarket often does not result in sufficient liquidity for venture capitalists to dispose of their stake in the business.

Reduction of Commitment to the Industry

Western countries are facing one of their most significant shifts in population demographics in decades. This is related to the "baby boomer" demographic, a population cohort born between 1946 and 1960, which is expected to retire between 2007 and 2011. In the United States alone, an estimated 75 million–80 million people will begin their transition to retirement. The baby boomer population worldwide is estimated to be at around 500 million people. For at least the next two decades, the proportion of the population that is over 65 will increase dramatically. The baby-boomer problem is exacerbated further by the baby-bust that followed the previous cycle. Consequently, the old-age dependency ratio (a ratio of the elderly population expressed in relation to the working-age population) will steadily rise. The group's life expectancy is also forecasted to exceed the current trend, with one in ten baby boomers expected to live to or beyond the age of 90.

There are two major implications for the venture capital and private equity industry. The first relates to the fact that pension funds, which are one of the largest contributors to the industry, will likely need to direct capital toward satisfying pension requirements. On the other hand, the existing working population will contribute significantly less into the pension funds' pool. The second implication relates to a wider economic prediction of a broader slow-down in economic activity and reflects a reduction in the general workforce. The result will be lower returns to the investment community, including to venture capital and private equity investors.

The two main demographic trends identified earlier point to a reduced allocation of capital to the venture capital and private equity industry, both in absolute dollar terms and as a percentage of the limited partners' overall portfolio. A reduced commitment to allocating capital toward venture capital and private equity is likely to affect larger players more than smaller firms. The smaller funds are likely to be targeted by limited partners, as they may better reflect the investment orientations of the limited partners (i.e., smaller funds tend to be more focused). In addition, investing into smaller entrepreneurial firms may be more rewarding financially when compared to seeking multibillion dollar deals.

Paradoxically, the trend of reducing allocations to venture capital may actually help the industry in the long-term. Lower amounts of available capital could ultimately result in a more selective approach to choosing investee firms, wiser investment choices, lower entry valuations for investee firms (less competition for deals), and better returns. Such a cleansing process may last beyond the normal economic cycles of the industry.

Index